ABOUT
DEVELOPMENT DIMENSIONS
INTERNATIONAL

Development Dimensions International (DDI) is a leading provider of human resource programs and services designed to create high-involvement organizations. Founded in 1970, **DDI** now provides services to more than nine thousand clients around the world, spanning a diverse range of industries and including more than four hundred of the Fortune 500 corporations.

DDI's products and services fall into three general areas:

1. *Assessment and Selection:* ensures that organizations select and promote team members and leaders most capable of working in high-involvement organizations.

2. *Organizational Change:* involves a wide range of consulting services and expertise in implementing teams.

3. *Training and Development:* includes proven and comprehensive skill-building systems for teams and their leaders.

DDI's corporate headquarters and distribution facilities are located in Pittsburgh, Pennsylvania, with regional training centers in Atlanta, Chicago, Dallas, Denver, Hong Kong, London, Los Angeles, Montreal, New York, Singapore, Sydney, Tokyo, and Toronto. International in the truest sense, **DDI** is represented in nineteen countries, and its programs have been translated into twenty-one languages.

For more information, write or call

DEVELOPMENT DIMENSIONS INTERNATIONAL
World Headquarters — Pittsburgh
1225 Washington Pike
Bridgeville, Penn. 15017-2838
Tel.: 800/933-4624

OTHER BOOKS BY THE AUTHORS
About Empowerment and Teams

Understanding the leadership implications of teams provides only part of the information one needs to implement teams successfully. To understand the complete picture of empowerment and teams, the following books are recommended:

101 Tips on Teams (Richard S. Wellins and Richard Schaff, with Kathy Harper Shomo. Lakewood Publications, forthcoming)

> This is a handbook, designed primarily for team members and leaders, that contains simple, practical tips for implementing successful teams.

Empowered Teams: Creating Self-Directed Work Groups That Improve Quality, Productivity, and Participation (Richard S. Wellins, William C. Byham, and Jeanne M. Wilson. Jossey-Bass, 1991)

> This is a how-to book on starting teams. It explores why empowered teams work, how they operate, and what's needed to make them survive and prosper. A particular focus of the book is how to get teams off to the right start.

HeroZ — Empower Yourself, Your Co-Workers, Your Company (William C. Byham, Ph.D., and Jeff Cox. Harmony Books, forthcoming)

> This sequel to *Zapp! The Lightning of Empowerment* deals with empowering yourself and with continuous improvement. It focuses on overcoming barriers to implementing change from the bottom up and working effectively with team members from all functional areas to accomplish projects. Written as a fable, it is easy and fun to read for individuals at all organizational levels.

Inside Teams: How 20 World-Class Organizations Are Winning Through Teamwork (Richard S. Wellins, William C. Byham, and George R. Dixon. Jossey-Bass, forthcoming)

> This book presents an insider's view of the successes and foibles of twenty of the top U.S. companies and their experiences with teams. It shows how managers can employ the positive aspects of teams while benefiting from others' experiences of identifying and solving team-related problems.

Team Leader's Survival Guide (Jeanne M. Wilson and Jill A. George. Development Dimensions International, forthcoming)

> This handbook guides leaders through the specific steps they must take to start, maintain, and advance self-directed teams. Designed as a practical companion to *Leadership Trapeze*, it provides the week-by-week prompting and coaching that leaders need to succeed in the challenging transition to teams.

Zapp! The Lightning of Empowerment (William C. Byham, Ph.D., with Jeff Cox. Development Dimensions International, 1988 [Reprinted by Harmony Books, 1991])

> This easy-to-read book, written in the form of a fable, provides an understanding of what empowerment is, why it is important, and what it takes to achieve empowerment — including the development of teams — within an organization.

LEADERSHIP
TRAPEZE

JEANNE M. WILSON
JILL GEORGE
RICHARD S. WELLINS
WITH # WILLIAM C. BYHAM

LEADERSHIP TRAPEZE

STRATEGIES FOR

LEADERSHIP IN

TEAM-BASED

ORGANIZATIONS

Jossey-Bass Publishers • San Francisco

Substantial discounts on bulk quantities of Jossey-Bass books are available to corporations, professional associations, and other organizations. For details and discount information, contact the special sales department at Jossey-Bass Inc., Publishers. (415) 433-1740; Fax (415) 433-0499.

For sales outside the United States, contact Maxwell Macmillan International Publishing Group, 866 Third Avenue, New York, New York 10022.

Manufactured in the United States of America. Nearly all Jossey-Bass books and jackets are printed on recycled paper that contains at least 50 percent recycled waste, including 10 percent postconsumer waste. Many of our materials are also printed with vegetable-based ink; during the printing process these inks emit fewer volatile organic compounds (VOCs) than petroleum-based inks. VOCs contribute to the formation of smog.

Library of Congress Cataloging-in-Publication Data

Wilson, Jeanne M., date.
    Leadership trapeze : strategies for leadership in team-based organizations / Jeanne M. Wilson, Jill George, Richard S. Wellins, with William C. Byham.
        p.   cm. — (The Jossey-Bass management series)
    Includes bibliographical references and index.
    ISBN 1-55542-613-1
    1. Leadership.   2. Work groups—Management.   I. George, Jill.
II. Wellins, Richard S.   III. Title.   IV. Series.
HD57.7.W54   1994
658.4'092—dc20   94-8620
                                                                      CIP

FIRST EDITION
HB Printing   10 9 8 7 6 5 4 3 2 1   *Code 9454*

The Jossey-Bass
Management Series

CONTENTS

Preface   xiii

The Authors   xix

**Part One: Leadership on the Trapeze:
The Transition to Team-Based Organizations**

1. Leading Teams: Conventional Wisdom
   Versus the New Realities   3

2. Teams as Competitive Strategy: Responding
   to the Forces Changing Organizations   17

3. Daring to Let Go: Stories of Leaders'
   Successful Transitions   38

4. From Commander to Coach: A Model for the
   Evolving Role of the Leader   57

5. Becoming the High-Involvement Leader:
   Learning New Skills, Tapping New Motivations   66

**Part Two: Making the Transition:
Getting and Giving the Right Support**

6. Beginning the Journey: Assessing Where You Are   87

7. Preteam Leadership: Buying the Concept,
    Overcoming the Fear, and Starting the Change   93

8. Preteam Safety Nets: Clarifying
    Organizational Expectations   128

9. New-Team Leadership: What to Do
    for Yourself and Your Team   153

10. New-Team Safety Nets: Demonstrating
    Organizational Commitment and Support   183

11. Mature-Team Leadership: Encouraging Focus,
    Direction, and Initiative   204

12. Mature-Team Safety Nets: Sustaining and
    Refreshing the Efforts of Mature-Team Leaders   234

13. Virtual Teams in Virtual Organizations:
    A Look at the Future   249

    Epilogue: Hang In There:
    The Change Is Worth It   265

    References   271

    Index   281

PREFACE

> At first you're pretty nervous, but you learn when to hang on and when to let go. And after a while it actually gets to be fun.
>
> Michelangelo, trapeze artist
> from his act
> *The Man on the Flying Trapeze*

Many leaders today feel like novice trapeze artists. Their organizations are moving to teams, and they're being asked to leap from the comfort and safety of one platform (their organizations' traditional culture) and get to another (self-directed teams). In the process, they have to let go of their old autocratic style and grasp a more empowering leadership approach.

Unfortunately, rather than being the exhilarating experience it could be, this leap is causing too many good leaders anxiety and heartburn. Why? We think the reason things are amiss in many organizations is that leaders often don't know what to do, and the organizations themselves don't know how to help.

PURPOSE AND AUDIENCE

We wrote *Leadership Trapeze* to help guide leaders and their organizations through the tremendous leadership transition that accompanies a move to teams. This isn't a book about the vanishing leadership role in team-based organizations, because we believe that the demands on leaders increase — not decrease — with the introduction of teams. Rather, our intention is to give leaders and their organizations all the tools they need to become less fearful and frustrated and more satisfied and successful in this very important role transition.

We felt compelled to write this book for several additional reasons:

- Leadership formulas of the past haven't always proved appropriate or sufficient for leading teams. Some, such as the old adage about "going along to get along," are downright counterproductive.

- On the other hand, much of the new conventional wisdom about team leaders is also off base. The popular notion that self-directed teams don't need leaders is a prelude to disaster.

- Most of the available advice seems to be directed at manufacturing supervisors, as if they were the only ones who have been affected by the introduction of teams. In reality, teams are springing up everywhere — in hospitals, government agencies, and even zoos. In each of these locations, there's an important and unique role for all leaders, including the support staff and union leaders.

- Very little has been written about how leaders' roles change when their teams mature. Because increasing numbers of teams are reaching maturity, specific suggestions on this topic are needed desperately.

- Finally, there's a lot at stake at this pivotal point in an organization's history. For leaders, their livelihood, their self-esteem, and the very concept of what they have to contribute are on the line. For organizations, the people they've invested years in developing (and who probably understand the technical processes better than anyone else) are at risk. We want leaders and their organizations to succeed in this transformation. When we look ahead to the future, we want to see significantly fewer casualties than we see today.

This book is written for those individuals who have played by the rules faithfully for years, only to find that the rules have changed. It is for all leaders of teams and would-be leaders of teams: white-collar, blue-collar, and no-collar leaders; leaders at the end of their careers and leaders who are just beginning; operations leaders and support professionals; leaders in management and leaders in unions. It's also written for everyone who has a responsibility to nurture their organizations' leaders: senior managers, human resource professionals, and front-line employees. In short, anyone who has a stake in leaders' success should benefit from reading this book.

The good news is that a growing number of leaders and their organizations are succeeding at this transition. We've tapped into their expertise in a number of ways. A national survey conducted by Development Dimensions International (DDI) on the changing role of the supervisor provided quantitative data from leaders in 90 organizations that have converted to self-directed teams. And our own clients, in more than 200 organizations where we helped create self-directed teams, provided many of the examples and lessons that appear throughout the book.

OVERVIEW OF THE CONTENTS

Leadership Trapeze is organized into two parts. Part One is descriptive; it paints a picture of the changing role of leaders. Chapter One explodes the most popular myths about leading teams. Chapter Two makes the case for why organizations need to change and shows how teams are being used to drive that change. To help readers appreciate the profound personal impact of this transition, Chapter Three tells the stories of five leaders coming to grips with the challenges of leading in the new team environment. Chapters Four and Five present our model for the new leadership role, complete with the behaviors required for success.

Part Two is prescriptive; it outlines exactly what leaders and their organizations need to do across three distinct phases of a team's implementation: preteam, new team, and mature team. The advice is further divided into suggestions for leaders (Chapters Seven, Nine, and Eleven) and recommendations to the organization about how to support leaders through each phase (Chapters Eight, Ten, and Twelve). We conclude the book with a look at the next generation of team leadership (in Chapter Thirteen) and our answer to the question, Is it all worth it? (in the Epilogue).

Throughout the book, you'll notice that some of the figures and illustrations are labeled *tools*. These are samples of some of the tools our clients have used to make this transition. We hope you'll be able to use them to guide your own journey.

As a leader in implementing self-directed teams, you're indeed on a high-flying trapeze. To be successful, you'll need the skills of a corporate acrobat. This book will help you develop those skills and enable you to become an accomplished performer in today's fast-changing business arena.

We hope that *Leadership Trapeze* will stimulate and enlighten you as much in the reading as it did us in the writing.

ACKNOWLEDGMENTS

We're grateful to our colleagues at DDI who did all the hard work while we wrote this book. We'd especially like to thank Bruce Court, Susan DeLuca, Rod Warrenfeltz, and the Strategies Team for slogging through earlier drafts of this work and offering insightful suggestions. And our gratitude goes also to Richard Gregory from Union Pacific Railroad and Jim Neal from Miller Brewing for their contributions to the sections of the book dealing with the role of union leaders.

Special thanks and a room at Woodville State Hospital are due to Kathy Shomo and her imaginary editor, Richard Bankert, for coordinating the views and writing of four people with, shall we say, strongly held views.

We'd also like to acknowledge Jody (Bodice-Ripper) Lang and Anne (Alchemist) Maers for their help in the creative process; Nancy Boyle, Carol Schuetz, and Phyllis Sproull for keeping us out of trouble; and Tammy Bercosky, Andrea Eger, Shawn Garry, Shelby Gracey, and Mary Szpak for giving up some of the best weekends in 1993 to turn our manuscript into something fit for human consumption. We are indebted to Mark Mosko and Susan Gladis who took our sketchy ideas and transformed them into understandable graphics.

Finally, we'd like to thank our friends at Jossey-Bass: Cedric Crocker for your patience and understanding (even though we could hear you holding your breath from three thousand miles away) and Bill Hicks for challenging our thinking and for not eating worms when we disagreed.

Bridgeville, Pennsylvania   Jeanne M. Wilson
March 1994   Jill George
                                     Richard S. Wellins
                                     William C. Byham

DEDICATIONS

To Sydney Wilson—the perfect test of my
leadership and empowerment skills.

—Jeanne

To my mother, Jan George—a model of shared
leadership at work and at home.

—Jill

To my father, Gerald Wellins, who taught me that
a family is much like a team.

—Rich

To my father, Edgar Byham—a natural leader
who knows when to let go.

—Bill

THE AUTHORS

JEANNE WILSON advises DDI's clients on creating high-performance, high-commitment work environments and, as co-leader of DDI's team practice, conducts research and development of new processes for implementing self-directed teams. She maintains her perspective by consulting with her own clients on team visioning, work redesign, leader assessment and development, and team performance reviews. Some of her recent projects have included implementing self-directed teams of sales and service professionals with Buick, redesigning an entire plant's processes and layout with Campbell Chain, and developing a team performance management system with Miller Brewing and Henkel/Emery.

Since joining DDI over ten years ago, Wilson has led groups in team member training, assessing team members and leaders against the new criteria for success in a high-involvement culture, and planning new plant start-ups. She is coauthor of *Empowered Teams* (1991, with R. S. Wellins and W. C. Byham), and her ideas about teams have appeared in *Industry Week, Total Quality Management, Service Quality,* and *Quality and Participation.* Wilson received her B.S. degree (1979) from St. Joseph's College, Indiana, in psychology and her M.S. degree (1982) from Purdue University in industrial/organizational psychology.

JILL GEORGE manages large-scale culture change and team implementations for DDI's multi-site clients. As a co-leader in developing DDI's teams consulting services, George has achieved results for DDI's clients by using sociotechnical systems–driven vision, design, role clarity, and team performance management interventions. She also assisted in the development of DDI's team training systems, which deliver the skills needed to operate effectively in a team environment. Some of her recent projects include redesigning the work-flow and team boundaries at UCAR Carbon's R&D facility and developing a joint union/management teams implementation at several sites within Union Pacific Railroad.

George received her B.S. degree (1985) from Virginia Polytechnic Institute and State University in psychology and her M.S. degree (1988) from the University of Tennessee in industrial/organizational psychology. She expects to complete her Ph.D. degree, also in industrial/organizational psychology, from the University of Tennessee in 1994. George has published and presented a variety of articles, which have appeared in *Training and Development Magazine, Quality and Participation, Total Quality Management,* and *Service Quality.*

RICHARD S. WELLINS is senior vice president of programs and marketing for DDI. He received his B.A. degree (1973) in psychology, his M.A. degree (1975) in experimental and social psychology, and his Ph.D. degree (1977) in applied social psychology, all from American University. Since joining DDI in 1982, Wellins has focused the majority of his time in the areas of new program development, research, and consulting. He formed DDI's start-up group, a special division responsible for designing team-based work systems for more than fifty new facilities around the world. He also led the development and launch of DDI's new teams training system, currently being used by more than two thousand organizations. Wellins also has consulted with numerous organizations, including Toyota, Laurentian Technology, A. T. Cross, and International Paper, in the areas of culture change, work-system design, performance management, and selection systems.

Wellins has published or presented numerous articles and papers in the area of high-involvement work teams. He is lead author of two nationwide research studies on teams: *Self-Directed Teams: A Study of Current Practice* (published with *Industry Week* and the Association for Quality and Participation) and *TQM: Forging Ahead or Falling Behind?* (published with Quality & Productivity Management Association and *Industry Week*). Wellins is the senior author of *Empowered Teams* (1991, with W. C. Byham and J. M. Wilson) and coauthor of *Inside Teams: How 20 World-Class Organizations Are Winning Through Teamwork* (forthcoming, with W. C. Byham and G. R. Dixon).

WILLIAM C. BYHAM is co-founder and president of DDI. An internationally known educator, consultant, and speaker, he is the author of more than one hundred articles, papers, and books. He received his B.S. degree (1958) and M.S. degree (1959) from Ohio University in science and his Ph.D. degree (1962) from Purdue University in industrial/organizational psychology.

Byham has received numerous awards for his innovative training technologies and for his commitment to research on the effectiveness of DDI programs. In 1989 he received the Professional Practice Award from the Society of Industrial and Organizational Psychology of the American Psychological Association, and in 1988 he was awarded the Distinguished Contribution to Human Resource Development Award from the American Society for Training and Development. He is past president of the Instructional Systems Association.

Byham is the author of *Zapp! The Lightning of Empowerment* (1988) and *Shogun Management* (1993), and coauthor of *Assessment Centers and Managerial Performance* (1982, with G. Thornton) and *Empowered Teams* (1991, with R. S. Wellins and J. M. Wilson).

LEADERSHIP
TRAPEZE

PART ONE

Leadership on the Trapeze: The Transition to Team-Based Organizations

Leading Teams:
Conventional Wisdom
Versus the New Realities

- "Who needs a boss? Not employees who work in self-managed teams" (Dumaine, 1990).

- "Middle managers and supervisors are likely opponents of the shift to self-directed work teams because their jobs are on the line. . . . You're making their worst nightmare come true" (Bednarek, 1990).

- "Naturally, some supervisors do not like the change because they don't want to give up their power. . ." (Denton, 1992).

- "The team manager is not supposed to tell anyone what to do or how to do it" (Houston, 1989).

If these comments are representative of the conventional wisdom circulating about leading teams, it's no wonder the phrase "self-directed teams" strikes fear into the hearts of unsuspecting supervisors and managers.

Today's team leaders often sign up for the leadership journey with the same uneasiness as the original sailors on the *Niña,* the *Pinta,* and the *Santa María.* Because they had no idea of what to expect, those sailors envisioned disasters of every kind — everything from encounters with giant sea monsters to falling off the edge of the earth. Equally outlandish misconceptions exist about leadership — especially the leadership of teams. These misconceptions flourish for two reasons:

■ *Positive leadership models are few and far between.* Chances are that a prospective team leader has never had the opportunity to observe an effective team leader in action. In the absence of any personal observation or experience, would-be leaders are forced to imagine or invent a role for themselves. This situation has resulted in some well-intentioned, but disastrous, mistakes.

For example, one new plant start-up struggled to establish a team environment on its own, without getting outside help or benchmarking against other companies that had moved to teams successfully. Not surprisingly, the leadership roles were poorly defined and the first group leaders had to create their own rules. Unfortunately, one of the rules they created was that leaders should never *tell* team members what to do. Instead, leaders were to *sell* the team on an idea or *ask* team members to comply; they were not to come right out and tell the team members what they wanted.

This system forced the leaders into all kinds of contortions to get things done. At the same time, it alienated team members, because they could see right through the game and felt that they were being manipulated. Even though this behavior was clearly frustrating to both leaders and members, the leaders clung to their misguided belief that this was somehow "the right thing to do" for teams. Today the plant has teams in name only, with a whopping 20 percent turnover rate among members and leaders.

- *There are plenty of "bad" team implementations out there.* One of the first things many organizations do in their pursuit of teams is to find out what others are doing. At first glance, this would seem to be a logical approach. But because the interest in teams has begun to accelerate only recently, there are many more fledgling implementations than there are mature, stable, successful team cultures. This means that many teams presumed to be "models" are actually very immature examples of teamwork in action.

At one site that had recently converted to teams, a plant manager stood up in front of a group of visitors and proudly announced that the plant had slashed two layers of supervision. Because he made this statement with such confidence and gusto, the visitors assumed his approach had been successful. What they didn't realize was that this implementation was still much too new for the organization to have experienced the negative consequences of such drastic actions.

Too often companies prematurely copy the early implementation decisions they observe in other organizations. And even when they begin to experience the pain of certain decisions, they assume it's a necessary part of the process (no pain, no gain) or that they haven't implemented a particular decision properly. They rarely stop to question their basic assumptions or decisions.

NEW REALITIES

The fear and frustration experienced by teams increase in direct proportion to the amount of misinformation circulating about the changing role of leaders. Obviously, then, we need to expose the myths. In this section, we examine the most common misconceptions about the changing role of leaders in team-based organizations. It's very important to sort out fact from fantasy. After all, there are enough real challenges out there that we don't need to invent imaginary ones.

The New Realities of Leading Teams

1. Empowered teams need good leaders.
2. Leaders gain power in the transition to teams.
3. Most leaders are capable of making the transition successfully.
4. New leaders must be direct.
5. Leaders need to relax — it's okay to make mistakes.

NEW REALITY 1: EMPOWERED TEAMS NEED GOOD LEADERS

The most common, most unfortunate misconception about teams is that they don't need leaders. The truth is that teams probably need *more* coaching, guidance, and attention in their early stages than the same individual contributors would need in a traditional structure. And the logical place for teams to get this help is from their leaders. If we arbitrarily strip out layers of supervision and support, we'll almost certainly wind up with floundering teams.

This is a particular problem with new facility start-ups. These greenfield facilities are conceived with the hope that they'll function with self-directed teams. The mistake they often make is to assume that "self-directed" means "leaderless."

One typical case involved a small high-technology plant in Pittsburgh. The top leaders of this start-up company envisioned a highly team-oriented culture in which all 100 team members would feel like "owners of the business." Based on their past experiences, the managers recognized that traditional supervisors often treat their subordinates in ways that leave the employees feeling very unempowered. The managers decided that their new facility would have none of that: teams would report directly to one of the top managers. This was a small operation, and the managers wanted to create a congenial atmosphere. They were investing a lot of time and energy in selecting the best possible team members. Surely these people could manage themselves, the managers reasoned.

A very short time after start-up, it became apparent that the plan wasn't working. The top-management group was very disappointed that the teams hadn't established goals for themselves and that the teams had failed to develop measurement methods for monitoring their performance. So, management created the position of production coordinator to act as a liaison between top management and the teams.

Six months later, the plan *still* wasn't working to the top leaders' satisfaction. Some team members had begun to "test" the system by coming in late, so another layer was installed to help monitor the situation. This time, shift team leaders were added.

When this arrangement didn't work either, top managers decided that the self-directed team concept had failed, and they reverted to a traditional culture. Yet if the group had had more leadership support for the teams in the beginning, the teams could have been trained to establish goals, monitor performance, and handle many of their own administrative issues. As it was, though, the team members were frustrated with managers for "going back on their promise" of empowerment, and managers were equally annoyed with team members for not acting more like owners of the business. All these problems could have been avoided if top managers had started with a clearer picture of the changing role of leaders within a team structure.

The crux of the problem is that leaders don't know what their new roles will look like after the implementation of teams. One way to solve this problem is to imagine the "box" of things leaders historically have handled in organizations. These responsibilities range from routine, reactive tasks (such as keeping track of employees' time off and monitoring quality) to more proactive tasks (such as developing an organization-wide supplier certification program or finding cost-effective ways to comply with government regulations).

In the move toward empowered teams, many of the leaders' routine or reactive tasks are eliminated or transferred to the team. This leaves the leaders with considerably fewer traditional tasks, which often leads organizations to believe that they can get by with considerably fewer leaders — or maybe none at all. What they fail to anticipate is that there are just as many new, value-added tasks needed to support the new teams. In most successful cases, leaders are left with considerably reshaped *but still substantial* roles. Usually the new roles lean more toward proactive tasks that add significant value to organizations and customers.

NEW REALITY 2: LEADERS GAIN POWER IN THE TRANSITION TO TEAMS

Power need not be a zero-sum proposition. It's easy to be confused about this concept, because so many organizational commodities appear to be zero-sum games: "The more money I negotiate for my budget, the less that's available for other departments" or "The more space my department takes up, the less space there is for you." Given this kind of thinking, it's understandable that most leaders try to protect what they have.

Power and influence, however, are *expandable* resources. It doesn't necessarily follow that the more power team members have, the less their leader has. In fact, the more power and influence a leader has, the better off the teams will be.

Consider the case of two different leaders in the same obstetrical ward of a large midwestern hospital. Carol was put in charge of the team in Unit A, and Alice took over a similar team in Unit B. Although Carol had worked for the hospital approximately the same amount of time as Alice, Carol was insecure in her new role. And because Carol was unsure about what she was supposed to do, she assumed a "back-seat" position with the team.

Carol felt uncomfortable providing direction for her team, so she waited until team members approached her with problems, questions, or suggestions. Even then, team members were generally frustrated with the outcome. Time after time, the solutions they came up with failed to be implemented because the team ran into roadblocks in other departments or higher up the hospital chain of command. At that point, however, team members were reluctant to go back to Carol because she had provided so little in the way of help or ideas in the first place. Gradually, Unit A lapsed into a pattern of mediocre performance and a sort of permanent learned helplessness. Their motto might just as well have been, "Oh, what's the use? Nothing ever changes around here anyway."

Unit B, on the other hand, became one of the top-performing units in the hospital. Even though they didn't always get what they wanted, team members had an unwavering belief in their ability to improve things. Much of this stemmed from their leader, Alice, who described her role as that of "a barrier buster." Team members went to Alice with the same kind of problems and complaints that the other team took to Carol; they left not only with the responsibility for improving the situation but with a commitment from Alice to help them with any obstacles they might encounter.

For example, when Hannah was working to solve a problem with the fetal monitors team members were using, she found that she couldn't get anyone from the supplier with real decision-making authority to meet with her. Alice stepped in and arranged a face-to-face meeting between Hannah and the supplier's technical director. She wielded similar influence to enlist cooperation and resources from other teams, support professionals, and even doctors. In no way did Alice's power diminish in her transition to becoming an empowering leader; rather, she turned it outward.

Traditionally, leaders exert their power internally by controlling subordinates. With the move to teams, however, most of that power needs to be exercised externally to influence support departments, suppliers, and other parts of the organization.

It's helpful to remember that a leader's real power comes from the ability to

- Enable process improvements.

- Attract resources.

- Remove barriers.

- Make things happen outside the team.

- Help team members realize their full potential.

NEW REALITY 3: MOST LEADERS ARE CAPABLE OF MAKING THE TRANSITION SUCCESSFULLY

When we've asked top managers of self-directed organizations how many managers were capable of making the transition, their estimates ranged from 80 to 90 percent. Most people agree that if supervisors really want to change, their chances of success are quite good.

Let's consider one typical example of what happens to existing leaders when an organization decides to move to teams. A 225-person packaging operation originally had the organizational structure depicted in Figure 1.1. In the new structure, the production and quality control managers were given technical consultant positions (at their old salary levels, but with no direct line responsibility), and four new team facilitator jobs were opened up for bid. A realistic job preview was provided for all candidates, and anyone who was interested participated in a facilitator assessment center designed to simulate the new job. Here's what happened:

- Four of the seven lead hands elected to return to team member status (in most cases, because of the reading and math requirements of the facilitator's job).

- Four nonsupervisory employees (two from the lines, one from maintenance, and one from production scheduling) and all three existing supervisors applied for the new facilitator jobs.

Figure 1.1. Original Organizational Structure at Packaging Plant.

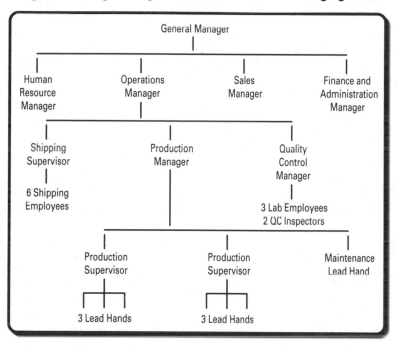

Of the ten participants in the assessment center, three were evaluated to be "ready now" (including two of the three existing supervisors), five were assessed to be "ready with development," and two were determined to be "not ready" (including one of the original production supervisors).

The company ended up with four team facilitators: two of the former supervisors, one former employee from maintenance, and one former lead hand. The production supervisor who was judged to be "not ready" was given a position in inside sales, which fit his skill profile quite well.

This situation is representative of what we find when we're asked to assess incumbent managers for development in organizations that are moving toward a more empowering culture. When incumbent managers are assessed against the standards of empowering leaders, on the whole 35 percent are "ready now," 45 percent could be "ready with development," and 20 percent are "not ready."

This breakdown is analogous to the triage principle that MASH units use in war to separate the incoming wounded into three categories: the 20 percent who are going to live whether they get medical attention or not, the 20 percent who aren't going to make it even if they do get medical attention, and the 60 percent who will live or die depending on the help they receive. As is the case with MASH units, organizations must focus their immediate development efforts on that middle 60 percent. Most current leaders will succeed in the new role once they get "medical attention."

NEW REALITY 4: NEW LEADERS MUST BE DIRECT

Successful team leaders loosen the reins; they don't drop them. Many others, in a misguided attempt to manage participatively, are so indirect that they appear manipulative. Consider the case of Tom, the president of a 200-person paper division in a large multinational company. A former consultant, Tom believed wholeheartedly in participative management. In fact, his paper plant had a long history of promoting an open and inclusive culture. When the plant decided to move to self-directed teams two and a half years ago, Tom decided that he needed to step up his own participative leadership behaviors and begin to treat his direct reports as a team.

His staff first noticed a change in their management-group meetings. After about a month, Tom's pattern became so obvious that his staff actually dubbed it the "Guess What I Think?" game. Here's how it worked. In staff meetings, Tom would raise a problem or issue for discussion. As his staff managers began offering solutions and alternatives, Tom would respond to each with a friendly "yes—but." ("Yes, but have you considered...?")

Finally, Tom would get around to asking a set of questions that inescapably led to a different solution — *his* solution. It became apparent that all along, Tom had had a preconceived idea about how to handle the situation and only pretended to want others' ideas.

Not surprisingly, Tom's leadership behavior caused a great deal of frustration for his subordinates; in fact, it all but extinguished their participation in problem-solving meetings. When Tom asked for input, the others simply waited for him to tell them what he was thinking. Tom was likewise frustrated: he couldn't understand why his subordinates didn't offer more of their own ideas.

The moral of the story is that it's okay for a leader to have thoughts and feelings — actually, people expect that. It's only when leaders focus on their own agendas to the exclusion of their teams' that everyone loses.

One way to think about this is that in a team situation, the leader's role moves from *giving directions* (telling people what to do or issuing orders) to *providing direction* (creating a vision of shared goals). Once everyone is committed to a common vision, the leader no longer has to sweat the small stuff. In this kind of scenario, everyone wins.

NEW REALITY 5: LEADERS NEED TO RELAX — IT'S OKAY TO MAKE MISTAKES

If you're harboring any illusions about making it through this transition unscathed, give it up. This is a long, complex, and difficult transition. Everyone makes mistakes. One thing that helps ease the transition is to relinquish two old, counterproductive beliefs:

- *When you don't know, don't ask.* It's virtually impossible for leaders to understand everything they need to know about leading teams *before* making the transition. In fact, it's almost guaranteed that we'll all find ourselves in new situations where we won't know what to do. Although it's probably acceptable to figure out what to do by trial and error, it will save considerable time and frustration if leaders consult trainers, facilitators, other team leaders, and even their bosses.

- *Don't look vulnerable (weak).* Almost all leaders feel vulnerable sometimes, so it takes a significant amount of
  energy to maintain a facade to the contrary. Why not just
  admit that the transition is a challenge and go on from
  there? One of the most effective behaviors for new leaders of teams is to *disclose* — in other words, to reveal their
  personal feelings to team members. When leaders say
  such things as, "I was worried that I wasn't giving you
  enough direction," it helps to build trust and improve
  relationships with the team. Why? Because leaders are
  showing that they're human, too.

The good news is that admitting and learning from mistakes will earn leaders the respect of team members faster than
almost any other type of behavior. This is hard for many
managers to believe — especially those who've spent years trying to hide, deny, or blame others for mistakes.

Consider the case of Frank, a plant manager at a 400-
person manufacturing plant that recently implemented self-
directed teams. An extremely bright and aggressive manager,
Frank worked hard to make sure his plant remained the top
producer in the entire division. As often is the case with
achievement-oriented people, though, Frank was viewed as
intimidating by those around him (especially the line employees at the plant, but also the other top managers). This reputation stemmed from behaviors Frank wasn't even conscious
of — behaviors such as cutting people off in midsentence,
thinking (and saying) that his ideas were better than others',
and raising his voice when he became excited.

About a year into the team implementation, when the
design team had structured and trained the first three self-
directed teams, the whole division was hit with a severe cash-
flow problem, causing belt-tightening at all the plants. Frank
reacted to this situation in his characteristic style: he focused
all his attention on solving the problem at hand. The result was
that resources previously promised to the teams were reassigned, a team compensation plan that had been in the works
was put on the back burner, and the design team suddenly

stopped meeting. As might be expected, team members' morale took a nosedive. Employees in parts of the plant that hadn't been converted to teams started saying, "We told you so. We told you this was just a fad." In no time, the new teams' improvements in quality and delivery began to evaporate.

When one of the design team members finally mustered the courage to approach Frank about the deterioration of the teams, Frank was surprised. He realized he had several options at that point: he could blame the shift of resources on corporate decisions, he could quietly begin to reinvest in the teams and hope they would pull out of their slump, or he could admit he had made a mistake.

The design team is still talking about Frank's decision to this day — about the afternoon he called them all together to admit, "I really fell on my butt on this one. The teams are so important to the success of this plant, and I let them down." It was such an unprecedented move that it permanently changed Frank's relationship with the employees. Because they believed him, team members trusted him more after he'd "opened up." In fact, it became something of a legend at the plant: the day Frank apologized. Because the rest of the plant took it as a sign that their leader cared deeply about the team concept, the implementation was saved.

Not all mistakes, of course, will be this dramatic; nor will all admissions and disclosures be met with such a positive response. But leaders can actually profit from their mistakes — and in more ways than one. Not only do mistakes present opportunities to show that a leader is human and to build trust with teams, they can result in deep personal insight and ongoing learning.

A classic example of such a mistake is what's become known as "the golf incident" in one western sales district that has self-directed teams. Don, the sales manager, had a limited number of tickets to a much-coveted golf outing. He turned them over to the team, with the suggestion that they give one of the tickets to a manager from another department. Because his suggestions had always been followed in the past, Don expected the team to comply with his wishes this time, too.

But the team had other ideas. Enjoying their newfound empowerment, they opened it up for discussion at a team meeting and decided to give all the tickets to hardworking team members instead. When they announced their decision to Don, he exploded. Why? He had already hinted to the other manager that he would be included.

Feeling completely unempowered by Don's response, the team also overreacted, slipping into a semipermanent pout. When Don realized his mistake and openly discussed it with the team, they were able to work out decision rules that everyone could agree on. As it turned out, this was a significant "aha!" experience for Don. It caused him to realize that he was overcontrolling on decisions of little consequence and wasn't as empowering as he had thought he was. Now when Don is in doubt, he'll ask a team member, "Is this one of those 'golf' things?"

SUMMARY

Making the move to a team-based culture isn't nearly as scary or difficult as it may seem, particularly if you don't fall victim to popular but misleading myths about leading teams. The realities are much more encouraging!

TWO

Teams as Competitive Strategy: Responding to the Forces Changing Organizations

In the last decade, the magnitude and speed of change the world over have had a dramatic impact on the workplace. Nowhere, however, has change had as significant an impact as on the role of today's team leaders.

WHY ORGANIZATIONS MUST CHANGE

To understand the profound changes required of leaders, first we need to understand the changes occurring in our organizations. Some of the major forces impacting organizational culture and necessitating radical change are overviewed here.

Change Force 1: Acknowledge the Knowledge Explosion

Knowledge, as Francis Bacon wrote, is power. And when there's an era of profound change, knowledge expands and increases in value and power. Today we live in such a time, and one of the greatest changes in our business world is the transformation of an industrial-based economy into an information-based economy.

In a 1990 *Harvard Business Review* article entitled "The State of American Management," Walter B. Wriston, former chairman of Citicorp and Citibank, writes about the accelerating pace of knowledge: "It is a simple fact that roughly 85 percent of all the scientists who ever lived on this planet are alive today. Knowledge is doubling every 10 to 20 years" (p. 80). Wriston notes that more than ever before, business relies on the talents and intellectual capital of its people.

In the workplace, teams represent one of the best vehicles for knowledge to develop into creative ideas that are put into action. The popular image of the solitary genius might be more myth than fact, because knowledge grows best where it can be supported and exchanged.

At Unisys Corp. in Pueblo, Colorado, where three-fourths of the highly educated workforce participates in self-directed teams, sharing ideas is key to constant-improvement efforts. On-site video conferencing enables teams to meet instantly with their customers, as needed, to share information and collaborate on issues. And old-fashioned conversation has its place, too: Melvin R. Murray, the plant manager, conducts "all-hands chats" with each employee ten times a year, and every other week he meets with groups of fifteen to twenty employees for informal information exchanges. Murray is the first to admit he has a tendency to "go overboard" with communication, but his commitment to sharing knowledge and information is working well: team members' ideas have helped this

Unisys operation achieve the reputation of being one of the ten best plants in America (Miller, 1993).

In the face of a knowledge explosion, how does a leader respond? Wriston writes, "The job of the manager today is very simple and very difficult: to find the best people you can, motivate them to do the job, and allow them to do it their own way" (1990, p. 80). In a word, this means *empowerment*.

Change Force 2: Do It Faster — Much Faster

Doing things faster applies not only to how quickly we take new ideas to market but also to how quickly we accomplish our internal processes and how promptly we respond to our customers. Sylvia Nasar, for example, has demonstrated that high-tech products going to market on budget but six months late will earn 33 percent less profit over five years than products going out on time but 50 percent over budget (Nasar, 1987). In their book *Competing Against Time*, George Stalk and Thomas M. Hout (1990) demonstrate how organizations that focus on speed (such as Wal-Mart, Atlas Door, Citicorp, and Thomasville) are able to outperform others in their industry significantly.

Oustanding examples of reductions in cycle time are everywhere:

- VF Corporation, a Fortune 500 company and producer of Lee Jeans, among other products, has reduced its manufacturing cycle time by 40 percent (Faltermayer, 1993).

- At Edy's Grand Ice Cream, with a total workforce organized around empowered teams, cycle time has been cut by 66 percent (Kirker, 1993).

- Air Products and Chemicals Inc., a manufacturer of polymer emulsions, has reduced the product development cycle at its plant in South Brunswick, New Jersey, from five years to nine to ten months (Benson, 1992).

- At our own company, Development Dimensions International (DDI), we're reducing the cycle time on new training system development by 50 percent, thanks to greater customer involvement and an empowered team approach.

CHANGE FORCE 3: IF IT's GOOD ENOUGH, MAKE IT BETTER ANYWAY

The elusive search for quality continues to be a major force for organizational change and a requirement for future competitiveness. Anyone who wants to talk about serious change should visit or read about those organizations that have won the Malcolm Baldrige National Quality Award or those that are in the process of applying for ISO 9000 (an internationally accepted quality standard that is now required to do business in Europe). At these companies, it definitely isn't business as usual.

Perhaps one of the strongest themes in quality is the concept of continuous improvement. We have shifted from a mindset of "If it ain't broke, don't fix it" to "If it ain't broke, fix it anyway." It is important to note that continuous improvement is not a top-down strategy; *everyone* in an organization must work at coming up with new ways to implement quality-improvement ideas every day. Dedication to quality must become an integral part of everyone's job, not an extracurricular activity.

The gains from strong and persistent quality efforts are impressive. An excellent example involves the 2,000 team members at Exxon's Baytown, Texas, chemical facility, who generate an average of 12 improvement ideas per person annually. This translates into an incredible 24,000 improvement ideas a year, many of which have contributed to significant results ranging from a six-sigma lead process capability to radical reductions in toxic waste emissions (Sheridan, 1993a). Similarly, at Honeywell, focused factory teams were able to significantly reduce internal defects and reduce warranty-related problems (Sheridan, 1993b).

CHANGE FORCE 4: ONE SIZE DOES NOT FIT ALL

Consumers have begun to develop highly individual preferences. The "one-size-fits-all" approach is disappearing rapidly, giving way to product variety—or its close cousin, total customization—in order to meet customer requirements.

In the past, banks used to offer services we could count on one hand; now some banks offer more than 100 different types of accounts (Noyelle, 1989). As another example of increased product variety, the number of items on typical supermarket shelves has skyrocketed in the last decade from 12,000 to 24,000. Recently, one of the authors visited a local grocery store and counted the number of different kinds of toothpaste (size, type of tube, brand, flavor, and so on). In all, there were fifty-three: travel sizes, stand-up tubes, baking soda brands, and even a kids' fruit punch flavor—with sparkles.

Some groups have moved to individual customer customization rather than mass market varieties. The Japanese and Italians, for instance, are putting the finishing touches on a system that will allow for individual upholstery orders differing in fabric, style, and size—all through electronic order systems (Berger, 1989). And the Japanese recently envisioned a system for producing cars that will allow individual preferences in sound systems, panel shapes, and lighting and seating styles through a networked CAD/CAM system that will deliver the vehicle in three days (Hall and Tonkin, 1990). Obviously, such changes have a considerable influence on how we manufacture and launch new products. A custom-designed car that can be produced in only three days is a long way from the Model-T concept: "You can have a car in any color you want as long as it's black."

CHANGE FORCE 5: MAKE IT CHEAPER

As we strive to improve our flexibility, speed, and quality, we still must pay attention to what remains one of the world's most important competitive measures: productivity. Customers not only demand products and services quickly and with impeccable quality; they also want them to be less expensive—or, to use a relatively new term, "value priced." Richard Rippe, Prudential Securities' chief economist, commented in a review of 1993's Fortune 500 companies that he's never seen a time when companies were more determined to control costs

(Faltermayer, 1993). Examples abound: consumers, no longer willing to pay the premium on famous OshKosh children's clothing, have forced the Wisconsin manufacturer to slash prices by 8 percent; and Compaq Corporation, faced with a highly competitive market, is lowering its PC costs by 23 percent (Kirker, 1993).

Other examples of dramatic productivity and cost improvements pop up every day. Varian Associates, Inc., at its Oncology Systems unit in Palo Alto, California, produces complex medical radiotherapy accelerators that are used around the world to treat nearly 73,500 cancer patients daily. J. Tracy O'Rourke, CEO, and Jim Younkin, manufacturing manager, both are committed to a culture of empowerment and continuous improvement. Focusing on the long-term nature of the change process, O'Rourke notes that "the sheer speed of change in our business makes it impractical for one person to make all the decisions needed to be competitive. Individuals must step forward in situations that call for their specific mix of skills and judgments." To achieve its objectives, Varian organized into self-directed work teams. The strategy has paid off not only with impressive gains in speed and quality but also with a 22 percent decrease in manufacturing costs over the past five years (Teresko, 1992, pp. 55–56).

Chrysler's Neon design team set some stringent speed, quality, and cost goals. From concept to production, the new car was launched in a little more than three years, shaving a year or two off normal U.S. model development time. As evidenced by supplier partnerships, benchmarking, and internal continuous improvement efforts, there is a strong quality ethic. (For example, the car carries dual airbags as standard equipment.) But quality alone isn't enough to compete. Chrysler is taking the car to market for production costs that are $500 *less* than any competing model, giving Chrysler some pricing room and the ability to realize a reasonable profit. The total budget for the ramp-up is $1.3 billion, a fraction of the $6 billion, six-year GM Saturn project. An important key to success is—and will be—the workforce. With cooperation from the United Auto Workers, ninety workers were employed to help assemble the prototype. So far, these individuals have suggested more than 4,000 changes to improve productivity and quality.

CHANGE FORCE 6: WE'RE DIFFERENT THAN WE USED TO BE

The forces shaping organizational change aren't confined to the economic and business climate alone; they also reflect changes occurring within the workforce itself. If we look around our own workplaces (and the world at large), we see a generation of people asking for—no, demanding—a far different approach to work than ever before. This means that companies hoping to compete successfully in the future will recognize that their employees' needs for challenge, respect for individual rights, entrepreneurship, trust, and democratic decision making reside not only at home but in the workplace as well.

As Walter Wriston points out, "Intellectual capital will go where it is wanted and stay where it is well treated. It cannot be driven; it can only be attracted" (Webber, 1993, p. 27). In *The Ultimate Advantage: Creating the High-Involvement Organization*, Edward E. Lawler (1992) goes so far as to say that it's the lack of synchrony between a democratic society and an autocratic workplace that has caused the high degree of labor strikes and litigation experienced in the United States.

Changing workforce values aren't confined to North America, of course. A recent European study showed that the younger European workforce—those workers from eighteen to thirty-four years old—places a far higher premium on values such as independence, imagination, respect, and responsibility than a comparable older sample. The same study shows increases over the past decade in the importance of values such as job interest, feelings of job achievement, and opportunities to use initiative (Harding, 1991). Even Japan, a country we all like to keep up with, is exploring ways to give its workforce more empowerment and accountability because of current economic conditions and changing workplace values (Neff, 1993).

THE RESPONSE TO CHANGE: TEAMS AND THE HIGH-INVOLVEMENT ORGANIZATION

A popular saying goes something like this: "If you keep doing what you're doing, you'll keep getting what you're getting." Given the enormous impact of the change forces on our organizations, we can't continue to conduct business as usual or, simply put, we soon won't have business to conduct.

Under current circumstances, hierarchical, autocratic, and functional organizations just don't work. Continuing changes in technology, market conditions, and internal processes require continuous learning, flexibility, and an almost fanatic dedication to continuous improvement on the part of the entire workforce.

We'll never increase our speed to market if we insist on ten, twelve, and yes, even sixteen layers of management in a 2,000-person manufacturing facility. Similarly, we'll never delight our customers when a front-line service person can't process a $10 refund without the approval of two people up the proverbial ladder (who in turn must refer to a 200-page policy manual to help guide their decisions). We'll never improve the quality of our products in a highly functional organization where work passes through twenty departments and then is scrapped by a special group of quality control inspectors.

A new workplace is emerging with an entirely new set of rules. The organizations referred to earlier, and thousands of others like them, have begun to make the dramatic changes essential to securing a promising future. While many different models are used to characterize this new workplace (Walton, 1985; Lawler, 1992; Peters, 1992), there emerges a strong central theme: organizations are shifting from autocratic, low-involvement, and low-commitment cultures to cultures that place a premium on empowerment and involving the workforce as true business partners.

One of the most prevalent and powerful paradigm shifts

we've seen in those organizations building new workplaces is the use of teams. In high-involvement organizations, teams are everywhere. Take, for example, Texas Instruments' Defense System and Electronic Group (DSEG), a 1992 Baldrige Award winner. The company's 15,000 employees belong to more than 1,900 active teams. Cross-functional teams are called together to solve customer problems. Product teams are formed to bring new technologies to market in record time. Self-directed, natural work teams are learning to take on more responsibility not only for the quantity and quality of their output but also for some leadership functions that formerly were performed by multiple layers of supervision. An equal dedication to the team concept can be seen throughout Tennessee Eastman Chemical, a division of Kodak and winner of the 1993 Baldrige Award.

Teams aren't merely departments or business groups. Rather, they're "a small number of people who are committed to a common purpose, performance goals, and an approach for which they hold themselves mutually accountable" (Katzenbach and Smith, 1993). Teams get the job done in a way that would be impossible for individual employees or managers, who are limited by their knowledge, skills, and resource bases. Imagine a single person reducing the development time of a new product by 50 percent. Impossible. But a team? It's been done dozens of times.

Although there are a lot of labels for teams, our experience with teams shows that they differ on three variables, which we call "the three P's." First, teams differ in terms of their *purpose* or mission. They might be natural teams that work together to produce a product or service, product development teams that are responsible for developing and launching new products, or quality improvement teams that solve tough customer problems. Second, teams differ in terms of their *permanence*. Natural work teams tend to work together on a day-to-day basis over an indefinite period of time, whereas a quality improvement team might meet twice a month, disbanding when the appropriate solution is found and implemented. Finally, teams differ in terms of the *power* they exercise. For example, a quality improvement team's responsibility might be limited to making recommendations to management about improving a process. On the other hand, a product development team might have a great deal of latitude, within specified time and budget constraints, in formulating a product they think best meets customer needs; they might also manage their own leadership functions, such as appraising and evaluating one another's performance.

SELF-DIRECTED TEAMS

Although the focus of this book is on leading one of the most powerful types of teams—self-directed teams (SDTs)—many of the concepts and tools you'll be reading about apply to all types of teams.

We define SDTs as groups of employees who are organized around a specific process, a product or service, or a group of customers. To varying degrees, team members work together to improve their processes, handle day-to-day problems, and plan and control their work. They're responsible not only for getting the work done but for sharing in the management of the team itself (Wellins, Byham, and Wilson, 1991).

At least three unique characteristics of an SDT distinguish it from other types of teams in more traditional organizational structures:

- Usually, SDTs are intact work groups of people who work together on a daily basis. In the vast majority of SDT implementations, a team assignment is long-term. (In terms of the three P's, there's a high degree of permanence.) However, as we'll see in the final chapter, members of a new type of team, called the *virtual team*, might work together on a day-to-day basis for a relatively short period of time, disband, and then be assigned to new teams.

- Often a company's move to SDTs requires a different way of organizing work—a shift from a functional, single-job orientation to a cross-functional, multiskilled orientation. Figure 2.1 shows the "before" and "after" of teams in a typical

Figure 2.1. Typical Manufacturing Facility Before and After Teams.

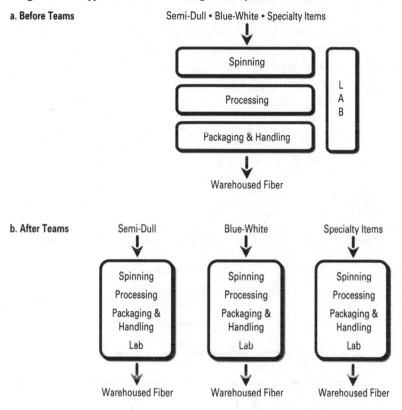

a. Before Teams   Semi-Dull • Blue-White • Specialty Items

Spinning

Processing

Packaging & Handling

L A B

Warehoused Fiber

b. After Teams   Semi-Dull   Blue-White   Specialty Items

Spinning
Processing
Packaging & Handling
Lab

Spinning
Processing
Packaging & Handling
Lab

Spinning
Processing
Packaging & Handling
Lab

Warehoused Fiber   Warehoused Fiber   Warehoused Fiber

manufacturing facility. In the case depicted here, people moved from jobs where they performed one function, regardless of the product they were producing, into teams that "owned" a particular product. Team members were expected to perform every function, including quality control and lab inspection tasks. Supervisors assumed other roles in the organization, ranging from team facilitators to technical experts. The manager became the "group leader," with responsibility for several teams.

Similar cross-functional designs have become prevalent in service organizations, such as insurance companies and hospitals. Before teams are implemented, work is functional; it's handed off from department to department. After teams are implemented, work is cross-functional; multiskilled associates are responsible for a particular product or group of customers. In the case illustrated in Figure 2.2, teams were organized to provide complete service to a geographic group of customers and the insurance agents who served them.

- An SDT is generally empowered to share various management and leadership functions, such as hiring, scheduling, budgeting, giving performance appraisals, and monitoring

Figure 2.2. Typical Insurance Company Before and After Teams.

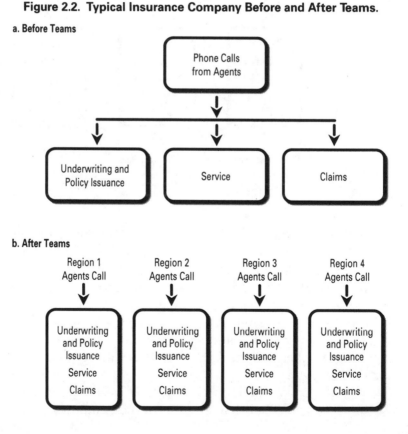

product or service quality. While the sharing of these tasks is by no means universal across teams or organizations, if many of the typical leadership responsibilities haven't been transferred to the team and if the roles and responsibilities of leaders haven't changed significantly, an organization probably isn't implementing SDTs.

In other words, self-directed teams require a complete transformation of the organizational culture. The list that follows contrasts the inner workings of an organization implementing SDTs with those of a more traditional organization. As this list shows, a move to self-directed teams requires a shift in systems and focus and, perhaps more important, in the roles of team members and team leaders.

Traditional Organizations	*Team-Based Organizations*
Information is tightly held and often confidential; it's available to and used by a select few within the organization.	Open information networks exist throughout the organization. Information sharing is seen as everyone's need and responsibility.
What the boss thinks and says drives performance. People are totally focused on what goes on inside the company.	What drives team performance is listening to and meeting the requirements of internal and external customers.
Work is organized around functions and departments. Common thinking is this: "What's mine is mine; what's yours is yours. Keep away from my turf."	Work is highly cross-functional, designed so that teams feel they own a customer or a product, not just a function or a specialty.
Power is retained by multiple layers of managers, who control the work of others while making all key decisions.	Responsibility and leadership are shared with those closest to the work.

Traditional Organizations	*Team-Based Organizations*
Jobs are narrowly defined. One person does one task and has very limited responsibility.	Jobs are defined more broadly. Multiskilling (where team members learn and perform several jobs) is common.
Rewards and recognition are based loosely on individual performance. It's the norm for managers to share in corporate financial success—but not others "down the ladder."	Rewards and recognition are shared and are based largely on organizational or team performance and on skill acquisition or application.
People's behavior and decisions are guided by rules, procedures, and policies.	Team behavior and decisions are guided by a strong and purposeful organizational vision, well-understood values, and clear accountability.
Quality control and improvement remain the responsibility of management or quality control experts.	Quality improvement is built into everyday work. It's everyone's responsibility and is practiced on a continuous basis.
The majority of work is accomplished by individuals who have little control over their work methods and processes.	The majority of work gets done in teams that have a great deal of latitude in deciding how to do their jobs in the best way.

MOVING TO SELF-DIRECTED TEAMS

The process of creating self-directed teams usually proceeds through four major phases—establishing the vision, designing the organizational structure, implementing the teams, and monitoring team efforts.

Vision.   The purpose of the visioning process is to identify the ideal future state of the organization. Typically, this effort is spearheaded by a steering committee composed of the top leaders in the organization, whose first step is to conduct an environment scan to assess market conditions, customer requirements, and competitive activity. Using this information, the steering committee reaches a consensus in four key areas:

- *Critical success factors* — key variables that will make or break the organization's future performance. In many consumer products companies, for instance, a critical success factor is "speed to market with new products."

- *Vision* — the direction in which the company is heading (and why that direction is important). This vision expresses the greatness toward which the organization strives and serves as a rallying point for all the organization's employees.

- *Mission* — the business the organization is in, as well as its goals.

- *Values* — how the vision will be achieved, including the attitudes, mindsets, and beliefs that affect how work is accomplished. Steering teams often work with all employees to reach consensus on the values and define "best practices" (specific behavioral expectations) for each of the values.

If it's determined that teams are an important mechanism for making the vision a reality, the steering committee might sponsor a readiness assessment to determine where the organization stands on key requirements for success with teams. Then, if the prospects for teams still look promising, the steering committee will define the parameters for implementing teams. Typical parameters include the scope and breadth of the initial implementation, "givens" in terms of how organizational systems can be changed, and any commitments about job security.

Design.   Once the direction and parameters are clear, it's necessary to develop a plan outlining the move from the current state to the ideal future state. Generally, this is the responsibility of a design team made up of members representing a diagonal slice of the organization, empowered by the steering committee to redesign the organization's structure and systems to create a high-performance/high-involvement culture.

Many design teams use a process called sociotechnical systems (STS) analysis to arrive at an optimal design. STS principles suggest that the organization's technical systems (layout, unit boundaries, and equipment arrangements) and social systems (hierarchy, roles, and empowerment) must be jointly optimized in the final design.

In the technical analysis, the design team maps out the organization's process, looking for variances and non–value-added activities (that is, activities that don't contribute to customer requirements or to the viability of the business). Once the non–value-added activities have been eliminated, the design team works to remove or control the key variances (that is, quality problems and errors or bottlenecks in the process).

The objective of the design team is to control variances as close as possible to their source and to ensure that team boundaries are drawn in such a way that each team controls all its own key variances. Consider, for example, the traditional manufacturing process, in which an out-of-spec part might be produced at a press because of temperature variation but not be caught or corrected until the part hits quality control. In a team-based organization, if temperature variation can't be controlled reliably at the press, the quality control function must reside within the team. This contributes to a design in which teams have maximum ownership over their own part of the business, significantly improved quality, and no frustration about inefficient hand-offs with other departments.

The goal of the social analysis is to ensure that the team design results in jobs that are motivating and rewarding for all members. Usually, the design team tackles this challenge by investigating the organization's current interaction and decision-making patterns, ultimately redesigning them for high performance and high involvement. Because decisions often are made dangerously far from where the work actually gets done, the design team creates an "empowerment schedule" to push decisions down to the lowest reasonable level. The empowerment schedule lists all the tasks and decisions that need to be made, as well as the specifics about when and how these tasks and decisions will be transferred to the teams.

The teams also need a mechanism or plan for handling their new responsibilities. One of the most popular approaches for sharing new leadership tasks is through a system of "star points." Leadership tasks are divided into several "points" of related responsibilities — one "point" might be responsible for coordinating the team's new training responsibilities, for example, and another "point" might manage all the quality tasks that the leader formerly handled for the team. Team members typically rotate through the points on the star so that all members learn the new tasks gradually over time. The benefit of this process is that it helps team members cover all their bases and become proficient at managing their own business.

Once the technical and social analyses have yielded an improved organizational design, the design team can move on to ensure that the systems are aligned to support the new structure. For example, information systems, facilities, compensation, and training must be redesigned to reinforce new behaviors and enable the teams and their leaders to be successful in the new configuration.

Implementation.   Most team efforts fail not in the planning or design phase, but in implementation. Teams mean change, and, for most of us, change represents a form of loss. In implementing teams, an organization must pay special attention to the needs and feelings of all those who will be involved. Constant communication will play a big role in successful implementations. Teams must get off to the right start by establishing their own charter. Training (usually lots of it) must be made available for both team members and their leaders.

Monitoring.   In our experience, no initial team implementation is perfect. An ethic of continuous improvement must be applied to the team concept from the very beginning. As the teams are being rolled out, the design team usually assumes responsibility for assessing the changing state of the organization against the ideal future state and suggests midcourse corrections. In some implementations, teams may be doing well; others may require additional support and facilitation. In addition, it's important to sponsor periodic renewal activities to celebrate progress and keep the organization focused on the original vision.

THE BOTTOM LINE

While representing little more than social experiments through the mid 1980s, SDTs have become one of the most viable strategies in the 1990s for building competitive organizations. In 1990 we conducted a survey revealing that 26 percent of North American companies use SDTs (Wellins and others, 1990). Not more than two years later, a similar study showed that the number had jumped to 35 percent (Gordon, 1992).

Is this another passing fad? We think not. SDTs will be around for a long time to come for two important reasons. *First, they work*:

- Self-directed teams at Westinghouse Electric Company in College Station, Texas, cut rework by 50 percent and reduced cycle time from twelve weeks to ten weeks (Wellins, Byham, and Dixon, forthcoming).

- Eastman Kodak Company's Customer Assistance Center teams in Rochester, New York, achieved a 100 percent improvement in service accuracy and doubled the number of calls handled per hour (Wellins, Byham, and Dixon, forthcoming).

- Wilson Golf Ball's Humbolt, Tennessee, plant teams helped productivity jump by more than 121 percent (McKenna, 1992).

- Hundreds of other organizations, including General Electric, Shenandoah Life Insurance, Motorola, Rank Xerox, and American Express, report dramatic gains in service, quality, and speed as the result of SDTs.

Second, they meet the needs of and mesh with the value systems of today's workforce. They provide a form of "turbo-empowerment" in which team members feel challenged, find their work meaningful, share in decision making, and develop a strong sense of identity with their organization and their customers. Overall, the trend is clearly toward increasing self-direction, as illustrated by the shift of tasks shown in Table 2.1. As teams become increasingly self-directed, important changes are required in the attitudes and behaviors of organizational leaders.

As this change occurs, there's a significant shift in task responsibilities for leaders with teams. Typically, teams assume responsibility for training others, managing daily operations, implementing process improvements, and keeping team records. Generally, leaders retain responsibility for rewarding the team, negotiating boundaries (in terms of expenses, time,

Table 2.1. Change in Percentage of Self-Directed Work Teams Responsible for Certain Tasks.

	1990 percentages	1992 percentages
Working with external customers	34	59
Setting performance targets	29	57
Budgeting	6	35
Training	33	55
Performance appraisals	17	37

Source: 1990 data, Wellins and others, 1990; 1992 data, Gordon, 1992.

and other resources), working on proactive plans for the team or the facility, and communicating the vision, mission, and values (George and Pavur, 1992).

A NEW ROLE FOR LEADERS

The degree of success we achieve in reinventing our organizations and successfully implementing teams depends on many factors, but perhaps none is as important as the transformation of leaders and leadership. To play by the new set of rules, especially those inherent in the self-directed team concept, requires considerable organizational change—change that won't happen unless it's championed by those who are "caught in the middle," our first-line leaders and middle managers. As organizations implement teams, these individuals must make a *personal* commitment to change.

The change isn't easy, but it's the challenge before us. As Kenneth Labich notes, "Managers are often directly on the firing line when a company begins experimenting with a new management method. They are asked to learn entirely new ways of behaving, and their worth to the company can suddenly depend on their ability or willingness to do something adults generally hate to do: change. The pressures can be intense, leading at times to a professional identity crisis" (Labich, 1989, p. 59).

It would be difficult enough to change decades of set values and behaviors in a *supportive* environment. Unfortunately, organizational empathy is often lacking, which makes the change process all the more difficult. According to *Fortune* magazine, "It's still open season on the American manager" (Dumaine, 1993, p. 80). Hardly a day passes without some former blue-chip company—such as GM, IBM, or Sears—dispatching another thousand or so employees to the corporate afterlife. In fact, the American Management Association recently revealed that, while managers make up only 5 percent of the workforce, they account for as much as 22 percent of the layoffs (1992).

SUMMARY

In spite of the difficulty of personal change, and in spite of the fact that organizations might be evolving toward high involvement faster than many leaders would like, thousands of leaders have begun a personal transformation — a transformation, as one manager tells us, from a "tyrannical, mean, and, shortly put, good-for-nothing leader to one who is empowering, trustworthy, dependable, and willing to stand behind the team."

In the next chapter, we'll look at the successful transformations of five leaders who had the courage and conviction to change.

THREE

Daring to Let Go: Stories of Leaders' Successful Transitions

The leadership transition isn't merely a matter of numbers and bottom-line results. It's also about profound personal change. It involves much more than acquiring new skills and competencies; leaders must learn to think and feel differently.

In this chapter, we tell the stories of five leaders' transformations. We look at how the leaders let go of deeply held attitudes and beliefs as they struggled to reconcile their expectations and experiences with the new realities of managing teams. We describe not just what happened but how it felt. As you'll see, these transitions represented periods of considerable introspection and personal growth for all five leaders.

CASE 1: SARAH

Milwaukee Insurance Group, Inc., recently celebrated its seventy-fifth anniversary. The company's primary business is property and casualty insurance, specialty lines coverage, and life insurance. It's grown from $2 million in premiums to more than $200 million in 1992, operating with 7,800 agents in seventeen states. The company now has almost 800 employees, with many organized into self-directed, natural work teams.

The culture at Milwaukee Insurance has always championed the values of people and leadership. Not surprisingly, Robert W. Doucette, who recently retired as president, echoes this sentiment. In his farewell letter published in the 1992 annual report, he said, "I have sincerely enjoyed the employees and agents that I have had the privilege to work with during my 47 years with the company. I have learned many things over the years. Most important, this experience has taught me that people, young or old, can respond to any challenge as long as it provides them with the support and leadership they need to use their talents most effectively" (p. 3).

Terri joined Milwaukee Insurance as a processor in 1985 and has worked for Sarah, her current manager, ever since. Rest assured, however, that Terri's early company loyalty wasn't inspired by Sarah's example. There were times not that long ago when Terri would pull her car into the company garage, see Sarah's car there, and experience a deep nauseous feeling in the pit of her stomach. There were even times when Terri wanted to turn around and go back home. Sarah, Terri told us, was "overpowering and demanding, with a total focus on getting policies out the door." According to Terri, Sarah was "unapproachable" and at times exploded into what Terri called "temper tantrums accompanied by throwing things at people." Sarah's boss described her as a "stereotypical autocrat."

Like Terri, Sarah has been with Milwaukee a long time—

more than fourteen years—having accepted a processing job right out of high school. She then advanced into a claims adjuster position and currently is a leader in the division that deals with specialty insurance for boats and with high-risk auto policies. Sarah describes herself as wearing two hats: she leads a team of policy processors and is also a work-flow process manager. In this second role, she's responsible for managing the entire policy-issuing process—from handling records to underwriting to processing and issuing policies.

Prior to the implementation of teams, Sarah thrived on the power and control that came with being a manager. Her style was to "do it my way or no way at all." As she looks back on her early years, Sarah recalls that words such as *tyrant* and *mean* were used to describe her. She vividly recalls her frustration when, despite her warning, employees continued to send stapled documents into a machine that automatically folded papers. Of course, this eventually jammed the machine. Sarah's solution was to call her employees into a room, throw stapled documents in their faces, and scream at them never to do it again. (Not quite as bad as the time she ripped the phones out of the wall because her subordinates were making too many personal calls!)

Sarah attributes her earlier style and behavior to a combination of factors. At the time, she felt pressured to focus almost exclusively on output, not people. In addition, Sarah enjoyed being the chief "problem solver"; she admits that she fostered a high degree of dependence in her people. As a new leader, she was set on proving herself. She felt the department belonged to her.

A few years after Sarah joined Milwaukee Insurance, the company started an ambitious quality improvement journey. A program called TCCP (for team operational efficiency, customer focus, cost containment, and technical proficiency) was established to initiate widespread participation through the use of teams. A second program, called Integrated Quality Management Systems (IQMS), also energized small teams of employees to evaluate and redesign by using support processes and systems (such as performance evaluations and bonus programs) to bring them more in sync with a total quality management (TQM) approach.

As time went on, Milwaukee Insurance began a natural transition to self-directed teams. In Sarah's department, teams began to assign their own work each day — a responsibility that used to be handled by Sarah. Team members also assumed responsibility for handling their own scheduling and dealing with interpersonal relationships and conflicts within the team. They cross-trained in the various processing tasks so that all team members were equipped to do each other's jobs. Recently, they implemented a new team-oriented appraisal system in which peer and self-appraisal constitute as much as 70 percent of the total evaluation.

This divestment of responsibility was a struggle for Sarah; she found it hard to let go. She enjoyed "calling the plays" and "knowing the next steps before anyone else." It didn't help that she felt that her employees were highly skeptical of her efforts to share responsibility as she was being trained and trying to change. According to Sarah, it took quite a while to demonstrate her sincerity. But the skepticism was two-way: she was uncertain whether her employees would accept new responsibilities. After all, they had learned to depend on her to assign and check their daily work.

In spite of her self-doubts and personal resistance to change, Sarah made a dramatic and successful transition. Why? Primarily because she finally realized that it was the best choice. The company was forging ahead with a new culture, and Sarah wanted to "march with the music." Over time, Sarah realized that she could trust her team members to do things with the same or higher work standards than she used to impose upon them. The work environment became less "me against you" and more "we're in this together."

You don't need to take Sarah's word, though, that the change has been a positive one. Terri sees the change as well. In Terri's words, "Sarah's made a 180-degree turn." According to Terri, Sarah has moved from being a punitive baby-sitter to a team coach. She has become more approachable and willing to help. She'll even roll up her sleeves and help with key punching and mailing if her team needs her. "She's become a better communicator," says Terri, "taking the time to keep the team informed." Sarah's boss has seen the change as well, describing her as "more of a coach, less hands-on, and willing to loosen the reins." The change is evident in Sarah's formal appraisal: input from her team is much more positive and consistent.

Sarah, of course, notices the change, too. She's far more relaxed at work. She refers to her team as a family; she watches over them while they watch over her. She feels that she's more open to risk taking, feedback, and new ideas. Instead of making all the decisions, she asks a lot more "what-if" questions. Recently, the organization asked Sarah to handle some of the work that was being done in the field. In the past, she would have demanded that her employees handle the increased load—period. However, this time she presented the request to the team to gauge their reactions (which turned out to be positive) and left it to them to find a way to handle the new responsibilities, while making it clear she was there to help.

Sarah admits she isn't perfect. Her toughest ongoing challenge is her "never-mind-I'll-do-it-myself" attitude. In other words, it's tempting for Sarah to want to jump in and solve problems or do a job herself. She's forever having to bite her tongue.

Sarah's advice to others making the change is to be open and flexible. After a while, she says, you can actually begin to have some fun. "If you go in with a positive attitude and are a bit laid back," she says, "you'll have a better chance of making things work." Sarah also realizes now that her new role provides her with *more*, not less, job security. Sarah knows that as Milwaukee Insurance continues to grow, the company will always need exceptional coaches.

Perhaps most important in all this change, however, are the feelings of Terri and other team associates at Milwaukee Insurance. Terri now loves going to work and views Sarah not only as a leader but also as a friend. That, perhaps, is among Sarah's greatest rewards.

CASE 2: JIM

Jim leads one of eight packaging plants that are part of International Paper's paperboard and packaging business. Not long ago, he made a difficult but successful transition from being a near-perfect autocrat to an effective coach.

Jim's interest in manufacturing might have come from his father, Bob, who worked for General Electric for thirty-nine years. Over the years, Bob learned a lot of lessons at GE, both as an assembly-line worker and as a manager. Perhaps Bob's most valuable lesson, however, was, in his own words, "that the guys in the factory can teach you an awful lot." It was a lesson Bob tried to teach his son early in his management career.

According to Jim, his father had been trying for years to tell him that most problems are management's fault; for the same number of years, Jim had argued with his father that the problems were the result of employees not caring enough about their jobs.

Jim's team of 130 employees manufactures paper cartons — up to ten million a day. (If you drink milk or juice, you've probably used an International Paper carton.) According to Jim, when he arrived at the company in 1984 "things were bad. By 1986, they only got worse." Costs were excessive, quality was substandard, and customers were upset. One senior manager called the place "a mess," and employees themselves admitted to widespread apathy. According to Jim, every day on the job was difficult. Considerable labor tension only added to the problems; the plant had two unions, and in 1986 one struck while the other crossed the line.

Jim reacted to his on-the-job stress with the leadership style he felt most comfortable with (and believed would work). According to Jan, a plate room operator, "Jim had absolutely no empathy for employees." His attitude was to "get it done at all costs." Dennis, another leader, remarked that "Jim used to go at the supervisors and pound on them, leaving them no choice but to do the same to others." Even Jim described himself as a boss "whose job it was to tell people what they were doing wrong." He added that the situation in the mid 1980s was a "war zone where the job and attitude of leaders was to keep the animals in line." Obviously, things needed to change.

Looking back, Jim says there were two catalysts for his decision to lead in a different way. First, in the mid 1980s, the company had begun a corporate-wide quality improvement process that stressed communication, involvement, and teamwork. Though there were difficulties at first, largely because of a bitter strike, the program eventually succeeded at building a culture based on trust and mutual respect. Second, Jim went through a personal experience that taught him a valuable lesson. One weekday he realized that in order to meet production goals, everyone would need to work overtime on Saturday. The employees resisted, not wanting to put in another stint of what was turning out to be a long stream of weekend work. Jim went into his "tyrant role," threatening to fire every employee who didn't show up. Guess what? No one showed up, and Jim couldn't fire everyone in the plant. For the first time, Jim realized that the employees were the ones who really controlled the plant—not the boss. He also came to the conclusion, somewhat sadly, that "rebellion was the only tool the workforce really had at its disposal to get the attention of bad managers."

Like many other leaders, Jim's initial reaction to high involvement and teams was skeptical. He viewed the change as "one more program to play" and was unconvinced that teams would work. Furthermore, he was worried about whether he would have the support he needed. After all, his past reward systems were "based on output and the number of people written up, not teamwork and quality." In fact, in the mid 1980s, Jim believed that others might think he was "kooky" if he believed in teams and joint problem solving.

Jim also feared the unknown. Even though the company had provided him with initial training, he could see that there was no cookbook approach to making a successful leadership transition. And, he worried that if the effort at corporate failed, a terrible work environment would get even worse.

In spite of these concerns, things did work out. International Paper's quality improvement process was a success not only at Jim's plant but throughout the corporation. The employees in Jim's plant began to evolve into natural, empowered work teams. Currently, they handle some of their own purchasing, the issuing of work orders for equipment, and scheduling. In 1989 there were eight quality control inspectors on the floor; today there are none. Team members often ask Jim for the keys to the company car so that they can visit a customer to listen, help, or solve problems.

Needless to say, this happy ending didn't just *happen*. Like anyone with ingrained habits, Jim struggles against relapse, waging a constant battle against his autocratic alter ego. For example, early in his career Jim thought that asking for help showed a weakness. He tended to want to jump right in with his own opinions and conclusions. Today he realizes that those closest to the day-to-day work more often than not are the ones with the "right" answers. For Jim, this realization has meant learning to seek and listen to the counsel of others and, perhaps most difficult of all, to reserve his own judgment.

Another battle Jim constantly fights occurs when he sees a production problem. Several times a week, Jim likes to go out on the floor to observe the production process. In the past, however, those floor visits were more like inquisitions. If he found something wrong (which, of course, was his objective), he would try his best to assign blame and take control of fixing the problem. Today, though, when Jim "manages by wandering around," he realizes that his job is to coach and encourage. On a recent plant tour, for example, Jim pointed out a carton-printing problem to a visitor. But instead of being annoyed, Jim described with pride how close the team members were to solving the problem.

Like all of us, Jim occasionally has an off day—a day when, for one reason or another, things just don't click. Jim has learned on those days to either pump himself up before a floor visit or sit on the sidelines, knowing full well the job will get done by the team.

Over time, Jim has learned to let go of the power he realizes he "never really had in the first place." Now he recognizes that he must trust his team and believes that they "really can do it better." In a very insightful statement, Jim explains that "the best thing about good leadership is that you don't always need to prove it."

The results speak for themselves. Scrap rate has dropped by more than 15 percent in the last three years, while labor productivity and throughput have improved significantly. Cost per ton produced has increased by less than 3 percent a year—one of the lowest increases among International Paper's packaging plants (or its competitors'). The two unions now work together with management and each other. Recently, they teamed up to develop a joint union logo that's used on a printed milk carton they proudly hand out to visitors; it describes the plant's history, purpose, and production process.

Jan and Dennis also see the change. Jan, the plate room operator, says she used to hate Jim and would go to work with the goal of making his life as miserable as possible. Today she feels the trust and spirit of "doing everything together." And Dennis sees an environment that's "more pleasant because of teamwork." One key change, Dennis notes, is that "people laugh a lot more today." Even Carol, Jim's spouse, has seen a positive change: "As Jim has learned to put his own ego aside, he's much more peaceful with himself."

One of the most interesting changes of all? Jim now writes to his father, sharing his experiences as a new type of leader. Now and then he even admits that he was wrong and his dad was right: everything wasn't the employees' fault after all!

CASE 3: PAT

Pat is a prominent manager at Cape Coral Hospital, a midsized facility in Florida. All the nurses and directors report to her, and she's widely recognized as being extremely competent in her job. In a typical day, she leads meetings, shares information, and makes decisions.

After following essentially the same routine for fifteen years, Pat found very little challenge in her job. She struggled with the fact that her work wasn't as enjoyable as it used to be. What's more, Pat had noticed that the routine nature of things had taken its toll on her staff as well. They had become dependent on her to make even the simplest of decisions. Frustrated because of the functional silos and boundaries built up in different areas of expertise, they relied on her to be the go-between. Furthermore, Pat was concerned that because her staff wasn't cross-trained, it was difficult to provide coverage during peak patient times.

Recently, Pat found herself at the helm of a hospital-wide transition to self-directed and patient-focused care teams. Through foresight and initiative, she introduced a culture change designed to restructure departmental barriers, empower managers and staff, improve technical and business knowledge, and move decision making to the staff responsible for delivering patient care. As a result of this culture change, Pat's work has become a rewarding challenge once again.

What was the catalyst for this culture change? In 1991 Pat and the top managers at the hospital took stock of their business. They found that because of changes in reimbursement policies, the hospital's profit margin had shrunk from 12 percent to 4 percent since 1981. In order to remain a viable business in the coming years, they decided that the work would have to be restructured to make patient care smoother and more efficient. They also realized that roles and responsibilities would need to change, so they decided to move to self-directed work teams.

Thus Care 2000 — the restructuring of patient-care delivery and staff roles and responsibilities — was born. The major drive of the vision was to establish staff members' and leaders' ownership of a care center and its patients. To do this, Care 2000 had to increase collaboration across fifty departments in the hospital and create seven reorganized business and care centers: three inpatient, one outpatient, one business center, one facility center, and one corporate services center.

The first major change for Pat was the move from director to coach. While this was a lateral move on the organizational chart, it was an improvement from Pat's point of view. According to Pat, "I would much rather be a coach to eighty people in a care center than a director of eight people in a traditional hierarchy. This gives me a chance to run a business and develop people."

Pat has been described by co-workers as someone who values the opinions of others; she's known for being fair and open to others' points of view. As a result, most people had become accustomed to approaching Pat directly with their problems — whether those problems involved patient concerns, family problems, or physician issues. They knew that Pat combined an empathetic approach with a can-do, take-action style of leadership. Because people were comfortable with Pat in her old role, they often went to her saying, "Tell me what I should do next."

Pat's challenge, given her strengths in the old role and her staff's reliance on her to solve their problems, was to find a balance between directing and empowering. Like most other managers making the transition from director to coach, Pat's behavior was inconsistent at first. For example, when working with an implementation team to prepare a hospital-wide communication event, Pat slipped into her old role by thinking, "My staff trusts me. I should be the one to deliver the communication." Even when her peers and staff expressed to her that they felt uninvolved and unempowered, Pat went ahead with her plan. She resorted to her old rule: when in doubt, take control.

In retrospect, Pat remembers many misconceptions about and many challenges in the move to empowered teams. "I thought it would be easier and that people would automatically see the benefits," she says. But that wasn't the case. Again and again, Pat had to produce data, examples, site-visit options, and conference calls with other hospitals where patient-focused care and empowerment were being handled successfully in order to provide validation for the work in Care 2000. Pat found that it took weeks for this information to sink in; then it took additional weeks of working together as a group before her staff finally realized that Pat wasn't going to jump in with all the answers. After several meetings at which she encouraged her staff to offer their ideas about restructuring and designing patient care, Pat could measure major changes in behavior and attitudes. She says, "It's fascinating to watch people blossom and take leadership where very little evidence of leadership skills existed before."

When people ask Pat's staff, peers, or boss what changes they see in her, smiles cross their faces. One of the directors reporting to Pat notes that Pat has learned to share the responsibilities of leadership. "Pat used to have a finger on just about everything: all the information, who was on first, and who was going out the door. In an eighty-six-bed hospital fifteen years ago, this was an easy thing to do. But today it's a different story. I think Pat has acclimated much better than most of the other care-center administrators, and my respect has grown even more for what Pat can do. She's given up a lot of different tasks, such as monitoring suppliers, reports, and meetings. Pat's really walking the talk."

At one point, when new beds were needed on the obstetrics unit, the implementation team approached the staff about developing a plan. The staff met, made decisions, and coordinated the move. In general, things went well, but several logistical details were overlooked. For example, phones and call bells weren't connected in time for the move because the staff hadn't involved Facilities Management early enough in the process. Pat says that "the benefit of having the staff learn the importance of cross-departmental coordination far outweighed the temporary inconvenience we encountered." Additionally, Pat notes that "what the staff learned from this experience will really 'stick,' because they learned it on their own."

When Pat is asked what it feels like to be in her new role as the care-center administrator, coach, and educator, she gives the following response: "The only thing I can say is that this stuff definitely works. The commitment has been great from the staff, and all we did was ask them to participate. They've really taken off with Care 2000. That enables me to focus on building our physician base and expanding our patient-care capabilities. This is the most challenging work I've done in fifteen years."

CASE 4: BART AND DIANE

Imagine working in a place where the air is permeated by the gentle smell of hops. Such is the life at the Miller Brewing Company in Ohio. The collegial impression is reinforced further by the campuslike setting: brick gates lead to a sprawling complex set among amber waves of grain. In the middle of this pastoral scene, people are hard at work producing millions of barrels of beer a year in a self-managed team environment.

The Trenton brewery began using the team concept when it opened in 1991. Today team members have responsibility for quality, safety, waste, housekeeping, and productivity. They also handle many personnel decisions, including selecting replacement technicians and team managers, scheduling overtime and vacations, and addressing performance issues. The technicians are represented by the United Auto Workers under an innovative labor agreement that replaces the traditional grievance process with an issue-resolution board.

With teams assuming so many important responsibilities, what's left for team managers to do? This is the story of two of Miller's team managers—what they do and how they feel about leading teams in a greenfield operation.

Ironically, Diane and Bart first met in 1980 at a premanagement supervisory training program Miller ran for three weeks in Milwaukee. After that, though, their careers took divergent paths. Diane rose through the ranks at one of Miller's can plants, moving up from Quality Control through supervision to arrive at a superintendent's position, in which she was responsible for half the plant. Bart also started out as a quality analyst, which he likened to "the quality police." "Their job was to run it; our job was to catch it," he says. Bart moved on to supervise Packaging and then Maintenance; finally, he was promoted to the position of maintenance engineer.

What motivated these two people, who were moving securely up the Miller ladder at opposite ends of the country, to apply for team manager jobs under this new concept being started up in Ohio? For Bart, it was his belief that teams represented the future for American industry, not just for Miller Brewing. He saw the change as a way to increase his "salability" for the future. Diane thought team management sounded like a perfect fit with her natural leadership style. In addition, it presented an opportunity for her to move from a can plant to a brewery. "After all," she says, "Miller isn't exactly known for manufacturing cans."

Diane and Bart were among the 30 team managers chosen for Trenton from the 300 who applied from Miller facilities all over the country. In the early days, each of the team managers took responsibility for one team on one shift. As the plant grew and extra lines were added, the managers' responsibilities expanded to encompass an entire business unit (all three shift teams in a particular area).

Bart is one of four team managers in the Core Maintenance Department in a system where there are also maintenance people on every production team. The maintenance technicians outside the core group actually run the equipment most of the time. That leaves the core maintenance group (thirteen mechanics and electricians) to handle peak demands and complex tasks that don't come up frequently enough on the production teams for their own maintenance team members to maintain their skills. The core group also handles common areas of the plant, such as the central chlorine system for the packaging lines and plant utilities. Originally, each of the maintenance team managers was responsible for one shift within the core group. But after six months, it became apparent that the core team was receiving mixed messages from the different managers, so they decided to reorganize. Now one of them manages the core group, and the other three serve as technical resources (to the brew house or the packaging lines, for instance).

Bart was the first to lead the core group. As he put it, "The technical resource role wasn't much of a departure from what I'd done in the past. I wanted to have experienced the challenge of managing and developing a team in this environment. That's what I came here to do."

And the environment *was* different. One major distinction was the element of trust. As Bart explained it, "In the other Miller plants, hourly employees couldn't be in the plants unless the boss was there with them, even if there really wasn't any work for the boss to do. So on the weekends, if two or three mechanics were there for a job, you had to be there, too, because no one trusted the employees to make the right decisions on their own. I had to lose a lot of the paradigms I came in with. For instance, 80 percent of what a line mechanic does, the operators can learn. I always kind of felt that way, but now I'm convinced."

Bart cited as an example the seamers in the Packaging Department (which are commonly viewed as among the most complex pieces of equipment in the plant). Four people came in on one weekend to repair the seaming levers, and only one was a mechanic. Not only did they repair the levers, but they finished "setting the seams"—something that at other breweries is done only by the most expert craftsman. "When I came in on Monday morning, the seams looked as good as I've ever seen them," explains Bart.

This was important to Bart because the core group was the closest thing to a traditional maintenance department Trenton had in the midst of the nontraditional culture they were trying to create. Bart also made a very early effort to establish a vision for the core group. "Most production people feel as if they're getting hosed by Maintenance; that Maintenance is a bunch of prima donnas." So Bart got the core group together to explain his expectations of a well-organized, customer-oriented maintenance group. He encouraged the group to envision what that would look like, and then he reinforced the vision with regular "fireside chats."

Bart's team members explain: "Bart gave a real sense of direction. Under him, the team always looked to get to a particular place. We always talked about purpose and *why* we did things."

The only times Bart got upset were when team members violated the vision. "The team used to kid me because I never showed any emotion in meetings." But there were times when Bart came down hard on team members. When one of the Packaging teams that hadn't used Core Maintenance very much called the core group to install some stainless steel piping, Bart saw a real opportunity to demonstrate good customer service. Because the job took too long and the work was poorly done, Bart confronted the team. He not only made team members fix the problem, but he took the time to reiterate that the core group was essentially a subcontractor—and needed to be the subcontractor of choice.

In addition to painting a vision for the core group, Bart wanted to help the group become self-managed. When the team members decided they needed an overtime policy, Bart encouraged *them* to develop it. He told the team that whatever policy they came up with had to meet two conditions: it had to allow them to satisfy customer needs, and the team had to view the new system as fair for everyone concerned.

Initially, the team decided on a traditional overtime system that involved charging everyone's hours. Bart didn't give this system much hope for success, but he remained silent, letting the team members draw their own conclusions. It wasn't long before the core group decided to try a different plan, in large part because the administration of this system had become a real burden. When the team approached Bart, he felt they were at the stage where they could learn more by working through the process themselves. So, he answered, "The path is more important than the result. You need to travel this road on your own."

Eventually, the team members learned that they didn't

need to track hours. As long as everyone had equal access to overtime, it didn't matter how many hours each person took. Now the overtime system is very simple, and the group administers it easily.

One of the team members elaborates on Bart's empowering style: "Bart never checked time and attendance. He just checked to make sure that the appropriate systems were in place." Another says, "Bart would come up to you and say, 'There's this problem.' Next thing you know, you were taking charge of the problem. At first I was a little scared, but I felt inspired. It was a challenge."

What's Bart doing now that the maintenance team is maturing? He says that he asks himself, "Overall, how well are they handling the vision?" and "What am I still doing that *they* could be doing?" "What supervisory responsibility do I still have that *they* could have?"

Meanwhile, back in Production, Diane is managing one of the packaging lines — three teams of seven people, one team on each shift. The interesting thing is that each of these teams is at a different stage of development. They all have different strengths and needs. One team works hard at making sound business decisions. Another is very focused on team issues, sometimes to the detriment of production. One team saves the sensitive issues for meetings Diane can attend. There is also a team that seems to need very specific direction in certain aspects of its responsibilities, while another needs lots of reinforcement.

How does Diane juggle three such different teams? "I have a master plan," she says, "for bringing them all up to the same level. Then I can help them all improve from there." Diane says that she focuses on one team's development at a time, and she refuses to allow team members to focus on shift production numbers; instead, she encourages them to focus on the line as a whole.

When Diane first started working with the teams, she spent a lot of time dealing with technical issues. She first became comfortable with the new technology herself, and then she helped the technicians, working alongside them on projects such as packer changes. Now she spends more time on team and individual development. "I attend a lot of the preshift meetings, and I try to sense when something's up," she explains. Diane's team members joke that she has extrasensory perception when it comes to team matters.

Diane also concentrates on coaching her teams to make better business decisions. One of her teams tells the story of the time team members were left with twenty-seven pallets of cans that had to be reworked as a result of a distribution mistake. They were so upset that they called Diane at home on a vacation day. Diane calmly listened to their concerns and then helped them think through the options, but she made it clear that the final decision was up to the team.

Unfortunately, Diane often works more than sixty hours a week. She views it as an investment in the teams' development. Although her team members marvel at her commitment, this schedule makes it hard for Diane to achieve much balance in her life. She jokes that her social life consists of two dogs with very strong bladders.

As Diane reflects on her job, she's pleased that every day she gets to do those things she liked most about her old job — primarily, managing an important segment of the business. Sometimes she worries that she's too specialized, focusing primarily on the development of the teams. And although she admits that this is what she does best, she occasionally misses the breadth of her old job (managing purchasing, scheduling, shipping, receiving, and even wastewater treatment). When asked if she regrets making the move, though, or if she would consider going back, she answers, "No. I like what I'm doing. I like the freedom and the feeling of building something from the ground up."

SUMMARY

All these leaders recount periods of doubt and concern. For most, it was a long and difficult transition; none of the transformations happened overnight. All five leaders found it particularly hard to let go and described the ongoing battle they still face to "let the team do it." But all of them have experienced moments of truth when teams have handled situations better than these leaders ever could have hoped. So in spite of the struggles, in the end they all say it was worth it.

In later chapters, we'll share the specific lessons these leaders learned as they worked their way through the phases of their teams' development.

FOUR

From Commander to Coach: A Model for the Evolving Role of the Leader

In an environment where we must have every good idea from every man and woman in the organization, we cannot afford management styles that suppress and intimidate. Whether we can convince and help these managers to change — recognizing how difficult that can be — or part company with them if they cannot will be the ultimate test of our commitment to the transformation of this company and will determine the future of the mutual trust and respect we are building. We know that without leaders who "walk the talk," all of our plans, promises, and dreams for the future are just that — talk [Welch and Hood, 1991].

We think this quote best summarizes what the changing role of the leader is all about. These particular words carry special meaning because they were not taken from a business book or a leadership speech; rather, they were part of a letter to shareholders contained in the first pages of General Electric's 1991 annual report. Written by Jack Welch, CEO, and Edward Hood, vice chairman, this message sent a strong signal to the entire business community: the dynamics of leadership style are no longer a taboo topic in the boardroom; instead, they're viewed by business leaders as vital to their economic success. What was considered a "soft" skill in the eighties is now being viewed as a "hard" skill—even by Welch, who used to be called Neutron Jack because of his autocratic style and propensity for eliminating people while leaving the buildings intact.

The previous chapter's case studies of transformational leaders—leaders who represent thousands of others facing similar challenges—reveal two common themes. First, leaders find themselves in the midst of dramatic changes in their own organizations. Not coincidentally, these changes are forcing a corresponding shift in their leadership paradigm. This new paradigm requires leaders to be more like coaches than commanders. Second, it's evident that the change, often difficult and slow in coming, must start from within. As Michael Taeger, vice president of operations for Curtis Screw Company, put it, "In moving to empowerment, leaders experience concerns and fear. I was able to accept it intellectually, but in my heart it hurt."

To help get through this change, leaders need a model of how their role evolves in a team environment. They need to know what new skills they must develop in order to succeed in their new organizational cultures.

Figure 4.1 shows how the role of a high-involvement leader changes over time. Level 1 represents the autocratic leader, rarely effective today in any work environment. Levels 2 and 3 represent the involving leader, best characterized by what is known as "participative management." Leaders at Levels 4 and 5 are truly high-involvement leaders; they share the leadership function with their teams, and team members are empowered to make decisions within established boundaries.

Figure 4.1. Five Levels of Leadership.

Autocratic Leadership
Level 1
Autocratic

Participative Leadership

Level 2
Central

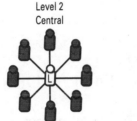

Level 3
Transitional

High-Involvement Leadership

Level 4
Partnering

Level 5
Highly Empowering

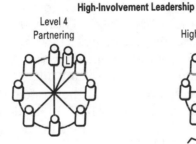

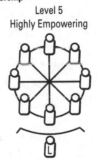

We find this figure particularly useful for two reasons. First, it reinforces a process of *evolution* rather than *revolution*. The leaders in our earlier case studies didn't change significantly in a week, a month, or even a year. Rather, the change was slow (and often painful) in coming. Second, the figure shows the relationship between the changing role of the leader and the changing role of the team. The "light space" in each circle represents leadership responsibility. As shown in Figure 4.1, the team member circles get "lighter" with the passage of time, indicating that team members are assuming more leadership responsibilities. Our belief is that the team and the leader need to be in sync as the organization progresses toward empowerment, because it's impossible to have truly empowered teams led by autocratic leaders. Similarly, it's difficult for empowering leaders to leverage their new style with highly resistant teams.

LEVEL 1:
THE AUTOCRATIC LEADER

Autocratic leaders are, for all practical purposes, becoming obsolete. They lead in a totally top-down style, with a heavy emphasis on command and control. Their focus is on getting the work done, no matter what it takes. They retain all authority and decision-making responsibility. They guard information, and communication flows in one direction only — downward. Employees function primarily as individuals rather than as teams and are expected to do what they're told; they have little control over what gets done or how it gets done.

This is where Sarah and Jim started in their careers at Milwaukee Insurance and International Paper. In fact, many of today's effective leaders were at Level 1 five to ten years ago. They were convinced that this approach to management was the right way to lead, and they were positively reinforced by their bosses for keeping on top of everything. Their workforce probably tolerated this style, and a handful of leaders might even have enjoyed it. In our interviews, autocrats were described as "stifling," "controlling," "tyrannical," "unapproachable"; they were generally said to have little time or empathy for those who worked for them. Several employees used the word *hate* to describe their feelings toward autocratic bosses.

We contend that the autocratic style of management,

which is no longer effective in most cases, is disappearing rapidly. Leaders trying to manage others by using this style find themselves, like dinosaurs, trying to survive in the context of new environmental realities. It's a style that simply doesn't produce long-term, consistent results, and the majority of the workforce will no longer put up with it.

LEVELS 2 AND 3:
THE PARTICIPATIVE LEADER

The majority of today's leaders fall into the participative leadership category characterized by Levels 2 and 3. They've recognized the need for change and have begun the necessary transformation. Participative leaders are still at the hub of the wheel, retaining the majority of decision-making responsibility. They take care of all team conflict, manage performance issues, and make key resource decisions. They still tend to get involved in the day-to-day work of their team members, assigning tasks, inspecting, and intervening when there are problems.

Participative leaders, however, are far different from their autocratic counterparts. They've begun to realize and feel the need to be more participative. As a result, they solicit input and ideas from their employees. (They still decide, however, if and how this input will be used.) They involve their employees on problem-solving teams and encourage them to make recommendations to improve the quality of the products and services they produce or deliver. Communication becomes more two-way, and open discussion and networking among team members begin to take place. Participative leaders are also more empathetic with their employees, realizing that participation and support can lead to better performance. At these two levels, leaders still focus their energy and attention primarily within rather than outside the teams, and they emphasize the task at hand rather than the development of people.

It's important to recognize that participative leaders, especially those at Level 2, are in a danger zone. At this level, many leaders simply stop moving forward; they've reached their comfort zone, and pushing further begins to feel painful. They're willing to share their base of power, but only to a point. "Who's *really* in charge?" is clearly a question in their minds. These leaders might think, "I don't mind asking for team members' ideas, but I'll still make the final decisions around here. After all, we don't want *them* to run the company."

Employees of leaders who've evolved to Levels 2 and 3 generally react positively, although somewhat skeptically, to changes in their work environment. They enjoy the sense of teamwork and collaboration, and while they still might not identify closely with their leaders, their mistrust and anger tend to dissipate. Two-way trust gradually increases as communication improves and information is shared.

Not surprisingly, though, employees often experience frustration at these stages. Enjoying their newfound taste of freedom, they sometimes stumble and fall as they try out new ideas and express increased initiative. Unfortunately, a great many of their ideas, while solicited, might be ignored, leading to a why-bother attitude. Many quality management programs end up stalled at these levels: employees lose interest because they're given the responsibility to come up with new ideas but have very little control over the implementation of their ideas; leaders fail to see the results they expected because they're too tied up with functional responsibilities, involvement in day-to-day activities, their own power base, and a belief that they still really do make the best decisions.

One last word of caution about participative leaders: many organizations confuse the participative leadership levels with the next two high-involvement levels. Too often, leaders consider themselves models of empowerment because they occasionally seek input from others and care, in a parental sense, about their employees. Pat, Bart, and Diane all began their transitions from a naturally participative style, yet they still had a lot to learn.

The key to moving to the next phase of leadership is to view Levels 2 and 3 as a resting place. You've driven up the mountain as far as most people go; now it's time for the tough climb. From here you have to get out of your car and walk.

LEVELS 4 AND 5: THE HIGH-INVOLVEMENT LEADER

The last two leadership levels are the ones most applicable to self-directed teams. At these levels, leaders are truly facilitators and coaches. They've internalized the belief that those closest to the job and the customers can "do it the best," and this belief is reflected in their leadership behavior. These leaders not only seek input from others; they also develop others' talents, skills, and abilities.

Level 4 and 5 leaders work toward building a committed team rather than a collection of individuals. Their challenge is to inspire their teams to focus on constant improvement, not only in their operational performance but also within themselves. As shown in Figure 4.1, the team is highly networked, with strong communication and information exchanges, especially at Level 5. A key role for leaders is to ensure that information flows within the team and that the team has access to other teams, suppliers, and customers.

At these highest levels, the team members themselves are also evolving. They've accepted (and may even relish) the responsibility they now have for the quality of their products and services. They also share many of the responsibilities that used to reside solely with their supervisors and managers. They might be hiring new team members, handling team conflict, scheduling their own work, or developing their own business plans and budgets.

Although Levels 4 and 5 are similar, there are key differences revolving around the role of the leader. At Level 4, many organizations still retain a formal and permanent leader within the team, even though the role of the leader has changed significantly. There are still the final vestiges of someone being "in charge." In contrast, the Level 5 leader moves outside the team and serves almost as an adviser to the team. The team itself assumes the majority of leadership responsibilities. This is accomplished by dividing responsibilities among team members, having team members serve as the team leader on a rotating basis, or some combination of the two approaches.

At Level 5, the leader's span of control—perhaps a better term might be "span of developmental responsibility"—increases significantly. In some cases, a leader might work with several teams, not just one. As AT&T Operator Services moved toward work teams, for instance, leaders were assigned as many as sixty team members to coach, compared with the twelve they used to manage. In some organizations, Level 5 leaders are *virtual team leaders*, providing guidance to one or more teams for a short period of time and then moving on to new teams. For example, a Level 5 leader might be asked to devote six months to a new-product launch team and then move on to spend the next six months with a process re-engineering team.

What happens to leaders as their teams begin to take on more and more responsibility? For now, suffice it to say that leaders at Level 4 and especially at Level 5 usually assume more, not less, responsibility. As Pat admitted, inspiring dozens of people is a far greater challenge than controlling a few. Leaders move out of their fire-fighting roles to more proactive roles; they look ahead for new business opportunities, spend far more time with customers and suppliers, and manage cross-functional processes. As Michael Taeger explains, his new job is to be an internal consultant, to help promote change, and to provide ongoing support for his company's change effort.

As leaders at Levels 4 and 5 begin to feel more comfortable with their new roles, they begin to see real payoffs. Teams feel a sense of ownership and pride. Trust is high among team members and between the teams and their leaders. Decisions reflect shared organizational values, not mandated rules. And the leaders themselves—believe it or not—enjoy their new roles a great deal more than before. Ironically, giving up the need to control and make all-important decisions results in a newfound sense of freedom for empowering leaders. Ed Lamb, a customer service manager in GE's lighting division, helped to champion a move to self-directed work teams. As he put it, "The past five years have been the most challenging, but also the most rewarding. There is nothing like seeing teams grow and develop."

SUMMARY

Becoming a high-involvement leader is a whole new game, and playing a new game means mastering an entirely new set of skills and motivations, not to mention getting even better at basic tactical skills. In the next chapter, we examine the skills that leaders must learn—and consistently practice—as they become increasingly empowering.

FIVE

Becoming the High-Involvement Leader: Learning New Skills, Tapping New Motivations

Painting a conceptual picture of team leadership is one thing. Getting there is an entirely different matter, requiring a complex set of skills and behaviors. In addition, it requires a change in basic beliefs and values. As shown in our earlier case studies, this transformation generally is a gradual process that requires years of practice and personal growth.

For the past two decades, we have studied the changing role of leadership through job analyses in more than 100 high-involvement organizations. These job analyses have allowed us to identify the skills, behaviors, and motivations for these changing leadership positions through interviews, direct observation, and surveys. Our data base includes organizations from all over the world that are in the process of moving to teams—organizations such as Toyota, Colgate Palmolive, Chase Manhattan, Bausch & Lomb, Hannaford Brothers, Saturn, ICI, AutoEuropa, Hill's Pet Products, and A. O. Smith.

Our research shows some interesting differences in the skills and behaviors required for effective leadership in the seventies versus the nineties and beyond.

WALK BEFORE YOU RUN

One of the authors of this book was recently busy doing some yard work when he heard a young child start crying in the street. Alarmed, he ran to offer some help. The child, a close neighbor, had fallen from his new fifteen-speed bike. Other than a scrape or two on the bike, everything was all right. After the child had calmed down a bit, he explained what had happened: he had been trying to shift the gears to go uphill when he lost his balance and fell. As it turned out, his new "high-gizmo" bike was the first he had ever owned, except for one with training wheels. We can't help but wonder if this child had learned to ride a simpler bike first (a three-speed perhaps?), had developed his sense of balance, and had built up his leg muscles before having to worry about shifting the gears, might he have made it up the hill? If he had had more practice, and more confidence in his abilities on a more basic model, would he have been more successful with the challenges presented by the new bike?

What does this story have to do with team leadership? If you browse through the dozens of books published on the topic of leadership over the past two years alone, you'll see that they all propose radically new, dynamic roles. From "habits of highly effective leaders" to "leadership, an inner greatness" to "mastering the new role," everyone is talking about how leadership has changed.

No doubt it has. After all, that's a major proposition in this book as well. The danger, however, in focusing on change alone: it's easy to forget that the "basics" are just as important to high-involvement leadership as are the advanced skills. Leaders should learn how to communicate and coach before worrying about high-involvement leadership, just as one should learn how to ride a basic bike before worrying about which of fifteen gears to use. Jan Klein and Pam Posey put forth a similar proposition in an article entitled "Good Supervisors Are Good Supervisors — Anywhere." They conclude that "top-notch performers do their jobs in much the same way, regardless of the work system or their formal titles" and assert that "it's time to debunk the myth that new systems require new and different supervisors" (1986, pp. 125, 127).

We propose that high-involvement leaders need two fundamental sets of skills. The first set, called *tactical skills*, generally is sufficient for those leaders at Levels 2 and 3 who don't plan to go (or aren't allowed to go) any further on their empowerment journey. These skills must be mastered in order for participative leaders to be successful; they also serve as a basis for moving on to the higher leadership levels. In our analogy, these are the skills required to ride the three-speed bike. The second set of skills, *strategic skills*, becomes essential to leading in high-involvement, team-based organizations (Levels 4 and 5). In essence, these are the skills required to race ahead with a new fifteen-speed bike.

Leaders need both tactical skills and strategic skills to ensure organizational sucess in a high-involvement culture. Each set of skills is reviewed in more depth in the pages that follow. Then, at the end of this chapter, Tool 5.1 is provided to help you self-assess your leadership performance in each skill area.

TACTICAL SKILLS

Tactical skills are the fundamentals of day-to-day leadership. They are essential leadership skills in any type of organizational environment, whether traditional or empowered, and provide a solid foundation on which to build the strategic skills needed in a high-involvement organization.

COMMUNICATION

Effective communication, both oral and written, remains a key leadership responsibility. While today's leaders might not need to be first-class orators or write elegant prose, they must be able to communicate information and ideas to others in ways that are clear and effective.

Communication involves more than just ability, though. We need to consider a leader's willingness and motivation to communicate as well. While it's true that some leaders' communication skills are disastrous, the majority of communication problems aren't related to a lack of skill. Rather, problems occur most often when leaders don't recognize the importance of communicating relevant information and when they hold on to information as a source of power over employees. Effective leaders communicate information about company performance, updates on new technologies, and customer data, for example, knowing that sharing such information fosters effective team performance.

MANAGING THE PERFORMANCE OF OTHERS

Effective leadership involves knowing how to manage individual and team performance. On a regular basis, leaders need to work with team members to establish performance goals and boundaries, to evaluate performance, and to provide balanced feedback.

Managing the performance of others also involves the ability and willingness to handle occasional problems with team members who are having difficulty performing their jobs or who aren't "living" new organizational values, such as teamwork and collaboration. Handling problems, however, shouldn't be the most frequent role for leaders. After all, the majority of our workforce wants to do—and does—a good job. For this reason, most of a leader's time should be spent reinforcing strong performers, keeping them motivated, and directing energy and resources toward their development.

The ability to manage performance is critical in a high-involvement organization for two reasons. First, even companies with self-directed teams leave the resolution of difficult conflicts or disciplinary problems in the hands of their leaders, at least initially. Second, although many teams have begun to establish their own goals, evaluate their own performance, and handle their own disagreements, leaders must help team members develop these skills by modeling and coaching the appropriate behaviors in the first place.

ANALYSIS AND JUDGMENT

Analysis refers to a person's ability to gather relevant facts, organize the information in a meaningful fashion, and look for cause-and-effect relationships. A counterpart to analysis, *judgment* involves making logical and effective decisions based on the analysis conducted. More often than not, poor judgment is the result of poor analysis.

Leaders today need analysis and judgment skills more than ever before. For example, TQM is rooted in the principle that decisions must be based on factual data. A statistical approach to quality improvement depends on the ability of team leaders and team members to be junior mathematicians. Analysis is not, by any means, all quantitative; leaders must also know how to ask the right questions of their peers, customers, and team members. They must learn to assess team performance and make decisions to help a lost team get back on track. Analysis and judgment also play a key role in the initial stages of empowerment: knowing when to hang on and when to let go.

As leaders move away from day-to-day team activities to concerns outside the team, analysis and judgment become even more imperative. For example, a team leader at Laurentian Technology in Canada (a company that manages information processing and storage) was asked to lead an effort to prepare a business plan for an entirely new service area. The project required that the team leader, along with the team, explore new technologies and market opportunities to make sound investment decisions. Needless to say, strong analysis and judgment skills were critical to their success.

COACHING

Successful team leaders are noted for their ability to coach others. Constant change means constant opportunities for growth and for helping teams succeed. Yet many leaders mistakenly look at coaching as a response that occurs "after the fact"—a skill to be used when someone hasn't measured up to expectations or when something has gone wrong. While coaching for performance improvement is crucial, the majority of coaching should be proactive. This means that effective leaders coach *before* the fact, helping to ensure their team members' success.

For example, when one of our clients' design teams was scheduled to make a key formal presentation to senior managers, the team leader recognized an opportunity to help the team with what could have been a difficult presentation (especially since it was their first). Thanks to this experienced leader's help, the team's efforts were quite successful. Had the leader ignored this chance to coach for success, the project's success—and certainly the team's esteem—would have been jeopardized.

Those coaches who are most effective have a tremendous gift for balancing, listening, and offering support *without removing responsibility*. Unfortunately, many leaders who honestly think of themselves as good teachers try to solve problems for their associates instead of offering support to associates who solve problems for themselves.

CHAMPIONING CONTINUOUS IMPROVEMENT
AND EMPOWERMENT

"If it ain't broke, make it better anyway" has become the new watchword for competitive success. Responsibility for service excellence and product quality has moved from the domain of management to the domain of all employees. This means that a major role of the team leader is that of first fostering an environment that respects and encourages people's ideas and contributions and then ensuring that the team has the support and resources necessary to turn ideas into action.

This competency, like some of the others, reflects both a motivation and a skill. It's a *motivation* because unless leaders truly believe that those closest to the job and the customer are in the best position to make improvements, it's unlikely that they'll seek out their team's input. It's a *skill* because it requires constantly seeking out the ideas of others. It's easy to support a *good* idea, of course. It's much more difficult to react constructively to an idea that seems flawed. If the leader shows any sign of disinterest—let alone utters such comments as, "That won't work around here" or "We tried that before"—it could be years before a team member ever approaches that leader again. The best approach is to help the team realize the pros and cons of a particular idea by posing questions. A word of warning, however: many ideas that leaders think are flawed aren't! Teams have a way of making the most improbable solutions work.

Getting ideas on the table is only the first step, of course. The key to success is providing the support to ensure that team members take responsibility for turning their ideas into action. The leader's role then becomes one of a resource provider, coach, barrier-buster, and cheerleader—not the person who does the doing. The real sense of team satisfaction and job empowerment comes not from being listened to but from playing an instrumental role in making things happen.

STRATEGIC SKILLS

While the tactical skills provide the basis for effective day-to-day leadership, the strategic skills account for the differences between average, middle-of-the-road, participative managers with lingering autocratic tendencies and those who've mastered the ability to lead effectively in high-involvement, team-oriented environments. Because the leadership of group or team performance is infinitely more complex than the direction of individual performance, strategic skills must be practiced well and consistently for leaders to move on to the fourth and fifth leadership levels.

LEADING THROUGH VISION AND VALUES

The terms *vision* and *values* are being used — and misused — by academics, politicians, and line managers alike to describe fundamental elements of effective leadership. While the concept of leading through vision and values is difficult to grasp and even more difficult to practice, it's essential to the success of team-based organizations.

In their research on leadership, Bennis and Nanus describe vision as something that "articulates a view of a realistic, credible, attractive future for the organization, a condition that is better in some important ways than what now exists" (1985, p. 89). James Collins, another expert in the area, is more down-to-earth: he likes to refer to vision as a "big, hairy, audacious goal" (Lee, 1993, p. 27).

Values, on the other hand, are the organization's basic precepts about its view of humanity, its role in society, what's important in both business and life, how business should be conducted, the way the world works, and what's to be held inviolate (Collins and Porras, 1991). Simply put, a vision is an end goal that helps paint a picture of where we want to go, while values help define the means by which we hope to achieve the vision.

If leaders focus on vision and values, will it really make a difference? Absolutely! In fact, new research recently conducted by James C. Collins and Jerry I. Porras demonstrates that visionary companies can outperform nonvisionary organizations by up to fifty-five times. How can this "touchy, feely stuff" help? No one explains it better than Robert Hess, CEO of Levi Strauss: "We always talked about the hard stuff and the soft stuff. The soft stuff was the company's commitment to our workforce, and the hard stuff was what really mattered: getting the parts out the door. What we've learned is that the soft stuff and hard stuff are becoming increasingly intertwined. A company's values — what it stands for, what its people believe in — are crucial to its competitive process. Indeed, values drive the business" (Howard, 1992, p. 135).

Frequently, leaders actually get involved in helping their organizations determine their vision and values, especially in start-up operations or at the beginning of a widespread team implementation. Far more important, however, is the role leaders must play in turning a fancy laminated index card, emblazoned with the organization's vision and values, into reality. This process starts with leaders' modeling the values themselves. Imagine the impact on every team member when the manager of a Corning plant helped shatter thousands of dollars of glass tubing that didn't meet customer specs. There was little doubt in anyone's mind that meeting customer needs and product quality were key organizational values.

But leaders' roles don't stop with modeling. Leaders must help each team member see and feel the relationship between the organization's vision and values and his or her own individual desires and goals. Leaders need to keep the organization's vision and values in the forefront of every team decision and action. Vision and values (not voluminous policy manuals) must be the beacons that guide day-to-day team behavior.

In their new book, *Reengineering the Corporation*, Michael Hammer and James Champy tell the story of a hotel doorman who immediately reimbursed a customer $150 for a radar device that supposedly had been lost in the hotel garage. The doorman didn't think twice, knowing he'd receive full management support (and the $150 back). The customer, who later found the device in his trunk, returned the money to the hotel with a note about the doorman's exceptional service. The customer, who will certainly stay with this hotel chain in the future, was a firsthand witness to the power of leading through vision and values (1993, p. 70).

BUILDING TRUST

While it's relatively simple to understand the practical importance of trust, trust can be difficult to achieve and very easy to violate. Take the case of Mike Walsh, a past CEO of Union Pacific Railroad, who focused the first ten months of his job on building an open relationship with more than 10,000 employees through "small-talk" sessions. Four months into his job, Walsh learned about a disturbing event: local leaders at one site had called a group of employees together for what was billed as a "safety meeting." Upon arrival, the employees were searched for drugs. Walsh flew to the site immediately, held another town talk, and apologized for what had happened. While there, he also learned about some safety issues in the "bunk carts" (where employees lived). With his managers' help, he immediately took care of the problems. The message was clear: let's begin to care about one another; let's begin to trust one another (Webber, 1993).

What leadership behaviors engender trust? The first is to "know thyself." Team leaders and managers must truly believe that the team will make the right decisions and that team members want to give it their best. In his new book on leading in a team environment, Kim Fisher relates a conversation with a Monsanto manager who told him that "the difference between successful and unsuccessful team leaders was more in what they thought than in what they did" (1993, p. 81). This isn't to imply that actions don't matter; rather, it affirms that if leaders truly believe in the value of their teams, the actions will follow naturally.

The second key trust-engendering behavior is a willingness to disclose information. It's always disturbing to employees when they sense that their leaders aren't telling them what they really think or feel. The more leaders share information with their teams, and the more they encourage employees to speak up without fear of retribution, the greater the bond of trust.

The third key trust ingredient is "walking the talk." Nothing violates trust more than saying one thing and doing another. In fact, leaders are better off saying nothing at all. They're particularly vulnerable when they talk about their belief in teams and high-involvement management and then continue to behave in autocratic ways. In his book *Leadership:*

The Inner Side of Greatness, Koestenbaum clearly describes the difference between thought and deed: "Truth is action. Truth is not what you say, but what you do" (1991, p. 191).

FACILITATING TEAM PERFORMANCE

Recently, we observed a team meeting at a consumer products company that's moving to self-directed teams but currently retains formal team leadership positions. At this particular meeting, the leader was supposed to facilitate, not direct or control. But the meeting, which revolved around overtime and housekeeping issues, was a disaster. Although the leader was far from autocratic, there was no agenda or clear group process, several team members refused to participate, and many individual contributions weren't even recognized. In discussing this meeting with the human resource manager, the leader said he thought a big part of the problem was that the company expected the supervisors who were becoming team leaders suddenly to manage their responsibilities through teamwork and meetings—but no one had provided the necessary training. The new team leaders knew *what* they were supposed to do but not *how* to do it.

Facilitating team performance, of course, is far more complex than simply managing meetings effectively, although it's often an important first step. Leaders must help get teams off to the right start by ensuring that team members have a strong sense of purpose, challenging goals, and clear boundaries and operating guidelines. Effective leaders also help tie the goals of an individual team to the overall vision of the organization. And finally, they keep the team going—perhaps the most challenging skill of all. Good team leaders know when to offer support and when to let go; they're masters at keeping the team motivated and challenged, and they're able to get the team back on course when it has stagnated or is experiencing internal conflict.

Leaders must also be proficient at recognizing ineffective patterns of interaction and decision making in their teams and know how to intervene in a way that builds the team's skills rather than causing team members to become dependent on the leader. Some leaders are so skillful at facilitating that their interventions are barely noticeable. This ability earned one of our clients the nickname Stealth Facilitator.

FACILITATING LEARNING

Bill Walsh ranks as one of football's coaching legends. During his career, his superb leadership skills helped turn Stanford University players and the San Francisco 49ers into winning teams. In a recent interview with *Harvard Business Review*, Walsh points out many of the similarities between successful business organizations and successful professional teams. "Management today," says Walsh, "recognizes that to have a winning organization, it has to be more knowledgeable and competent in dealing with and developing people. This is the most fundamental challenge" (Rapasort, 1993, p. 112).

Like all good coaches, Walsh recognizes that winning the game isn't as important as consistently winning season after season; he knows that continuously developing players' skills and refining their approach is the key to success. A winning team respects the needs of its members and is committed to helping team members develop.

Helping people learn and develop is essential to a high-involvement team, whether in a corporate boardroom or on a football field. With the move to empowered teams, individuals have more responsibility for "running the business." They may be expected to cross-train, learning a whole range of new jobs. Team members are expected to know their customers and continually explore ways to meet customers' needs better and faster. They're also expected to learn leadership skills, such as training others, making hiring decisions, and giving performance feedback. Sharing job and decision-making responsibilities must rest on a foundation of learning, development, and growth.

The critical job of team leaders, then, is to create an environment and culture that support learning and growth. David Garvin, who's studied the role of management in a learning organization, puts it like this: "There must be time for reflection and analysis, to think about strategic plans, dissect customer needs, assess current work systems, and invent new products. Learning is difficult when employees are harried or rushed; it tends to be driven out by the pressures of the moment. Beyond a doubt, organizations and their leaders need to increase the time their teams spend on learning—inside the classroom and out" (1993, p. 91).

Of course, it's more than just the amount of time devoted to learning; it's also the approach. In an article on the new "nonmanagers," Brian Dumaine talks about the Socratic approach: "An old-school manager often told people what to do, how to do it, and when. A new-style manager asks the questions that will get people to solve problems and make decisions on their own" (1993, p. 82). Today effective coaching discussions are marked by leaders' *how*, *what*, and *why* questions rather than by such statements as, "That's a crazy idea" or "It won't work around here." The major advantage of this approach, of course, is that team members learn underlying critical-thinking skills that they can apply to other situations. As Charles Manz and Henry Sims point out in their book *Superleadership*, the outstanding high-involvement leaders are the ones who use their skills to teach others to lead themselves (1989).

A final element in facilitating learning relates to the culture that leaders create within teams and the organization as a whole. This concept is highlighted in *The Fifth Discipline*, by Peter Senge. According to Senge, leaders must "work relentlessly to foster a climate in which the principles of mastery are practiced in daily life. That means building an organization where it is safe for people to create visions, where inquiry and commitment to the truth are the norm and where challenging the status quo is expected" (1992, p. 172).

Facilitating learning means building a culture where risk taking is encouraged, failure is seen as a positive learning experience, and people are open to others' input, thoughts, and ideas.

BUILDING BUSINESS PARTNERSHIPS

At International Paper's Philadelphia packaging plant, team members are assigned to key customers. Their job is to get to know the customers, find out what their needs and expectations are, and ensure that their needs are met. To carry out this part of their job successfully, team members must go beyond teamwork by forming partnerships with their customers, other plant team members, suppliers, and the company's sales division. At International Paper, forging internal and external alliances to accomplish business goals has become the rule, not the exception, in doing business. The concept of building partnerships has moved from the exclusive domain of the boardroom right down to the floor.

The complexity of today's work world means that we do very little alone. Team members must interact with one another and with members of other teams. Functional silos are being replaced by teams that manage cross-functional processes. And with a move toward higher spans of control, employees must take the initiative to obtain the information and resources they need to get the job done without having to go up and down the organizational ladder.

Like the other strategic skills, building business partnerships involves both skill and motivation. Team leaders must begin by giving up some deeply ingrained beliefs that their success and job security depend on how well they protect their turf. Leaders must look outward and realize that their turf isn't their own department or team but is the entire organization and the organization's customer base. They must also give up another deeply ingrained belief: that they're in competition with their peers and that making someone else look bad makes them look good.

Like electricity, partnerships can act as a powerful source of energy for an organization. Initially, new teams tend to be rather internally focused, concerned with getting the work done, learning new job skills, and sharing leadership responsibilities. At this stage, team leaders need to act as a conduit of energy to and from other parts of the organization. They need to spend time developing partnerships with customers, suppliers, and other teams in order to maximize the effectiveness of their teams and the entire organization.

As teams mature, an even more important leadership role in building partnerships is to install "outlets" for the team—coaching them to form their own partnerships. This can mean helping team members tear down the visible and invisible walls that separate them from other teams. For a company such as General Electric, this means encouraging a group of team members to hop on a transport plane to visit a key customer. For Serta, a leading mattress manufacturer, it means encouraging an operator to work closely with a supplier in developing a new piece of equipment. For Laurentian Technology, it means linking up team members with hardware suppliers to make purchase recommendations on hundreds of thousands of dollars' worth of equipment.

SUMMARY

The job of the high-involvement team leader can take years to master. From effective coaching to building trust, successful team leaders must put their own drive for continuous improvement into high gear. To determine your own skill profile, use the checklist in Tool 5.1 to gauge your strengths and developmental needs. As we'll see in Part Two, strategic skills enhance tactical skills, and both sets of skills become an essential part of helping teams mature.

Tool 5.1. Self-Assessment for Leadership Skills.

TACTICAL SKILLS

Communication

	Developmental
Strength	*Need*
☐	☐

Orally expresses ideas effectively in individual and group situations, adjusting the complexity and tone of the message to the needs of the audience.

☐ ☐ Ensures that team members get the information and data they need to perform their jobs effectively.

Managing the Performance of Others

Developmental
Strength   *Need*

☐ ☐ Helps gather and give feedback that guides and motivates team member performance.

☐ ☐ Helps the team and team members establish realistic performance expectations.

☐ ☐ Reinforces, recognizes, and celebrates positive accomplishments and performance.

Analysis and Judgment

Developmental
Strength   *Need*

☐ ☐ Through probing and questioning, seeks out information that identifies underlying problems and opportunities.

☐ ☐ Takes overall team and organizational views into account when making decisions.

☐ ☐ Reaches logical conclusions and makes decisions that usually have positive outcomes.

Coaching

Developmental
Strength   *Need*

☐ ☐ Actively seeks ideas and suggestions from team members for performance improvement.

☐ ☐ Collaboratively describes alternatives and builds on good ideas.

☐ ☐ Provides support without removing responsibility for actions.

☐ ☐ Offers time to discuss and share ideas in advance of events, situations, and opportunities to ensure successful performance.

Tool 5.1. Self-Assessment for Leadership Skills, Cont'd.

Championing Continuous Improvement and Empowerment

Strength | Developmental Need

☐ ☐ Allows team members to take reasonable risks, realizing and accepting the fact that not every idea will work out.

☐ ☐ Provides the necessary resources and tools to the team to allow team members to turn their ideas into action.

STRATEGIC SKILLS

Leading Through Vision and Values

Strength | Developmental Need

☐ ☐ Leads by example, consistently modeling the organization's values in everyday actions.

☐ ☐ Consistently helps shape team priorities and actions consistent with the organization's vision and values.

☐ ☐ Helps the team understand the what and why behind the organization's vision and values and connects those to the team's mission and goals.

☐ ☐ Takes time to consistently and frequently reinforce and recognize team members who behave in a manner consistent with the organization's values.

Building Trust

Strength | Developmental Need

☐ ☐ Honors commitments and personal contracts with others.

☐ ☐ Models trustworthy behavior. Is willing to discuss sensitive issues, admit errors, and take action when others aren't behaving in a trustworthy manner.

☐ ☐ Communicates openly and honestly. Doesn't send mixed or sugarcoated messages.

☐ ☐ Shares thoughts, feelings, and rationale.

Tool 5.1. Self-Assessment for Leadership Skills, Cont'd.

Facilitating Team Performance

Strength	Developmental Need	
☐	☐	Helps each team member understand the roles he or she plays and how those roles are linked with the goals of the team and organization.
☐	☐	Helps mature teams maintain performance through new challenges, developmental opportunities, and enhanced responsibilities.
☐	☐	Helps facilitate the team process by ensuring that all team members are heard, keeping meetings on course, helping reach consensus, summarizing actions, and so on.

Facilitating Learning

Strength	Developmental Need	
☐	☐	Helps the team and team members prepare development plans for both current and future responsibilities.
☐	☐	Establishes and encourages a "no-blame" environment so that teams can learn from events and processes that have run into difficulties.
☐	☐	Allows the time and resources for training and development on and off the job. Truly views development as worth as much time and effort as "getting the work done."

Building Business Partnerships

Strength	Developmental Need	
☐	☐	Encourages the team and team members to develop collaborative relationships with other teams, departments, managers, and internal customers.
☐	☐	Prevents the team from becoming isolated from the rest of the organization. Discourages actions that foster team elitism to the degree that it detracts from total organizational performance.
☐	☐	Always looks for ways to bring the "outside" in to the team. Encourages cross-team meetings, supplier/customer visits, and so on.

PART TWO

Making the Transition:
Getting and Giving
the Right Support

SIX

Beginning the Journey:
Assessing Where You Are

The leadership transition isn't unlike a white-water rafting trip we all took recently. Our guide for the trip spent quite a bit of time on shore describing the river and what to expect. He introduced us to all our safety equipment and then tried to convince us that we really would have fun. When we couldn't stall him with questions any longer, he marched us down to the river and insisted that we get in the water.

We've reached that point in the book: you're in the water! We've described the leader's new role, why it's important, and what it is—and isn't. Now it's time to show you how to paddle. In the second part of the book, we provide practical advice to leaders and their organizations on exactly how to succeed in this journey.

Throughout Part Two we write directly to "leaders," those of you who are first- and second-level supervisors; most of our suggestions are directed to this pivotal leadership level. We use the terms *manager* and *management* to refer to the top-level decision makers in an organization — those individuals to whom you, the team leaders, report.

In our experience, you and your teams will go through three distinct phases in the teams' implementation: preteams, new teams, and mature teams. This chapter describes each of these phases and provides a checklist to help you determine where you are in your implementation. The remainder of the book provides guidance about how you and your teams can advance through these phases successfully.

PRETEAM PHASE

The preteam phase begins when the organization first considers teams; it ends when teams are formally chartered and have held their first meeting. On average, this first phase can last anywhere from four to twelve months. At the beginning of the preteam phase, leaders and employees are holding their first discussions about empowered teams. By the end of this phase, everyone will have developed a clear vision of what teams can accomplish. In addition, the organization will have put into place a design for how teams will operate to turn the vision into a reality.

During the preteam phase, you might find yourself asking questions such as, "Will I have less influence than before?" "Will I work myself out of a job?" "Will I be forced to assume a less important role?" It's natural to focus on your personal concerns at this stage. In fact, almost everyone reacts this way. As you become more confident and comfortable with the new role, however, you'll find that you're able to expand your focus to help the teams with their concerns and development.

You're in the preteam phase of evolution if you're

- Becoming aware of the need to change.

- Completing an organizational readiness assessment to determine your organization's cultural strengths and developmental areas.

- Defining organizational values to drive behaviors toward a more empowered culture.

- Still not sure that teams will work.

- Responding to other skeptics who are wary of the team concept.

- Unsure about what your new role will be.

- Reconfiguring roles and responsibilities at all levels so that individuals have more decision-making ability.

- Redesigning departmental boundaries so that teams have ownership of their work and can control errors or variances within their own team boundaries.

- Focusing on your personal needs and role.

If six or more of these statements apply to you, you're probably in the preteam phase of evolution. Chapters Seven and Eight will be particularly helpful to you as you work through forming teams.

NEW-TEAM PHASE

The new-team phase begins with the first team meeting and ends approximately one year to eighteen months later. In the beginning of this phase, you'll spend a significant amount of time getting your teams started by developing a team purpose statement, goals, and clear roles and responsibilities. Shortly after start-up, you'll find yourself spending 40 to 60 percent of your time coaching team members to handle responsibilities that used to be routine parts of your old job, such as scheduling vacations, assigning daily tasks, and monitoring production. By the end of the new-team phase, you'll assume a few new tasks yourself. These responsibilities might range from increased involvement with budgeting to completing a market analysis for a particular segment of the business.

You're in the new-team phase of evolution if you're

- Helping team members work together within new boundaries.

- Transferring responsibilities to team members according to an empowerment schedule.

- Developing team goals in alignment with your organization's vision and values.

- Struggling to resist the temptation to slide back into the comfort of your old role, especially during crisis situations or technically complex problems.

- Spending 40 to 60 percent of your time coaching and developing team members.

- Seeing attitudes and behaviors becoming aligned with the team concept.

- Looking for more information to share with your teams about the business, customer complaints, profitability, and related matters.

- Focusing more on team needs and roles than on your own.

As a general rule of thumb, you're in the new-team phase if six or more of these items apply to you. Chapters Nine and Ten will be most helpful to you in moving successfully into the next phase: mature teams.

MATURE-TEAM PHASE

If your teams have been operating continuously for eighteen months or more and are handling most of their new responsibilities successfully, you're probably in the mature-team phase.

The key elements that distinguish mature teams from new teams are competency at handling new responsibilities, proficiency at solving interpersonal problems, willingness to continue working together, and ability to maintain predictable levels of high performance. If these elements aren't present, your teams haven't matriculated fully into the mature-team phase.

Many leaders in the mature-team phase begin to feel as if all their traditional responsibilities are being handled by the teams. Then what's left for a leader to do? Plenty! Not only does your coaching role continue as teams assume more complex tasks; your role also expands significantly as you spearhead special projects related to marketing, research and development, engineering, outside vendors, or multiple-department teams. Not only will such projects broaden your experience, but they will also increase your value to the organization.

In the new-team phase, your focus shifted from self to team. In the mature-team phase, your focus expands to include both the team and the organization. Your new responsibilities require you to keep one eye on maintaining your high-performance teams and the other eye on organization-wide projects. Unlike the other two phases, the mature-team phase has no ending point. That's because mature teams never stop developing. They're on the road of continuous improvement.

You're in the mature-team phase of evolution if you're

- Being more proactive, spending as much as 80 percent of your time on strategic customer or product/service improvements.
- Working with teams that generally handle their new responsibilities successfully.
- Coaching teams to assume more advanced responsibilities, such as budgeting, peer review, and salary increases.
- Watching your teams produce at peak levels.
- Maintaining quality levels at an all-time high.
- Noticing that doubts about the team concept have all but disappeared.

- Stretching to take on roles outside your department or facility.

You've made it to the mature-team phase if at least five of these items apply to you. Chapters Eleven and Twelve will help you maintain your high-performance teams.

SUMMARY

Leaders will find Chapters Seven (preteams), Nine (new teams), and Eleven (mature teams) particularly helpful because these chapters contain practical advice to help you navigate successfully through the phases. At the end of each chapter, special sections are devoted to the unique needs of leaders in support departments and unions.

Chapters Eight, Ten, and Twelve focus on the organizational support you will need in the three phases of evolution. These chapters are written primarily for managers who are in a position to coach and develop leaders of teams. For those who are considering the next step beyond self-directed teams, the final chapter focuses on the challenges of leading the teams of the future — virtual teams.

SEVEN

Preteam Leadership: Buying the Concept, Overcoming the Fear, and Starting the Change

Much of your success with teams will depend on what you and your organization do—or don't do—in the preteam phase. If you skip key steps for your teams, yourself, or your boss in this initial phase, you'll end up feeling uncomfortable and ineffective in the long run. If you follow these important steps, however, you'll be well on your way to working yourself into new challenges on the job—and perhaps the most rewarding opportunities you've ever had.

WHAT'S HAPPENING
IN THE ORGANIZATION?

At this early stage, leaders in your organization are making the case for change. Even though the decision has been made to move to teams, all the ramifications of that decision won't become clear for many months. It's unlikely, for example, that the organization knows exactly how leaders' roles will change before team boundaries are redefined and a final design is approved.

What should be clear, though, is the overall vision for teams—how far and how fast the organization intends to move down the empowerment continuum—and some compelling business reasons for the change. Companies choose to move to teams from a variety of different starting points. Some may be under the gun, using teams as a last-ditch effort to salvage efficiency and regain customer satisfaction. Others may be operating at all-time high quality and satisfaction levels but think they need teams to stay ahead of the pack.

Promega was in this second kind of situation. As a mid-sized biotechnological supplier experiencing a 40 percent growth rate, Promega's leaders anticipated an increasing need for the company's products. With such a high rate of growth, managers were concerned that the organizational structure would become overly bureaucratic, decreasing their ability to respond to market demands quickly. Having decided to convert to work teams, they used the preteam phase to begin creating awareness about how teamwork could serve as a competitive advantage in the areas of research and development, marketing, and production. Leaders quickly realized that collaborative work teams would maximize the sharing of knowledge, thus giving them an edge over traditional competitors using similar technology.

A large distilled beverage company made the case for change in a different way. When a manager asked his boss, "Why should we change? Aren't we fine the way we are?" his boss responded, "Our competition is coming out with new products over the next five years, and two of our product lines no longer will be in production. I envision that yours will be one of the two. What other motivation do you need?" A harsh question? Perhaps. But it spurred the manager to work on developing a plan to use teams in order to become more competitive in the future.

No matter where your organization starts in the preteam phase, the very thing you as a leader need to do is to understand—and, more important, *accept*—the business reasons behind the change. Once you personally accept what the organization is trying to do and why the change is critical to success, you'll be able to move on to determining how you can make the changes happen.

HOW LEADERS FEEL

Whether an organization is enjoying record growth or has large-scale improvements to make, it's natural that leaders feel concerned about the changes occurring in the preteam phase. Even leaders who are willing to make the change have fears about the implications of moving to teams. In our study of team leaders (George and Pavur, 1992), leaders expressed three major fears in the preteam phase: team members who would be unable to handle increased responsibility and decision making, not knowing how teams work or how to coach and develop them, and being held accountable for negative team performance.

FEAR 1: TEAM MEMBERS WON'T BE ABLE TO HANDLE INCREASED RESPONSIBILITY

In some cases, this fear is legitimate; in others, it's nothing more than a convenient excuse. It's also important to differentiate between an inability to handle increased responsibility and the lack of motivation to do so. We shouldn't be surprised if, after years of watching others in the organization be punished for taking risks or making mistakes, team members are reluctant to stick their necks out. But with support and encouragement, most employees will learn to welcome challenge and variety in their work. In fact, one Harris poll ("What Workers Want," 1988) showed that while 77 percent of employees want the freedom to decide how to do their own work and to participate in decisions, only 28 percent of employees feel they have it. Another point worth noting is that only 37 percent of the executives surveyed think their employees *want* more freedom.

In our years of diagnostic interviews in organizations making the move toward teams, we've noted a consistent, natural phenomenon: the tendency to blame other levels.

- Senior managers invariably point to first-line supervisors (whom they characterize as being irrationally resistant to change); they say employees want more responsibility but supervisors won't let it happen.

- Front-line leaders, on the other hand, fear their managers' inability to give up control and employees' unwillingness to accept more responsibility. Supervisors say they'd be willing to give up control but managers won't let it happen and employees aren't ready for it.

- Employees doubt the commitment of *all* levels of management.

The obvious observation here is that no group sees itself as part of the problem! So before you start doubting others, you might want to examine your own thinking. If employees aren't embracing their new responsibilities, you might want to ask yourself these questions:

- Have I given employees the big picture so that they can understand why they're making changes and why these changes are important?

- Have I helped employees develop the skills they need to tackle new tasks?

- Have I accepted the case for change myself?

FEAR 2: LEADERS DON'T KNOW HOW TEAMS WORK OR HOW TO COACH AND DEVELOP THEM

The fear of not knowing exactly what to do is particularly frightening if you've been rewarded for decades for being a tough, no-nonsense *manager*. Now your organization is telling you to be a *coach*—perhaps without adequate direction, advice, or models.

This happened to Robert, who'd always assumed he was a good coach. After all, he'd been coaching his son's Little League team for years. The kids seemed to like him, and he usually had winning seasons. Robert assumed that if he was a successful coach on the playing field, he must be a good coach at work, too. This false sense of confidence led Robert to bypass the training his company offered on coaching and developing teams. Instead, he approached his assigned team at work with the same kind of enthusiasm and pep talks that had fired up the Little Leaguers. When his motivational speeches didn't have the desired effect, Robert assumed that he must not have been peppy enough, so he doubled his efforts. He worked very hard to find creative ways to "inspire the troops." He bought everyone team sweatshirts, called impromptu "huddles" when a major customer complained, and even held a pep rally at the end of the first quarter. He was devastated when, at the end of the period, his team gave him low ratings on coaching. It took several meetings with his boss before Robert understood that what his team members wanted was help in developing their own ideas, not just a team barbecue.

In this example, Robert *thought* he understood teams—and didn't. In other cases, leaders are afraid because they know they *don't* understand how teams work. To confront the fear of not knowing how teams work, you need to develop a personal action plan to increase your knowledge about teams and your proficiency with coaching.

FEAR 3: LEADERS WILL BE HELD ACCOUNTABLE FOR NEGATIVE RESULTS

This third fear is essentially a fear about losing control. Many leaders fear that their teams will make all the decisions but that they themselves will be punished if those decisions don't pan out. This was evident at one government agency that had just announced a move to empowered teams, when one supervisor stood up in the announcement meeting and blurted out, "Oh great! *They're* responsible for the vacation schedule! And who do you suppose is going to be blamed when our overtime costs go up? Me, that's who!"

Luckily, such fears about loss of control and misplaced accountability are largely unfounded. While you might feel uncomfortable at first, most leaders of mature teams report that they have as much control as ever before. But it's a different type of control.

As leaders progress through their careers, the relationship between personal effort and control over results becomes increasingly remote. When we begin our careers as individual contributors, the assumption is that the harder we work, the better the results. This leads us to believe that we have *direct control* over our results. When we become leaders in a traditional culture, suddenly it's no longer possible to do everything ourselves; even if we work very hard, we can only partially influence departmental results. We can try to accomplish goals through others only by telling them what to do. This is a form of *control based on authority*.

When organizations attempt to create an empowering culture and we become leaders of teams, the relationship between our efforts and departmental results becomes even more distant. If we attempt to do everything ourselves, we end up with poor results and a weak, ineffective team. In the end, we accomplish our goals only by developing a shared vision and goals. This is *control based on commitment*. Adapting to this type of control is a hard adjustment for most leaders to make. Unfortunately, some of us never unlearn that early lesson: the only way to achieve results is to do the work ourselves.

Interestingly, much of the control that leaders felt as traditional managers probably was illusory. As one former supervisor from Tennessee Eastman put it, "I was kidding myself. I could issue commands, but my subordinates could always find creative avenues of passive resistance. Machines would mysteriously break down, tools or supplies would be unavailable, or the other person you needed to process an order was on his or her break." In the long run, it's more effective to rely on control based on *commitment* rather than control based on *authority*.

SKEPTICISM ABOUT
THE TEAM CONCEPT

According to Cummings and Huse (1989), there are two kinds of resistance: personal-level resistance and organizational-level resistance. *Personal-level resistance* refers to the fear that your existing skills and contributions may not be valued in the future and that you might have difficulty learning to function effectively in a team-based environment. *Organizational-level resistance* is caused by ingrained procedures, the cost of changing the status quo, fear of costly mistakes, and old-school behaviors that have been reinforced for decades.

The most common causes of resistance become apparent when you compare the comfort of the old role to the changes required in the new role. On a personal level, we see the following:

Old Role	*New Role*
Large knowledge base of how to do the job.	Lack of knowledge about next steps and how to get results through teams.
Very few new tasks or large-scale changes.	Need to learn technical process changes, redesigned jobs, leadership and culture-change skills.
Years spent building and maintaining the status quo.	Lack of involvement or history of investment in work teams.

Old Role	*New Role*
Low tolerance for change.	High tolerance for change.
"I'm successful as long as I keep doing what I've been doing.	"Will I have a job if I change what I'm doing? Will I have a job if I *don't* change?"

On an organizational level, the following differences often cause resistance:

Old Role	*New Role*
Decades of praise and rewards for old-school behaviors.	Little evidence of reinforcement for the new behaviors yet.
Decades of rigid steps to follow.	New procedures and steps that are less clear.
Many policies guiding acceptable behavior organization-wide.	More fluid policies and a strong set of values that allow leaders and team members more freedom to meet customers' needs and improve the quality of work life.

WHAT TO DO FOR YOURSELF

Don't make the mistake many other leaders have made in the transition to teams: focusing solely on team development and ignoring their own development. Before you can help your teams prepare to take on new responsibilities, you must prepare yourself.

You also need to understand clearly the vision for the team implementation. If you don't understand the vision, it will be difficult for you to explain it to your employees. Clarify your understanding by asking the following questions:

- How far do we expect to go with teams?
- What decisions will members and leaders make in the future that we aren't making today?
- What types of training and development will be offered to me and my team?
- How fast will teams be expected to take on new tasks?
- Is participation voluntary?
- What happens if an employee or a leader makes a poor decision?
- What's my role?
- What's top management's role?

Next, you need to get comfortable being uncomfortable. You'll learn that stretching yourself beyond your current comfort zone is a sign that you're doing things right. The tension will provide a catalyst for learning more about teams and how they work, thus equipping you to play an effective support role. Many leaders in the preteam phase find it helpful to do some or all of the following:

- Attend conferences on empowered teams and compare war stories with other leaders who've been in the trenches and made the transition successfully. This is what made the difference at Seattle Metro. According to Tracy Peterson, the director of finance, "The supervisors learned that the change we were promoting was not flaky, but rather a goal of American industry. . . . That's the value of getting out of your own backyard" (Peterson, 1993, p. 70).
- Visit other sites that are implementing teams. Find out how these leaders handled their concerns.
- Look around you and determine who the best coaches are. Identify what they do that you don't do, and begin adopting their successful techniques.

■ Learn more about the organization's implementation plan and develop a personal transition plan so that you'll be prepared for what's coming next. (Later in the chapter, Tool 7.1 provides an example of a personal development plan.)

You can use your newfound knowledge to change not only your actions but also some of your personal attitudes and beliefs — what Kim Fisher (1989) calls the "invisible elements" of the team leader role:

Invisible Elements	*Visible Elements*
Vision	Behaviors
Values	Style
Assumptions	Language
Paradigms	Etc.

To be effective in your new leadership role, you'll need to change from the inside out — in other words, the "invisible" elements need to lead the way. This means that you'll need to change your personal values and beliefs and model them sincerely for your employees to see. Aligning your personal values and beliefs with the organization's is critical because what's on the inside (those invisible elements) will drive your outside behavior. Consider the following example:

> An employee comes to you saying the quality of the motor parts doesn't meet specifications; therefore, according to the company's driving value of quality, those parts should not go out the door.

$\downarrow$

> You think to yourself, "I still believe that the way I've always worked produces the best results. We've gotten away with less-than-perfect parts in the past. I also think

employees should do as I tell them, since I have the most experience."

↓

You say, "Sandwich the bad parts in between the good parts and ship them out."

Changing your beliefs about leadership is much like changing your beliefs about diet or exercise: you know what works for you. Some people are persuaded by reading the advice of experts. Others like to talk to people who have tried a different approach to see how they succeeded. Some are persuaded only by trying it themselves—actually changing their behavior and seeing how it feels. Still others are persuaded by logic, analyzing the need to change and then following the logical "next steps."

This is how a plant manager at Pexco handled it: he mapped out the process for all the tasks required in the billet preparation cell. He and his leadership team found that there were more than eighty tasks being done in that cell alone! Based on this finding, the leadership team agreed that there was no way they could manage three cells in the old-school, high-control way. So they agreed that the most productive way to work would be to empower employees to manage the cell operation details.

Finally, cement your new beliefs by analyzing how you spend your time at work. Assess how much time you spend inspecting your employees' work and completing time and attendance reports. When most leaders conduct this mini-analysis, they discover that they're spending far too much time (50 to 70 percent) on reactive, administrative, and fire-fighting tasks—activities that add little or no value, or that employees could do with training. If your analysis shows similar results, begin reallocating your time. Map out a plan for changing how you spend your time as you move into the new-team phase. Then help yourself visualize your intended changes by creating pie charts that show how you used to spend your time compared with how you plan to spend it in the future. Figure 7.1 shows one leader's pie charts.

Figure 7.1. One Leader's Allocation of Time.

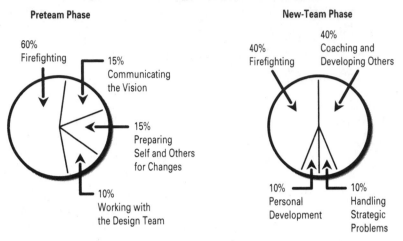

Preteam Phase

60%
Firefighting

15%
Communicating
the Vision

15%
Preparing
Self and Others
for Changes

10%
Working with
the Design Team

New-Team Phase

40%
Coaching and
Developing Others

40%
Firefighting

10%
Personal
Development

10%
Handling
Strategic
Problems

WHAT TO DO
FOR YOUR EMPLOYEES

Once you've become personally acclimated to the preteam phase, it's time to prepare your employees for the changes they'll face. The steps outlined in this section will help you prepare your employees to operate as a team and prevent them from unnecessary struggling later on.

One of your first and most important jobs is to explain the organization's vision for teams in a way that's both understandable to and motivating for employees. You'll need to help them understand how the vision statement will impact their day-to-day lives, serving as a translator of sorts for such terms as *vision* and *values.*

At Pexco, for example, the driving value is "a passion for continuous improvement." The way leaders at Pexco operationalize the driving value is to say, "We won't send out bad tubes just to make production numbers." If technicians discover a work method or materials that are producing tubes with poor surface finishes, they're expected to pull engineering, purchasing, and maintenance resources together to take action to improve the product.

Another way to help employees internalize the vision is to keep it simple. Consider reducing the vision to a few key words that everyone can remember. For example, a lengthy vision statement might be reduced to the three C's: customers, continuous improvement, and commitment to employees. At UCAR Carbon's Factory A, the vision is an easy-to-remember acronym, CLIMB, which stands for continuous improvement, long-term focus, involvement of everyone, meeting customer needs, and bias for action.

In order for employees to appreciate your organization's vision fully, you'll need to guide them through many of the same steps the top managers of your organization took in creating the vision originally:

- Sensitize them to the pressures the organization is facing, both externally and internally. Discuss where your organization stands in terms of customer satisfaction, competitive position, cost of operation, quality rates, and expected growth.

- Discuss the differences between where your organization is now and where it needs to be. What kinds of changes are required to remain, or become, competitive? What are your customers' quality requirements today; what will they be next year? Showcase a competitor's product and customer testimonials about why they buy your competitor's product. (For example, at Bausch & Lomb's contact lens division, customers reported preferring smaller blister packs to vial packaging. So, when smaller blister packs were introduced at Bausch & Lomb, employees understood why the new packaging was key to their success.)

- Describe how employees will benefit from the changes. Not surprisingly, if employees understand how changes will appeal to their own self-interests, they will be more motivated to change than if they're merely told what to do. Let employees know how they'll be involved in designing, reviewing, and implementing the changes. Find out if they will receive any financial rewards as a result of working in teams (for example, stock options, pay for skills, or team bonuses). Remember that it's your job to let employees know how taking on new responsibilities will increase their job security and offer new opportunities for them.

■ Establish a link between individual values and the organization's values. For example, most employees take pride in doing their jobs well, an internal value that can be linked to the organization's value of constant improvement.

In addition, remember to actively manage communication about the change. In other words, practice myth control! The more information you can provide about the changes, the more comfortable your employees will feel. If you can't answer a question, "I don't know" is an acceptable answer—if you add, "I'll find out and get back to you." And then do just that.

In spite of your best efforts, some employees will still resist change. And left unresolved, resistance can prevent effective teams from developing. When redirected, though, energy formerly used in resistance can be channeled to drive the culture change and to build teams.

According to Peter Block (1981), many leaders' initial reaction is to *combat* resistance, which can prevent employees from going through the natural reaction cycle that's critical to their acceptance of change. Instead of allowing resistance to be expressed as a natural process, leaders sometimes try to rub it out, thus increasing the resistance. Attempt instead to channel resistance into productive behavior by trying the following:

■ Give your key resisters important responsibilities directly related to the change. For example, put them in charge of collecting ideas for a cross-training plan or visiting a vendor to learn about new equipment you're considering purchasing. Because skeptics often feel little personal investment in the change and lots of investment in the status quo, you need to create more involvement in the team concept by giving them meaningful tasks. Even resisters will find it hard to criticize changes if they've been involved in designing the changes.

- Take your key resisters to visit other companies that are using teams successfully so they can see the team concept in action. Design team members from Cape Coral Hospital went on a site visit to a hospital in Oklahoma. Before the visit, several Cape Coral directors were highly skeptical of making proposed changes in the radiology and cardiopulmonary departments; in addition, some of them were reluctant to work on the design team because of a long-standing rift between support departments and nursing departments. After the site visit, though, not only were the design team members excited about the work-flow improvements they had seen, but they enjoyed traveling with each other so much that they returned a more cohesive group.

- Ask your worst skeptics to make a presentation to other employees about the planned changes in your area. This will put the skeptics in a position of responsibility, authority, and visibility to others; most employees—even skeptics—consider presentations an honor and will try to represent the group to the best of their ability.

WHAT TO DO
WITH YOUR BOSS

Most preteam leaders report that not all their struggles are with their employees. In fact, your boss might be your greatest challenge! As you learn to be an effective team leader, your boss might be learning right along with you. You shouldn't assume that your boss has coaching and team-leadership behaviors down pat. You might even encounter situations where you're coaching your boss as both of you make the transition to your new roles!

One of the most helpful ways to ensure that you and your boss have common expectations about the development of teams is to establish regular progress review meetings. The focus of these one- to two-hour meetings in the preteam phase is to establish and review a development plan that you can use to ensure that you both are clear about what's expected of you and that you receive feedback and recognition as you make small approximations to your new role. One example of a leader development plan is provided in Tool 7.1.

You'll find it helpful to take initiative for personal development, looking for opportunities to become more effective in your new role. You should initiate agenda topics for meetings with your boss (and, of course, be prepared to discuss those topics) so that both of you will become more confident about your ability to succeed.

Be sure that one of your standing agenda items is receiving feedback from your boss. In the preteam phase, you might feel uneasy about asking your boss for feedback. However, if you avoid asking for feedback because it feels uncomfortable, you risk the chance of receiving worse feedback later on. By agreeing with your boss to include feedback as a standing agenda item, you ensure that feedback will become part of your progress review routine and you won't have to ask for it. After several meetings, the feedback process will become much easier—for both of you!—and it will prepare you for giving and receiving more direct feedback in later team phases.

KEY BEHAVIORS

The enormity of the change you're facing can feel overwhelming in the preteam phase. By focusing on a few key behaviors,

Tool 7.1. Sample Preteam Leader Development Plan.

	Now	Next
What My Employees Need	• Introduction to the organization's vision and values • Better understanding of internal partners' requirements • More exposure to "external reality"—that is, competitive information and customers' needs (for example, customer letters and returned products)	• Overview of the team concept
What I Need from My Boss	• Opportunities to work with customers on-site • Clear direction about what I have authority to do in implementing work teams • A clear picture of how I should spend my time • Time to attend training on communication, coaching, and delegation	• Specific feedback on my development plans • Help in brainstorming ideas for problems I encounter • Updates on what the steering committee has decided
What I Agree to Do	• Sign up for twelve hours of leadership skills training • Schedule regular biweekly progress review meetings and be prepared with agendas and brief updates • Start a development plan for all the employees in my department	• Visit other self-directed sites and complete a brief trip report • Explain the organization's vision and values to all my employees

though, you'll boost your confidence and improve your chances for success later on.

COMMUNICATE

You can facilitate everyone's transition through the preteam phase by reliably communicating information as new decisions are made. Early on, you'll need to develop a communication strategy that conveys the most important information in a way that's easily understood by your teams.

As a good rule of thumb, communicate any important piece of information at least three times. This approach makes it almost impossible for your listeners to misunderstand your message. Another tip is to vary *how* you communicate by using different media — for example, written, visual, and face-to-face communication. Whether you elect to use electronic mail, voice mail, signs or diagrams, bulletin boards, or in-person conversation, remember to communicate frequently and effectively. Communicate as if your life depended on it. (It does!)

Above all else, be consistent in conveying your message from person to person or group to group. And watch out for status symbols — titles on name badges or special lunching places, for example — that communicate the wrong message. You don't want your teams to get the idea that "we're all equal, but some of us are more equal than others."

DEVELOP FLEXIBILITY

Show that you're flexible and open to new ideas by doing the following:

- Think creatively about how work is organized. Identify barriers to empowerment in your own area that reduce employee decision making and satisfaction. Recognize inefficiencies and non–value-adding activities in your existing work methods.

- Use brainstorming techniques to generate ideas.

- Stop yourself before rejecting ideas. Think first of ways an idea might be implemented; then evaluate its merit. If you find yourself thinking, "That's not the way we do it around here," use that as a signal to *continue* rather than stop.

ASK FOR HELP AND ENCOURAGE INVOLVEMENT

When in doubt, get involved and involve others. You'll want to include other key stakeholders who impact your area — such as engineers, accountants, or purchasing specialists — because these support professionals can help analyze your work processes and develop increased responsibility in your employees.

BUILD TRUST

Building trust is imperative to making any change a success. It is especially important during the uncertainty of the preteam phase. You can help build trust by acknowledging others' contributions during discussions, redirecting a discussion when someone's esteem is threatened, and not minimizing or ignoring others' feelings and concerns. Remember that the most important thing you can do to build trust is to ensure that your actions are consistent with your organization's values. Actions really do speak louder than words.

DON'T PANIC

As you experience change and commotion in the preteam phase, remain calm. It will all come together as the new organization is reconfigured and takes shape, and you'll be ready to handle new challenges as your teams get started.

ANTICIPATE SAND TRAPS

Any number of barriers can crop up during the preteam phase of evolution. Knowing what kinds of traps to anticipate will help you feel more comfortable in the role, and thinking through ways to extract yourself from the sand traps and put yourself back on the fairway will increase your chances of success.

Faulty Self-Perception

Too often leaders think they've given up control and are being good coaches when others perceive them as controlling, traditional leaders. You're in this trap if

- You do all or most of the talking in meetings.

- People come to meetings unprepared because they know you'll run the meeting and take care of follow-up details yourself.

- People don't give you honest feedback—that is, they sugarcoat the feedback they give you so that almost all of it is positive.

If you see these things happening to you, consider

- Reminding yourself that this is normal. The preteam phase is a difficult transition at first, because your role hasn't been completely redesigned and your teams haven't been formed officially.

- Assigning meeting agenda items to employees ahead of time, letting them know that they're responsible for specific topics.

- Asking for feedback in a way that will make it easy for people to respond honestly.

- Admitting that you might be a "closet" controller. Stating this fact yourself may elicit more open feedback from others.

Inevitable Setbacks

When you've experienced an empowerment setback, it's important to acknowledge your backsliding. Teams are particularly sensitive to unempowering situations in the preteam and new-team phases. They may react by thinking, "Aha! This stuff is only talk."

You've probably had an empowerment setback if

- Employees are talking behind your back.
- Employees clam up in meetings.
- Employees stop responding to your suggestions that they become more involved.
- At a meeting to redesign a process or to clarify a role, you feel that you must take control before it gets out of hand.
- You go to a meeting and neglect to involve your employees in the outcome of the meeting.
- You overlook opportunities to involve employees in preteam activities (such as working with the design team to define team boundaries or collect baseline data).

You can counteract an empowerment setback by

- Admitting that you made a mistake.
- Admitting that you temporarily slid back into your old role.
- Discussing what happened with the individuals involved. Generally, people readily acknowledge how difficult it is to be consistent as a coach, especially early in the transition.

YOUR OWN SKEPTICISM

If you are inadvertently contaminating others with your skepticism, you're causing unnecessary fear and resistance among your employees. You're in this trap if

- You joke about proposals for the new team structure. This happened to one insurance company manager we know when he commented in public that the team implementation could mean all team members could become underwriters — the equivalent, for this group, of implying that just anyone could become a heart surgeon. This sarcastic comment threw gas on the resistance fire. The employees overhearing this comment weren't amused, and the underwriters were irate. One of them asked, "Do they think just *anyone* can do this job?" Employees can't always tell when you are joking and when you're serious, so be careful.

- You neglect to address the changes or implementation plan in your meetings, or you give either one of them a two-minute spot on your agenda.

- You take pot shots at the proposed changes. One manager for a large beverage company grumbled throughout an open-house session intended to introduce the team concept to employees. Every ten minutes or so, he would say something like, "Our managers won't let us make decisions, so why should we empower our employees?" or "Why should we form teams to help us improve operations? Our product costs can be reduced only by pennies as it is. Marketing is the high expense for this company. We should put the marketing people in teams." While his concerns were important, they should have been voiced with the steering committee — not with the employees.

If you fall into this trap, you'll want to

- Educate yourself. Visit successful implementations. Skepticism often comes from ignorance.

- Communicate your statements and questions as constructive concerns, focusing on the solutions, not the problems.

- Take time each week to plan specific ways to reinforce the culture change.

LESSONS LEARNED

If you feel as if you're struggling, consider these lessons learned from leaders who've made the transition successfully:

- "Be patient. Remember that people won't see the benefits of change right away. Light bulbs will come on, though, as you repeatedly explain your change plans" (Pat, Cape Coral Hospital).

- "Look at things in an open-minded way. Don't start by being negative about the change process. Recognize that change can have many advantages for you, your team, and your organization" (Sarah, Milwaukee Insurance).

- "Don't skip the training basics. It's essential to show your commitment to the change process by attending the training sessions you want others to attend" (Pat, Cape Coral Hospital).

- "Train team members and leaders together, or at least concurrently" (Jim, International Paper).

- "Trust that if your employees are given the proper guidance, they'll make good decisions for the company and its customers" (Sarah, Milwaukee Insurance).

- "Keep a list of what you've learned through the preteam phase. Look at it periodically. This will give you a feeling of mastery" (Jeff, DDI).

- "Don't expect the team environment to be a utopia. There are still problems; they're just different" (Diane, Miller Brewing).

- "Practice frequently, but start where you know you'll be successful—only ten feet off the ground at first. Be sure you're prepared—with safety nets, spotters, and harnesses. When you get used to it in your head, take it up to the next level" (Michelangelo, trapeze artist, from his act *The Man on the Flying Trapeze*).

PRETEAM LEADER JOB PROFILE

In the preteam phase, your job should take on the characteristics outlined in Exhibit 7.1. Since your job probably hasn't changed radically yet, you can use this time to prepare your-

Exhibit 7.1. Job Profile for Leaders in the Preteam Phase.

Time spent on reactive tasks	60 percent
Primary tasks	• Clarifying the organization's vision so that employees internalize it • Modeling the vision for employees • Providing employees with time for training and redesign tasks
Behaviors required for success	• Communicating, communicating, communicating • Becoming flexible and open to new ideas • Asking for help • Encouraging involvement • Building trust • Refraining from panic
Priorities/problems	• Dealing with skeptics • Creating motivation for change • Analyzing how you spend your time; begin shifting away from fire fighting to proactively developing your team • Working on a development plan for the next steps
Parts of the job that are most satisfying at this phase	• Participating in the creation of a new structure and culture • Helping shape the organization's future • Unleashing your own potential (as well as employees') • Learning new and valuable skills

self, your employees, and even your boss for the changes that will occur with the formation of teams. Planning and preparation now will make the start-up of teams infinitely easier.

SELF-CHECK

Consider how you spent your time last month. Then use the checklist found in Tool 7.2 to determine whether you're

Tool 7.2. Self-Check for Leaders in the Preteam Phase.

Last month . . .	*Done*	*Not Done*
I learned more about the team concept through reading, visiting sites, and seeking information from steering and design teams.	☐	☐
I showed my commitment by following through on changes I said I would make.	☐	☐
I tried to understand everyone's feelings about the team implementation and provided support and coaching.	☐	☐
I refrained from whining or complaining about the changes.	☐	☐
I honestly considered new ideas that I initially thought were radical.	☐	☐
I made time for employees to work on the changes.	☐	☐
I spent time thinking about how I could change, and I took action to make some changes.	☐	☐
I signed up for a training course (for instance, on coaching or on leading change).	☐	☐
I figured out which behaviors are strengths for me and where I need to develop.	☐	☐
I made "feedback from my boss" a regular meeting item.	☐	☐
I developed a next-step plan with my employees.	☐	☐
I communicated all the information I could about the change.	☐	☐
I served as a communication link between the design/steering teams and my own team.	☐	☐
I tried to understand individual team members' feelings about the team implementation, providing coaching and support as needed.	☐	☐

effectively changing your role in the preteam phase. Periodic self-checks will keep you on course.

SPECIAL CONSIDERATIONS FOR SUPPORT PROFESSIONALS

One of the primary goals of a team-based organization is to redesign the work so that decisions are made at the point where the service is delivered or the product is manufactured. This goal is next to impossible to achieve, however, if support professionals (engineers, human resource staff, and marketing personnel, for example) are left out of the redesign effort. Most organizations, unfortunately, separate the support professionals from the employees who work within the core process. As a result, there are two factions that have little interaction with one another. This creates handoffs, delays, errors, and suboptimization.

According to Edward E. Lawler, staff professionals need to "provide information and expertise to the actual decision makers, not make the decisions or become obstacles to change and innovation" (1992, p. 72). This approach represents a radical change for those support professionals who have been reinforced over the years for creating impenetrable technical towers. In a team environment, support professionals must share their knowledge with the teams "on the line" in order to reduce cycle time and minimize cross-department handoffs. Thus the support professional's role becomes that of an educator, coach, and facilitator.

As organizations implement teams, we find that support professionals often have three general concerns: the type of work they'll do, the technical expertise required, and availability of ongoing support when there are problems.

For instance, at one chemical plant that was moving to teams, there was considerable debate about including maintenance specialists on each of the operations teams. While the design team believed it was important to ensure that each team had at least one member who could handle equipment emergencies, the maintenance department resisted the idea because they believed such a "split" would dilute their technical expertise. Eventually, the problem was solved by retaining a very small core maintenance group with highly specialized experts and deploying one maintenance generalist on each operations team. The generalists ultimately reported that as they trained the rest of their team members to handle routine maintenance activities, they actually had plenty of time to practice and develop their technical skills.

Many support professionals also are concerned that their lack of core-process knowledge will weaken their credibility in working with the teams. Accountants and human resource professionals gravitate to their own areas of expertise; consequently, their knowledge of the technical aspects of the business may not be strong. Initially, they can feel at a loss working with core-process teams.

Support professionals who have made the transition to a team-based environment report numerous reasons why the change worked to their benefit. According to a research study of 542 technical professionals from fourteen companies, a majority of support professionals reported a preference for working in a team-based environment as opposed to a traditional, isolated environment (Beyerlein, Beyerlein, and Richardson, 1993). The most frequently cited benefits of working as a support professional team member (the average tenure on a team was 1.3 years) included "more trust, acceptance, less competition, better design decisions, and better problem resolution" (p. 16). Furthermore, the majority of respondents reported being satisfied or extremely satisfied with the following:

- The amount of personal growth and development they get in their jobs (45.5 percent; only 10.7 percent were dissatisfied or extremely dissatisfied).

- The feeling of worthwhile accomplishment they get from doing their jobs (56.4 percent; only 5.8 percent were dissatisfied or extremely dissatisfied).

- The amount of independent thought and action involved in doing their jobs (63.1 percent; only 3.4 percent were dissatisfied or extremely dissatisfied).

- The amount of challenge in their jobs (57.9 percent; only 3.8 percent were dissatisfied or extremely dissatisfied).

So, in spite of their initial concerns, support professionals who had made the preteam transition reported very favorable results.

What can support professionals do to help make the transition in the preteam phase? The more active they are in exploring how the organization and their role will change with the move to teams, the more comfortable and successful support professionals will be as leaders. So they should stay involved! Here are some steps support professionals can take to advance their role:

- Sign up for a team overview session. Learn more about how teams are implemented and what steps are being taken toward teamwork in the organization.

- Get involved in preteam activities. Join a design team or volunteer to be part of a visioning session. The more involved support professionals are, the more they can use their technical knowledge to support the change and design their future role.

- Visit other support professionals at a team-based site. Ask them what their role was like before teams and what it's like now. Use others' experiences to help create a new support role that works for the organization.

- Create new relationships with team leaders and team members. Support professionals should consider moving their desks out on the floor near the rest of the team so that interactions become more frequent and more comfortable.

- Remember that without help from support departments, the teams will be unable to make decisions and control errors. Support professionals' role in the organization will become even more important as teams assume new responsibilities in the later team phases.

SPECIAL CONSIDERATIONS FOR UNION LEADERS

Union leaders need to make some philosophical decisions early in the game—namely, are they going to be sparring partners or waltzing partners with management in the move to teams? If they choose a partnership with management, they must play an active role in designing and implementing teams in a manner that results in a "win" for employees.

Consultants who specialize in assisting organizations in their shift to teams note that union leaders tend to "make decisions concerning the team concept and employee involvement activities with limited understanding about what these processes involve, a lack of adequate time to examine the proposed changes, and limited experience with the process of implementing and monitoring the changes" (Lazes, 1993). Thus union leaders have three important tasks in making an educated decision: investing the time to know and understand the subject, clarifying how their role as a union leader will be affected, and assessing the potential benefits of a team-based organization.

The following issues are of particular concern to union leaders:

- *Joint training.* Handled effectively, joint training can be a tremendous benefit for employees. For example, the United Auto Workers (UAW) and the big three automakers, as well as the Communications Workers of America and AT&T, have established model joint training programs. In these cases, union and management leaders co-developed the training curriculum. On a smaller scale, companies such as Johnson & Johnson

Medical have set up joint supervisor and steward training. In Johnson & Johnson's case, the training was pi-
oneered at a 700-person plant outside Dallas, represented
by the United Textile Workers of America. The program
was developed in cooperation with the stewards and
supervisors, bringing these two groups together for the
first time. The program teaches a collaborative problem-
solving process that calls for supervisors and stewards to
work together in identifying and resolving problems at
the lowest organizational level (Cernero, 1991).

■ *Work redesign.* If the company is considering redesigning
the workplace by using sociotechnical systems (STS) processes, there are many potential benefits for workers. For
this reason, it's worth union leaders' time to study other
long-standing implementations to determine the implications for their workers. One example of a positive STS
implementation occurred at Shell Sarnia, which advanced to the point that the managers, workers, and
leaders of the Energy and Chemical Workers Union
voted to switch from an eight-hour shift to a twelve-hour
shift—all without amending the contract (Hoerr, 1991).

If the company is considering work redesign, a typical early step is to establish a design team. In most cases,
the design team becomes a powerful group. As such, it
can be a source of strength or a source of competition for
the union. At Corning in Erwin, New York, the design
team (which, by the way, had at least 75 percent union
members) was able to obtain key executives' signatures to
appropriate changes in manufacturing processes to support the team design, totaling $3.5 million. Now union
officials focus their role on securing more business for the
plant from corporate headquarters (Kullburg, 1993).

■ *Team-based conflict resolution.* Once established, teams
often take part in the organization's conflict resolution
process. As leadership responsibilities are transferred to
the team, conflicts erupt not between team members and
leaders (as in the past) but among team members. Union

leaders must decide which is in their members' best interests: traditional notions of submitting grievances or a team process that enables them to handle some of their own conflicts. In addition, they have to maintain the line between conflict resolution and discipline or corrective action.

- *Seniority rules.* Originally established to ensure fair and equitable treatment, seniority can get in the way of team decision making. Many team members prefer to make decisions about issues such as scheduling, job rotation, and access to training on some basis other than seniority. When Xerox was forced to reduce staffing, for example, workers had to bid into teams to avoid layoff. Those team members who had volunteered for teams to begin with had developed specific skills and working relationships, and they wanted the teams' integrity to be protected. They didn't want membership on the teams to change just because of seniority rules, so they opted to change the seniority system (U.S. Bureau of Labor Management Relations, 1988).

- *Job classifications.* To avoid status differences and promote cross-training, many team implementations coincide with a reduction in the number of job classifications. Again, union leaders need to decide where their membership stands to gain the most: from the preservation of multiple classifications or from greater use of the workers' skills.

- *Compensation.* A move to teams almost always causes a reevaluation of the compensation system. Some of the most popular alternatives are gainsharing, pay for skills or knowledge, and team-based bonuses. Each of these alternatives comes with its own set of advantages and disadvantages and deserves very careful study.

Unfortunately, an international union might not be much help to local leaders when it comes to making these important decisions. As Frank Rothweiler, international representative for the International Union of Operating Engineers, put it, "They have a lot of other priorities, and many of them have been out of the workforce for a long time" (Sheahan, 1993). Union leaders' best approach might be to learn from other local union leaders who've lived through the shift to teams.

Union leaders can use their knowledge to ensure that teams are implemented effectively. For instance, one of the first steps in a redesign process is an environment scan—an analysis of business conditions and customer requirements. This tool has the potential to be viewed as a waste of time in the headlong rush to "get those teams up and running." But consider the consequences of bypassing the scan. A shipyard (represented by eleven unions) that was trying to establish multicraft teams based on what were considered to be state-of-the-art models in Sweden and Japan completely neglected the fact that the market for new ships and repair work was declining rapidly (Sheahan, 1993). They learned the hard way that finding ways to reduce scrap is of little use if you have no customers. In retrospect, the change effort would have been better served if the teams had focused on exploring new markets.

At this early stage in a team implementation, union leaders must be prepared to field a barrage of questions from their constituents. These questions range from the uninformed ("We're not going to implement 'self-destructive teams,' are we?") to the suspicious ("You're getting in bed with management on this one, aren't you?"). This is a time when independent research of the issues will be most useful.

Finally, just as managers have had to jettison some of their old beliefs, union leaders have to rethink some of theirs:

- "You manage; we grieve."

- "The union proposes; management disposes."

- "The gains one party makes invariably come at the expense of the other party."

None of these old views is consistent with the new roles that are necessary for leading a successful team implementation. Making teams work for the union membership requires union leaders to be actively involved in the implementation; they can't simply react to management's plans. Union leaders should remember that in order to influence the implementation, they must have clear goals about what they hope to accomplish for their workers.

The best way to make sure the bargaining unit's best interests are represented in the preteam phase is for union leaders to be involved on the steering committee. Steering committees set the direction, values, and behaviors expected of all employees. At Corning, where twenty-eight U.S. factories are converting to team-based production, the American Flint and Glass Workers Union and management set joint direction via a clearly worded philosophy statement called "a partnership in the workplace." Part of this statement includes six key values that address both employee and union rights in the workplace (Hoerr, 1991). Similar joint agreements that clarify vision, goals, and expectations for the future have been developed at Scott Paper with the United Paperworkers International Union (1992) and at Magma Copper with the Steelworkers International Union (1992) (Charlier, 1992).

Steve Wyatt, education director of the UAW's Region 1A, has pinpointed five reasons for union involvement that highlight the importance of the union's role:

- It's the union leaders' right to be involved.

- Management is too important to leave to managers.

- Involvement provides more opportunities to advance the union agenda (in joint meetings, training, and design team activities).

- Union leaders gain access to important information about the company's welfare and decisions.

- Involvement can help democratize the union by increasing members' skills at participation and increasing the

union's relationship with members who don't have regular contact with the union to resolve discipline issues
(Sheahan, 1993).

Many unions report extraordinary results from teams,
for both the union and the employees. For instance, the
results of a longitudinal study conducted by Fields and
Thacker of organizations with joint union-management
partnership efforts showed that union commitment wasn't
"busted" (Fields, 1993). The study measured loyalty to the
union, responsibility to the union, willingness to work for the
union, and belief in unionism. The participants were surveyed
three times, with a twelve-month span between the first and
second times and a thirty-two-month span between the second
and third times. By the second survey, loyalty to the union and
responsibility to the union had increased significantly, while
willingness to work for the union and belief in unionism
remained the same. Fields and Thacker assert that union
officials engaged in employee involvement activities produce
improved attitudes toward the union. Employees support
union leaders who are actively involved in joint union-management employee involvement interventions.

The results within individual organizations are encouraging:

- At Magma Copper's San Manuel, Arizona, copper refinery, teams reduced production costs by 13 percent. The
  joint culture-change process reduced a $400 million debt
  to $220 million. As a result, the company was granted
  enough credit to open another operation (Charlier, 1992).

- Corning's Erwin, New York, plant began its team implementation in 1989. Today the company reports 56 percent better quality, zero customer shipments missed this
  year, 51 percent fewer safety incidents, all start-up goals
  met within eight months, and 25 percent lower production costs. The design team was able to pay back the
  redesign investment in nine months. The plant has had
  no layoffs in two years and is now hiring new employees.

■ At Scott Paper's Mobile, Alabama, paper mill, members of the United Paperworkers International union and the International Brotherhood of Electrical Workers are members of production "asset" teams throughout the operation. Together, these teams have increased productivity 100 percent in the chip cooker and digester areas. Even the teams' equipment vendors didn't think such impressive results were possible.

SUMMARY

Leaders' work in the preteam phase will have a significant impact on effectiveness and job satisfaction when teams are actually rolled out. Because the new-team phase will be hectic and demanding, leaders must take advantage of the time to prepare now.

EIGHT

Preteam Safety Nets: Clarifying Organizational Expectations

At this point in the transition, leaders are perched on the precipice of a seemingly perilous maneuver: letting go of one style and attempting to latch on to another. It's the organization's responsibility to provide the safety nets that give leaders enough confidence to let go.

Six key strategies will prepare and strengthen leaders for roles in a team-oriented culture: senior-management support, role clarity, career options and learning paths, assessment and feedback, training, and employee support. It's important not to skip or neglect any of these strategies, because without them, some leaders might never move from their old platform, and others might not make it safely to the other side.

SENIOR-MANAGEMENT SUPPORT

Many top managers who look back on their first steps in building a team-based culture have a common regret: in the move to teams, they neglected to involve "middle" leaders at the very beginning. Typically, organizations establish a vision for a team-based culture that originates with the top facility or division managers and doesn't involve the other leaders. Then, with the vision in mind, these senior managers often jump to a focus on what the team members will do to get results. Eager for employees to take on greater responsibilities, the organization gears up to provide employees with hours of skills training. In the process, they often neglect to involve leaders in creating a change blueprint. It's no wonder, then, that many leaders resist the team concept—they were left out!

A far better way to begin a team-based culture is for top management to involve leaders from the start. Leaders should be involved in all phases of the team-building process: the vision, the design, the implementation, and maintenance of the team-based culture. This will establish more consistent support at all levels of the organization.

As the company moves through the phases of its team implementation, top managers should consider involving leaders in the following ways:

- _Vision._ Consider including leaders from all levels on the steering committee. Leaders can help that committee assess organizational strengths and needs, provide specific examples of parameters or boundaries teams will need, and provide a realistic estimate of what targets should show improvement (and by when). Often leaders are the company's most knowledgeable resource for starting a baseline of key performance indicators before the teams are actually implemented. They can identify which specific quality, production, and safety measures are appropriate to track, thus enabling the organization to compare its preteam and postteam performance.

Leaders also can be involved in the creation of the vision through visioning conferences, which are meetings with fifty or more employees designed to focus everyone on the organization's current situation and elicit input on the ideal future state (Weisbord, 1987). Leaders can be instrumental in facilitating these sessions (Pasmore, 1993).

- *Design.* No design or implementation team is complete without leaders as members, because leaders provide both technical knowledge about the process and organizational insight into how things get done. To ensure that leaders' expertise is not ignored, some design teams create a special "study group" to address leader concerns and issues. The design team can work with leaders in designing leader roles, providing knowledge of work teams, and conveying critical information about the move to teams.

- *Team member basic training.* Much of the training in the preteam phase focuses on developing team awareness and interpersonal skills, covering such topics as what it's like to work in teams, how to participate in meetings, and how to value others' skills and perceptions. Many leaders make excellent trainers, because they're able to link team principles to real-life situations, and they're often available to deliver training sessions on short notice. At Corning in Erwin, New York, for example, leaders are certified to be team skills trainers. They deliver training whenever time becomes available, such as when machines break down.

Early in the process, top-level managers must decide what level of leader involvement will be needed to implement the vision and design effectively. If a high level of leader involvement is sought, top managers must model the team process with the leaders, including them in key decisions. "The result is fully buying, as opposed to just 'buying in' or 'going along,'" according to a senior manager at Union Pacific Railroad. A low level of leader involvement may contradict the principles of the team process (high involvement, inclusion, and open communication) and can result in fear, resentment, or resistance.

The following continuum illustrates the different levels of involvement. We recommend that organizations promote at least a medium level of leader involvement across all phases of team implementation.

Low Involvement

- Leaders give feedback on the vision, design, and implementation strategy that someone else developed.

Medium Involvement

- Leaders sit in on selected vision, design, implementation, and monitoring sessions and provide input.

- Leaders from affected redesign areas serve as members of the design team.

- Leaders are assigned to help align organizational systems with the team concept (facilities layout, information systems, and so on).

High Involvement

- Leaders co-facilitate key vision, design, or implementation meetings.

- First-line leaders are members of the steering committee.

- Leaders identify organizational performance indicators that will improve with the team implementation.

- Leaders are actively involved in the facilitation and development of new teams.

Obviously, not all leaders will jump at the invitation to become highly involved. In our experience, we have found that as many as 30 percent will resist involvement in the change effort, and many others will be skeptical. Even if the leaders resist, keep the invitation to become involved open.

In an intensive three-year study of new managers, Linda Hill (1992) found that most leaders attributed their motivation to become leaders to the opportunity to exercise power and control. Would-be leaders assumed that they would gain much desired autonomy to do what they thought best and that they would no longer be burdened by the unreasonable demands of others. In reality, though, these motivations come into direct conflict with the requirements of a team environment — one in which leaders are often besieged with demands and must consult others before taking action. Thus, one of the greatest barriers to leaders' becoming more empowering is the primary motivation that attracted them to the job in the first place.

Fortunately, there are many ways to influence leaders' motivation. For example, managers can begin by clearly addressing the most common personal-level contributors to fear and resistance. To do this, managers must expand leaders' knowledge about how to get results with work teams, describe how their jobs will change, and ensure some sense of job security.

Sometimes, leaders hear rumors that they might not have a future job with the company as a result of teams, so they might well be concerned that they're working themselves out of a job. This can create feelings similar to that of trapeze artists who've just swung into the center circus ring, about to let go, but with no bar to grasp. Without a bar for their outstretched hands, leaders will hold on to their trapezes for dear life — and then swing back to their original positions.

At Union Pacific Railroad, the steering committee made it clear that leaders would continue to have meaningful positions in the organization, although these positions wouldn't always look like the positions they held before teams. The steering committee agreed to develop career options for leaders as a first step in the change process (and worked with the supervisors' union on that task). The committee also made it clear that no one would lose a job because of the team initiative (assuming, of course, that poor performance wasn't an issue).

Once leaders' job security issues have been addressed, the organization must describe *how* leaders' jobs will change and the likely consequences of the change. According to Jerald M. Jellison (1993), an effective way to approach this step is to think about an altimeter. Discussing how leaders' jobs will change at the 30,000-foot level certainly will trigger resistance, because leaders are given only a cloudy description of competencies they should focus on (such as becoming a better coach, taking more initiative, and being more customer-focused). Even at the 20,000-foot view, the terrain is unclear (with talk of facilitating involvement). Although these descriptions imply action, they don't let leaders know with any specificity what to do. At the 10,000-foot level, "become a better coach" is explained as "don't always tell them what to do." While these statements provide more specifics, they still leave room for the artful dodgers of the world to resist them.

In order to see true behavior change, then, managers must get to ground-level descriptions with the organization's leaders. Describe exactly what actions the organization wants its leaders to perform. For example, ground-level descriptions of coaching for preteam leaders might include the following: "Find three ways to reinforce your employees before you leave each day" and "Ask at least one open-ended question in every employee discussion you have today."

Managers also need to find ways to personally support the leaders' role change. A key problem in the preteam phase is that top-level managers are seen as being too busy to provide clarity, resources, and advice to their leaders. When top managers support the leaders' new role only in 30,000-foot words and on paper rather than through actions, very little meaningful change will occur.

At one contact lens manufacturer, almost no change occurred in leaders' behavior even after a year in the new-team phase. A formal audit of the team implementation that surveyed all leaders showed slow acceptance of the new role — a reluctance that was attributed by the leaders surveyed to a lack of top-management involvement in the process and too little coaching about role clarity.

Some of the best ways top managers can support leaders are these:

- Reinforce leadership behaviors that even remotely resemble the "right" thing to do; that is, reinforce or shape leader behavior when leaders act according to their new role.

- Encourage leaders to meet regularly as a group to discuss how things are going. As one agenda item, leaders can compare their development plans and find out what's working — and not working — for other leaders.

- Remember to deal with emotions and feelings, not just rational thinking. Empathy and understanding will go a long way!

- Share more of the "big-picture" information — the kinds of things that typically stop at top managers' desks. Of particular interest to most leaders are topics such as changing suppliers, acquiring new business, and introducing new products or services.

- Free leaders from some of their former tasks in order to give them time to work on the vision, design, and implementation of teams. Leaders who want to be involved often have too many other priorities that tie them to their old role.

ROLE CLARITY

Perhaps the single greatest contributor to leaders' resistance is a lack of role clarity or lack of involvement in defining what the new role should be. "You're taking something away from me" is a leader's initial reaction. In the preteam phase, leaders need to understand that their role will expand, not shrink, over time. One of the best ways for leaders to arrive at this understanding is for the organization to involve them in defining their new role.

At Magma Copper, a unionized mining facility that began the move to a team-based culture in 1988, all the supervisors and stewards gathered together for a three-day role-definition session. Early in the session, they were given interpersonal skills training (tips on maintaining others' self-esteem, showing empathy, and involving others to get their ideas) to help them with their task. They had one requirement from management: come up with a new role that describes what responsibilities they should hand off or keep and where their roles should expand. At first the leaders were skeptical, thinking that management eventually would come in and tell them what to do. But that didn't happen. Later, when they presented their new role ideas to management and their suggestions were accepted, the leaders felt terrific (Lewis and Elden, 1992).

If leaders haven't defined how they'll spend their time differently one month, six months, and one year from now, chances are they have no idea of what the organization expects them to do. Leaders will feel that their role is important and clear if they work through a process such as this one to achieve role clarity:

Step 1. Leaders prepare a list of tasks for which they're responsible now.

Step 2. Managers provide a list of projects and tasks that leaders need to do more of in the future (for example, handling problems across shifts or creating a supplier certification program).

Step 3. Managers help leaders identify tasks they currently perform that don't add value to the viability of the business or the customers' requirements. Categories of non–value-added tasks might include reviewing other people's work, completing paperwork and re-ports, stockpiling materials, and reworking materials or reports.

Step 4. Managers provide leaders with criteria to help them decide which of their remaining tasks can be handed off to team members, which they should re-tain, and which new tasks they should take on. (Exam-ples are shown in Exhibit 8.1.)

Step 5. Managers and leaders use pie charts (like the one shown in Figure 7.1) to visualize how leaders will allo-cate their time in the new role.

Step 6. Leaders and managers use a role agreement as a reminder that leaders will be involved in more chal-lenging work as their teams develop. (A sample agree-ment is presented in Tool 8.1.)

Step 7. Leaders communicate with employees, staff pro-fessionals, and managers about how their roles will change and what implications the new roles will have for others. This last step is particularly important, because a recent study of six manufacturing sites using self-directed teams indicated there was significant dis-agreement between managers and team members on the role of team leaders (Hutzel and Varney, 1992). Obviously, it would be extremely frustrating for team leaders to feel caught between the conflicting expecta-tions of their managers and team members.

Organizations need to remember that their culture change will succeed only if leaders support the changes. And leaders are much more likely to support the changes if they understand and feel comfortable with their changing role. Keep in mind that in the old role, at least people understood what to do—even if they didn't like it.

Exhibit 8.1. Changing Leadership Responsibilities.

Consider *transferring* any responsibilities that

- Team members can handle now (or with training).
- Are highly structured or for which standard procedures are well developed.
- Require a lot of time and prevent team leaders from doing the parts of their job that only they can do.
- Tap underutilized skills and abilities of team members.
- Require detailed, up-to-the-minute knowledge of what's happening on the job.
- Team members could handle if they had more information and understanding of the big picture.

  Examples might include tasks that involve

  - Monitoring work flow.
  - Assigning jobs.
  - Tracking performance.
  - Identifying quality improvements.
  - Filling out work orders.
  - Scheduling.
  - Monitoring safety.
  - Resolving interpersonal conflicts.

Consider *keeping* any responsibilities that

- Managers think the leaders should handle personally.
- No one else can reasonably learn. (Some specialized responsibilities, for example, might take years to learn to handle.)
- No one else has time to complete. (Some responsibilities require so much time away from the work itself that team members might not be able to complete them by specified deadlines.)
- The team can't handle yet (because they aren't mature or cohesive enough).

  Examples might include tasks that involve helping team members

  - Increase their skill and competence levels.
  - Learn how to make decisions and solve problems.
  - Maximize self-leadership capabilities.
  - Take full responsibility for their performance.

Consider *adding* responsibilities that

- Will help team members gain confidence and competence in their new roles.
- Involve more strategic, big-picture tasks that leaders always wanted to get around to but never had the time for.
- Will help solve problems or improve performance across teams.

  Examples might include tasks that involve

  - Implementation of new work-flow strategies.
  - Coaching and support of new work teams.
  - System/process improvement projects.
  - Coordination with other organizational units.
  - Strategic planning.

Tool 8.1. Sample Role Agreement for a Group Leader in a Bank.

As a group leader, I agree to do the following:

- Spend at least 40 percent of my time coaching team members and team coordinators in managing their day-to-day activities (scheduling work for the day, cross-training) and in other activities that will help them reach higher levels of empowerment.
- Help the team develop team skills (conflict resolution, consensus decision making, balanced participation) by using team tools in each meeting.
- At every team meeting, provide assistance and knowledge about the problem-solving process.
- Monitor the team's interactions, give feedback, and make suggestions for improvement. I agree to assess the team's current state, strengths, and needs and provide feedback at least quarterly.
- Act as an as-needed adviser in recommending tools for the team.
- Work with management and team members to implement new services for customers.
- Coordinate activities between groups.

Signed:

_____ Group Leader

_____ Division Manager

CAREER OPTIONS
AND LEARNING PATHS

In the preteam phase, it's critical to involve leaders, especially the naysayers, in creating their own career options and learning paths.

Organizations can begin by emphasizing that leaders will have *learning paths* in the organization, not *jobs*. Leaders need to understand the fact that functional jobs are changing. The answer to the question, "What happens to my job?" lies in a leader's ability to move along a learning path, not in retaining a narrowly defined job. Leaders' value to the organization increases in direct proportion to the breadth and depth of their experience, so that someone with one year of experience repeated fifteen times is not as valuable as someone with fifteen years of varied experience.

Even in the preteam phase, it's helpful for leaders to understand what their options are. If the organization has been perfectly clear about the new role expectations, some leaders may choose to opt out now. In our experience, there are a variety of reasons for this reaction. Some may not want to expend the energy necessary to change their leadership style. Others may not feel capable of making this change. But most will realize they can contribute significantly if the organization matches them with the right position. Some typical assignment options follow:

- A series of special projects with external suppliers, customers, or new team installations.

- Assignments as technical project leaders. Some leaders naturally gravitate to the technical aspects of the work and so would be effective at coordinating incoming work or sponsoring process improvements.

- Assignments as full-time team consultants or facilitators working to keep teams on track and trained as they mature.

- Staff positions in areas such as purchasing, human resources, scheduling, or engineering.

At this point, managers won't know which leaders *can't* make the change to their new role. They might not even know yet who *won't* make the change. But organizations can reduce the impact of those who can't or won't by providing leaders with meaningful career options and involving them in establishing a learning path that appeals to their self-interests and strengths.

ASSESSMENT AND FEEDBACK

When we surveyed the practices of more than 500 self-directed organizations, we found that 72 percent of supervisors were successful in adjusting to their new role, but most of these supervisors were only *somewhat* successful, as shown in Figure 8.1 (Wellins and others, 1990).

Leaders in the self-directed team organizations we surveyed were rated best at providing teams with resources (such as space, tools, and staff) and on coaching teams to work together more effectively. They were seen as least effective at providing overall direction for the team, providing necessary business information, and recognizing team contributions.

These findings are critical, because leaders' effectiveness is closely tied to the bottom-line impact of teams on the operation. Specifically, team members were most satisfied— and quality and productivity were highest—when supervisors and group leaders were effective at providing overall direction for the team, providing the team with resources, providing the necessary business information, coaching teams to work together, and recognizing team contributions (Wellins and others, 1990). To maximize the impact of teams and their success at new tasks, leaders must begin a process of assessment and feedback against the requirements of the new role.

In the preteam phase, involving leaders in assessment

Figure 8.1. Success of Supervisors' Transition.

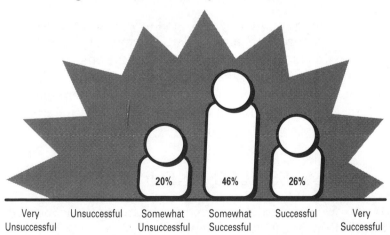

| Very Unsuccessful | Unsuccessful | Somewhat Unsuccessful | Somewhat Successful | Successful | Very Successful |

can be complicated. Early on, leaders may not be used to being assessed or receiving developmental feedback. Even those who are might be highly sensitive to negative feedback. And some might not have a clear understanding of what they're being assessed against. For these reasons, one of the most effective things the organization can do is to provide a yard-stick of the new criteria for success in the form of a behavioral job description.

We've found that leaders understand the behaviors re-quired in the new role when those behaviors are compared side by side with the behaviors required in their current role. Managers can use a mini–job description to increase leaders' understanding of what behaviors will be important in the new role. Before teams, a typical job might have looked like this:

Production

- Schedule output.
- Make assignments.
- Inspect quality.
- Order parts and materials.
- Deal with downtime.
- Call maintenance.
- Follow up on shortages.
- Approve decisions.
- Address quick-fix issues.
- Give directions on how to complete a task.

Administration

- Schedule vacations.
- Conduct performance reviews.
- Complete reports.
- Control inventory.
- Maintain safety standards.

- Schedule training for employees.
- Prepare contingency plans for downtime.
- Orient new employees.
- Monitor attendance.
- Inspect work stations for cleanliness.

After teams, that same leader's job description might look like this:

Leadership

- Keep goals in front of the team.
- Provide guidance without removing responsibility for action.
- Alert the team when it strays off course.
- Help the team think through alternative issues.

Production

- Develop expertise in quality manufacturing.
- Work with operators to refine team layout, design, and function.

Training

- Work with the team to identify both job-related and interpersonal training needs.
- Work with the team to develop a cross-training plan.
- Make sure team members are trained properly in the necessary technical skills.

Team Dynamics

- Diagnose team dynamics.
- Counsel team members when interpersonal conflict occurs.
- Encourage team members to examine how they work together.

- Help build teamwork among team members and with other groups.

Task Support

- Make sure the team has the resources it needs to get the job done.
- Interact with the technical staff to ensure proper support.

Coaching

- Coach the team to function in your absence by seeking involvement.
- Develop leadership capabilities of team members.
- Help the team become as self-sufficient as possible.

Once leaders see what new behaviors are required, they'll be in a better position to assess their own skills and readiness for change. A simple self-assessment can provide leaders with a rough idea of how they stack up against the profile for the new role. (See Tool 8.2 for a sample self-assessment form.)

This simple self-assessment process has benefits for both the organization and its leaders in the preteam phase. The organization benefits because the process increases the leaders' willingness to participate in training and apply new skills on the job; the leaders benefit because going through the assessment process themselves helps prepare them for receiving more in-depth feedback from others in the new-team phase. Additionally, the process gives leaders an opportunity to improve in areas where they know they're deficient. They can use this information in their own personal development plans.

TRAINING

In the preteam phase, the organization's culture might resemble a hardened, dried-out plot of soil in which nothing can

Tool 8.2. Self-Assessment Form.

---

1 = I don't do this at all.

2 = I do this, but I'm inconsistent in how well I do it.

3 = I always do this effectively.

Key Behaviors

Promotion of Culture Change/Teamwork

1 2 3   • Use skills and tools learned in training in and out of meetings.

1 2 3   • Talk positively about the culture change.

1 2 3   • Pitch in to help other team members.

Encouragement and Reinforcement

1 2 3   • Encourage skill building.

1 2 3   • Provide reassurance.

1 2 3   • Talk positively about the department outside the department.

Interpersonal Skills

1 2 3   • Maintain or enhance self-esteem.

1 2 3   • Listen and respond with empathy.

1 2 3   • Ask for help and encourage involvement in and out of meetings.

1 2 3   • Willingly accept feedback.

Trust

1 2 3   • Talk directly with people you have concerns with.

1 2 3   • Keep confidential or damaging information confidential.

1 2 3   • Acknowledge mistakes you make and learn from them.

Guidance

1 2 3   • Provide helpful suggestions and insight rather than taking over.

1 2 3   • Provide resources and information rather than step-by-step instructions.

1 2 3   • Encourage others to voice their opinions rather than swaying others to your opinion.

---

grow. Sprinkling a few drops of water on leaders won't turn this dried-out plot into a garden that's easily cultivated. Rather, we recommend an "even-soaking" approach to training: leaders should be given awareness and tactical skills training throughout the preteam phase.

At this stage, it's important to build leader awareness and ability in the tactical skills and behaviors discussed in Chapter Five: communication, managing the performance of others, analysis and judgment, coaching, and championing continuous improvement.

How the organization handles the training process is just as important to leader success as *what* is covered in the training. We offer the following tips from organizations that have survived the preteam phase:

■ *Awareness first.* Leaders will feel much more comfortable and confident moving into their new role if they understand why the organization is moving to teams. What are the business reasons for going to teams, and what impact does the change have on leaders? Providing leaders with a context for change will make training more meaningful and easier to apply to the job.

A government agency's taxation center began its transition to natural work teams by making the case for change with the leaders. Leaders knew that the center, as a government agency, was in no danger of being shut down as a result of competition, so at first they didn't feel motivated to change the culture or their role. When the steering committee reviewed the backlog of reimbursements, though, as well as the volume of changes in the tax laws, the leaders realized that they wouldn't be able to keep up without making significant changes. In this case, forecasting the state of the business provided the incentive for leaders to change.

Awareness of team concepts also should cover how teams are implemented, the tasks they perform, how often they meet, how jobs are redesigned, and how systems and policies change to align with the move to teams. One effective method for clarifying basic team concepts is to describe both effective and ineffective examples of team implementation. These examples allow everyone to discuss red flags and risk points.

Of course, the *best* way to clarify team concepts is through a visit to a company with a mature-team implementation. The most important consideration in selecting a site is that leaders have a chance to talk to the leaders there. It really doesn't matter if the other site is in your industry; even if it's not, leaders will come away with interesting lessons from those who've made the transition successfully. Before the actual visit, it's helpful for leaders to prepare questions about how teams were implemented at the visited site in order to help clarify their understanding of key issues.

Be sure to include leaders in the basic team orientation training with the employees. Both leaders and employees in the preteam phase want the security of knowing that they all heard the same message. In addition, during joint training, leaders will be able to get a read on how willing their employees are to embrace the team concept. This knowledge will enable leaders to strategize how to work with potential resistance and build trust and rapport.

■ *Space training across the entire preteam phase.* Leaders who receive a solid week of training in one dose often don't retain much of what they were exposed to. It's far better to give leaders time to absorb and apply the new concepts and skills. Although training times vary (depending on how much training individual leaders need), we find eight to sixteen hours a month a useful guide. An example of a preteam training plan is provided in Exhibit 8.2.

■ *Balance conceptual and practical training.* Be sure to mix conceptual training with some practical, hands-on training (such as technical cross-training or work-flow process mapping). We've found that leaders can get overloaded easily with conceptual information about the change to teams. Leaders seem to get more excited about conceptual training when they can immediately apply it (for example, in work-flow redesign or in meetings with their employees).

Exhibit 8.2. Sample Leader Training Plan for Preteam Phase.

May	June	July	August	September	October

• Big picture: Why are we moving to teams?	• Process mapping
	• The basics of empowerment: How to lead in a culture change
	• Team orientation:
	  1. How teams are implemented
	  2. Examples of teams in other companies
		• Additional technical training (if needed)
		• Changing role of the leader
			• Overcoming resistance to change
			• Developing collaborative relationships
				• Coaching
				• Resolving conflict
				• Encouraging initiative
				• Giving and receiving feedback
					• How to start up a team:
					  1. Purpose
					  2. Ground rules
					  3. Roles and responsibilities
					  4. Goals
					  5. Measures

■ *Include other participants.* Try to create a mixed group of leaders, support professionals, and union officials during preteam training. This accomplishes a couple of key objectives at once. First, going through training together helps to break down barriers among the groups; it also helps individuals develop a better understanding of one another's needs and constraints. Second, all leaders will feel involved from the start; this will help prepare them for their role in the team concept early on.

■ *Lay the groundwork for team start-up.* At the end of the preteam phase, leaders can use their tactical skills to prepare for team start-up meetings. These meetings are designed to get the teams off on the right foot by facilitating early agreements on how the teams will operate.

Typically, the team start-up process includes the following steps:

1. *Identifying the type of team.* We all know how confusing it is to differentiate between cross-functional teams, natural work groups, and self-directed teams. Leaders need to be clear with employees about how these teams are different, which team they're striving to be, and how the team will benefit employees and the organization.

2. *Developing a team charter.* Leaders can begin to prepare themselves for the new-team phase by learning how to develop a team charter with employees. The team chartering process will help the leader and the team define such things as the team's purpose, operating guidelines, scope of authority, roles and responsibilities, and performance measures. (A sample charter is provided in Tool 8.3.)

3. *Identifying training and development needs.* Leaders can begin to increase employees' ownership in the change process by getting them to assess their own training needs. Leaders will need the organization's help in assessing current skill levels and creating training plans with the team.

Tool 8.3. Sample Team Charter.

Purpose	To provide a quality product to our customers on time every day.
Tasks	• Fill customer requests daily without material being returned as a result of quality errors. • Set short- and long-term goals for improving timely and accurate service to other areas and for improving team performance through method development and/or changes. • Develop and improve working relationships and communication with fellow team members and associates. • Cross-train all team members to handle each task in the unit. • Handle preventive maintenance of equipment.
Boundaries	Team members can make improvements in their own work areas, provided that orders continue to go out on schedule, the entire team has reached consensus on a given improvement, the cost of the improvement is within the team's budget, and the support team is kept informed. All other changes or decisions must be approved in advance by the support team.
Measures of Team Success	• This year, decrease the amount of time spent looking for materials by 30 percent. • Reduce scrap to 1 percent of total volume shipped.
Training	• Each team member must be familiar with all tasks on the team before co-training other members. • Each team member is expected to complete training in team skills, interaction skills, and quality action skills.
Ground Rules	• Respect one another and value differences. • Don't talk negatively about people; instead, give immediate face-to-face feedback. • Accept feedback; don't become defensive. • Always look for ways to improve. • Have fun.
Meetings	• The entire facility will meet quarterly to review the previous quarter's performance and the requirements for the coming quarter. All team members will attend. • Meeting leaders will be elected by the team every six months. • Teams will meet for five minutes each morning and longer (twenty to thirty minutes) every two weeks.

These start-up meetings are important because two of the key characteristics that distinguish high-performing teams from low-performing teams are clear operating guidelines and clear role definition (Sundstrom and others, 1990).

EMPLOYEE SUPPORT

Believe it or not, employees also can help support leaders in the preteam phase. Unfortunately, most organizations neglect to use employees as a resource in helping leaders to be more effective. Yet, there are many important steps managers can take to encourage employee support.

Managers can help employees understand that it is unrealistic to expect their leaders to change overnight. While many leaders might honestly want to change, it is often a long and difficult transition.

It also takes time to complete the transition of transferring tasks to the team. This was a somewhat disappointing realization for some of the enthusiastic staff at Cape Coral Hospital, who expected Pat and other administrators to hand off decisions about scheduling, purchasing new furniture, and hiring new employees on the unit right away. According to Pat, "We had to explain all the planning involved in handing tasks to care teams. . . . It requires information, clinical readiness, and training. Besides, we had to get used to giving decisions we were used to making to teams and getting ourselves ready to do the coaching once the task was handed to the staff."

In addition to some coaching on patience, employees should receive training about their new roles and responsibilities. Many employees tend to see empowerment as a one-way street at first. They can immediately think of what leaders need to do—they might offer such observations as, "Leaders need to do more coaching" and "Leaders need to stop doing walk-around inspections"—but they usually have a more difficult time identifying what they themselves should do. Employees need to learn to consider more than one alternative when confronting a problem, share their expertise with others, and receive feedback about their interpersonal and team skills. If employees are actively working on becoming more empowered participants in the business, leaders' jobs will prove considerably easier.

TOUGH SITUATIONS
THE ORGANIZATION
MIGHT ENCOUNTER

As managers work with preteam leaders, several tough situations are likely to crop up. Here are a few common problems and potential solutions.

LEADER RELUCTANCE

What happens if leaders continually refuse invitations to get involved with the design team or to attend vision meetings, citing crises on the floor as excuses?

What could be causing the problem? Leaders might be trying to call your bluff, thinking that you won't confront them on the matter. Fear of the unknown or lack of commitment also might be getting in the way.

What might the organization do? If managers have asked for their participation repeatedly with no response, try confronting leaders directly in a nonthreatening and esteem-maintaining way. In addition, consider including attendance and participation at design team meetings as performance management goals—worth, say, 20 or 30 percent—so that leaders will take participation seriously and receive credit for contributing.

INADEQUATE PLANNING

What happens if leaders underestimate how much planning and structure are required to launch teams? They are taking no steps to prepare, because they don't understand the magnitude of the change.

What could be causing the problem? Most likely these leaders simply have no experience with self-directed teams.

What might the organization do? Try comparing a team's launch to a new-equipment or new-product launch. Just as there are effective ways to introduce technical changes, there are specific steps to follow for the introduction of teams. Ask leaders to consider the consequences of poor planning: role ambiguity, internal conflict, production losses, resistance, and lack of management support. Involve leaders in shaping the roll-out plan so they will understand the steps required to launch teams.

EXCESSIVE RETICENCE

What happens if leaders seem to be going along to get along? They aren't voicing *any* concerns about the implementation.

What could be causing the problem? They may be afraid that you're going to shoot the messenger. There also might be some lingering, passive resistance.

What might the organization do? Ask challenging questions and disclose concerns to provide a model and encourage leaders to ask questions and voice their own concerns. In addition, managers should close each implementation meeting with the leaders by asking each leader to share at least one question or concern.

SUMMARY

A tremendous amount of organizational support is necessary to prepare leaders for the successful introduction of teams. As with many things, the pay-me-now-or-pay-me-later principle applies. Time spent preparing leaders for change in the pre-team phase will significantly reduce the number of problems the organization will experience in the new-team phase.

NINE

New-Team Leadership:
What to Do for Yourself
and Your Team

Before empowered teams, Texas Instruments had two manager tracks: one was a technical manager, and the other was a people-watching manager. Texas Instruments decided that people-watching managers weren't a good use of managers or money because they were watching people who were already competent. I used to be one of those people-watching managers.

Texas Instruments did away with the people-watching managers and created new roles for them. Because I was able to coach teams to be self-managing, I'm now responsible for new product applications with research, development, and marketing. I spend most of my time with potential customers in the private sector devising packaging equipment that we used to use in the

defense industry that now can meet automobile manufacturers' needs.

This is the most challenging and interesting work
I've ever done. If I hadn't let go of the day-to-day tasks, I
wouldn't be where I am today. My stock in the company
went up because of empowered teams. It's the best thing
that ever happened to me [manager, Texas Instruments,
North Dallas Facility].

Testimonials such as this from leaders who've made the transition successfully and are enjoying more rewarding opportunities by empowering others are becoming increasingly
commonplace. This chapter will help you join the ranks of
leaders who've survived — and thrived — in the new-team
phase. It contains tools to help you chart your progress and
suggestions for how to cope with changes occurring within
your organization, your teams, and yourself.

WHAT'S HAPPENING
IN THE ORGANIZATION?

The new-team phase is a time when all the organizational
planning completed by the steering and design teams comes
together. New teams are starting to get off the ground, and
everyone is anxious about the potential benefits.

Generally, this is the most exciting phase for leaders and
team members. It's as if the organization had started putting
together a large puzzle in the preteam phase, finding the edges
and corners so that the puzzle began to take shape. Now, in
the new-team phase of evolution, more pieces of the puzzle
are being filled in and it's easier to see the entire picture. The
major pieces of the puzzle that come together by the end of
this phase are observable team results, plenty of opportunities
to apply the skills learned in training, and a definite sense of
whether you're suited to leading in a team environment...
or not.

HOW LEADERS FEEL

Leaders often are surprised to find that they feel different about leading teams once they're actually in the thick of things. Expectations from the preteam phase don't always pan out. We've collected some typical leaders' reactions, ranging from those who are totally optimistic to those who just can't seem to make the transition.

THE EUPHORIC OPTIMIST

You're a euphoric optimist if you can't help but see positive results everywhere you look. Pat, from Cape Coral Hospital, describes how the transition felt in the new-team phase: "It's working! This team stuff really does work! The training was the key for me. I feel as if I've grown tremendously in the last six to eight months. I'm even more excited about the staff's growth. They've taken on scheduling, leading meetings, and resolving operating and interpersonal conflicts. It's amazing!"

THE CAUTIOUS REALIST

If you see some results but are still worried about what's around the next corner, you're a cautious realist. Jim, a development engineer at UCAR Carbon's Parma, Ohio, research and development facility, is an optimist, but with a reality check thrown in. After three months in the new-team phase, he had this to say: "Yes, we're seeing some positive changes. However, the technicians could do better on completing their assignments between meetings. The engineers could do a better job of not beating on each other during team meetings. It's working, but we have a ways to go." According to Jim, he felt alternately optimistic and hesitant — comfortable at times and out of control at other times.

THE PRIVATE WARRIOR

John, a leader selected for a team facilitator role at a customer service center, never felt completely at ease with the coaching role. Even though he was an effective facilitator, he said, "It felt like having to ask permission to blow your nose." Within a matter of months, John found a different role that was much more comfortable for him—one where his technical and analytical skills could shine; he volunteered to become a member of a reengineering team that planned to expand the restructuring to other parts of the service center.

THE INCONSISTENT BACKSLIDER

Chris, a manager of a steel mill start-up, believes that he's a good coach of his teams. Others see his backsliding more than he does. He's frustrated by feedback that he dominates meetings. Chris's perception is this: "I've been through designing teams before, so I know the right approaches to take." Some backsliders feel as if they phase in and out of their new role: one day they're effective coaches involving others; the next day they backslide into despotism. Others, like Chris, might not see their own inconsistencies.

WHAT'S NORMAL?

Many leaders find themselves vacillating back and forth among all these reactions, which is perfectly normal in this stage.

Former supervisors (even euphoric optimists) have visions of becoming like the Maytag repairman, and they're surprised to discover that there seems to be *more* to do after the formation of teams than there ever was before.

Gene Grimm, a former supervisor and one of the first team facilitators at Campbell Chain, reported that he was much busier after the introduction of teams. Early on, the teams hadn't yet picked up any administrative or leadership responsibilities from Gene, so he needed to invest time in training them in those areas as well as in team and technical tasks. The team members had their own doubts and questions—especially one team, whose members required an extraordinary amount of Gene's time and attention.

Actually, most supervisors who make this transition report that their jobs become more difficult, at least at first. One

Figure 9.1. Stress and the Changing Leadership Role.

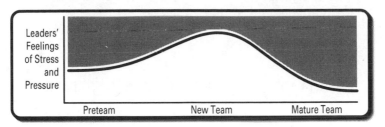

of the coaches at AT&T's Denver Works put it this way: "Some people said that our jobs would be easier when we became coaches because the teams would do all the work. We've found just the opposite to be true. Now we do two to three times more work" (*Commitment Plus*, 1992, p. 3).

That extra work generally results in an increase in leaders' stress in this phase. If we plotted supervisors' typical reactions to their changing role as leaders, we might see something like the wave shown in Figure 9.1.

When asked about the reasons behind the temporary initial increase in stress, leaders attribute it to various causes:

- "It was as if I had to concentrate on what I was doing much more, whereas before I was pretty much on auto-pilot. After being a supervisor for fifteen years, I had the traditional management style down pat. Facilitating teams didn't come naturally to me at all" (former supervisor, now a team coordinator at a hand tool manufacturer).

- "What made it hard was that I had to focus on two things at once: changing my own behavior at the same time I was trying to help team members cope with the change" (sales manager responsible for three self-directed teams).

- "Even though we've been in teams for two years now, my job keeps changing. It's not like the old days when what I did in 1985 was just like what I did in 1975. Now I'm

taking on some stuff that my boss's boss used to do"
(former general foreman in a steel plant).

WHAT TO DO FOR YOURSELF

A concrete plan of action for the new-team phase will help you
survive some of the stress and ambiguity associated with this
phase.

The first thing to focus on is your coaching skills. This
was the number-one barrier leaders themselves reported in our
nationwide survey of team leader practices: their own lack of
coaching skills (37 percent) (George and Pavur, 1992). If you've
already participated in coaching skills training and feel that
you need additional help, you might want to try consulting a
coaching mentor—someone whose coaching skills you respect. You can arrange to observe this person in coaching
situations, and you can ask him or her to observe you. It's
usually most effective to ask the mentor to work side by side
with you over an extended period of time; that way, the person
can give you feedback not only on your coaching skills but also
on any coaching opportunities you might have missed.

You also might want to ask the mentor to give you
feedback about whether you might be creating status differences when you coach team members. It's important to avoid
developing a small cadre of members within the team that you
rely on to handle the more challenging tasks. In a research
study conducted with 106 manufacturing teams in a large
motor manufacturing facility, teams whose leaders provided
information and latitude to a small group within a larger team
had significantly less communication, coordination, and cohe-
sion than teams without status differences. Furthermore, leaders who created status differences in their teams and didn't
provide adequate coaching support had teams that were significantly lower in team satisfaction, willingness to remain on
the team, and ratings of team performance than teams whose

leaders didn't create status differences and who provided adequate coaching (George, 1994).

The second greatest barrier for the former supervisors in our study was "team members who resisted my efforts to assist the change to teams" (34 percent). Try not to become discouraged if your initial involvement overtures are rebuffed or ignored. Early in the game, your attempts to transfer responsibility and coach team members are likely to be met with lukewarm responses. After all, this behavior is new to others, too. They still might be wondering what you're up to. Try your coaching tactics at least three times before giving up or changing strategy.

If you still don't seem to be making progress, try confronting problems directly. In new teams, inexperienced team members often keep their thoughts and feelings to themselves, because they don't want to rock the boat or appear resistant. This is what Larry Hirschhorn calls "going along to get along" (1991). Your job is to encourage conflict to surface constructively. Don't try to sweep it under the rug, avoid it, or deny it. If you do, it'll come back to haunt you and do more damage to your team later on.

One member of a new team in a commercial policy section of a large insurance company didn't want to be thought of as a troublemaker after the team had reached consensus on when meetings would be held, so he didn't explain to the team that the agreed-upon meeting times were almost impossible for him to meet. After he had missed several meetings and wasted his own and other people's time reviewing what had gone on in previous meetings, the leader raised the issue at a meeting. When pressed, the team member explained that he couldn't meet with the team at the agreed-upon times. Without the leader's help in putting the problem out on the table, the team probably would have continued to waste time and be frustrated.

Although you should be tough on problems, be patient with teams. New teams often experience temporary periods of "going in circles" when they might not use all their new skills. They might seem to run into the same problems over and over, without getting much better at solving them; their meetings may be awkward and ineffective at first. Remember that these problems are often only temporary. With your coaching, your teams will pull out of the difficult times and get back on course.

WHAT TO DO FOR YOUR TEAMS

Teams are very needy at this stage in their development, requiring almost all your time and attention. Don't despair. Things will get better! Typically teams work through a predictable process of dependence (when they rely heavily on your help), counterdependence (when they seem to reject everything you say or do), and then independence (when they become quite cohesive internally but competitive with other groups). With the proper support, eventually they'll arrive at a realization of their interdependence and start working effectively with internal and external partners. As their leader, you can expedite their development in a number of ways.

First, always keep the big picture in front of the team. While working in the trees, team members can lose sight of the forest. Encourage them to check what they're doing against their charter. Describe what's going on on other shifts and in other departments. Share other teams' goals. Describe the results other teams are getting, and explain how their successes impact your team.

Ruthlessly evaluate your delegation behaviors. Are you passing on tasks and decisions to the team? At this stage of evolution, it's not uncommon for team members to feel that they can handle more responsibility than you're giving them. If left unaddressed, these feelings will escalate into full-scale complaints about being unempowered. What you'll need is an objective way to discuss and evaluate how much responsibility the team can handle. For this purpose, many leaders use a team delegation grid similar to the one illustrated in Tool 9.1.

Obviously, you'll want to try letting the team handle as many responsibilities as possible when the consequences of

Tool 9.1. Team Delegation Grid.

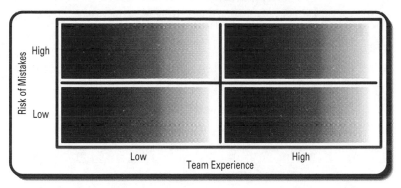

failure are low. Low-risk situations — even situations the team doesn't have much experience with — are great opportunities for development. In our experience, most conflicts occur because the leader overestimates the consequences of making a mistake or team members overestimate their experience. If you find yourself feeling reluctant to turn over a particular responsibility to the team, check to be sure you are not succumbing to any of these common excuses:

- I have the background and experience, so I can do it better.

- Teams take a lot of time, so I can do it faster.

- This assignment has high visibility with top management, so I'll do it to look good.

- This is a risky decision, so it's my anatomy on the line.

- The team isn't ready to do this yet (translation: "I enjoy doing it myself").

If there's any uncertainty, the grid shown in Tool 9.1 can help you and the team discuss situations objectively and then agree on appropriate degrees of empowerment.

Once tasks and decisions have been delegated, you'll need to help team members understand the context for what they're doing. Use your knowledge to ensure their success with new tasks. Help your team answer important questions such as these:

- How long will the task take? What's an appropriate completion time?
- Who needs to be involved and why?
- Who should be kept informed and why?
- What are the resource requirements and parameters in terms of money, time, and so on?
- What are the expected outcomes, and how will they be measured?
- Where should team members go if they need help?

Once the team is comfortable with their new responsibilities, your primary job is to provide resources and remove roadblocks. For example, you might help your team obtain the necessary approval for assigning people to overtime, provide a technical troubleshooting guide, or help locate technical specialists when necessary.

In addition, you should look for opportunities to coach the team and individual members when they're trying something new or something particularly difficult and when they run into problems. When you coach, concentrate on asking open-ended questions to encourage the team to develop solutions themselves. It's tempting to revert to *telling* your employees what to do. (After all, you know all the answers!) But if you continue to *tell* all the time, you'll end up with employees who have a hard time thinking for themselves. In a team-based environment, it's much more effective to ask questions:

- What was the last thing you tried?
- How will this impact the next phase of the process?
- How does this meet your customers' requirements?
- What's likely to happen if you do this?

- What will your next step be?
- How does this relate to other projects?
- What results do you think you'll get from this approach?

Remember to balance your approach, though. Asking *too* many open-ended questions can lead employees to think that you've already got the answer and that your goal is getting them to come up with *your* answer instead of their own alternatives.

You can tell that you've reached expert coaching status if you can successfully back off and jump in at the appropriate times. This skill is one of the most difficult to master, but it will make a huge difference in your effectiveness as a leader of new teams. The list that follows shows some examples of when to back off and when to jump in:

You should back off *when...*	*You should* jump in *when...*
The team has clear goals and objectives.	Objectives and goals are ambiguous or nonexistent.
The team uses an agreed-upon process to gather data and generate solutions.	The team regularly runs into brick walls and gets sidetracked or begins to shut down.
The team has assigned an internal facilitator to monitor the process.	The team prematurely charges ahead (that is, team members jump to a solution before gathering data).
The team is struggling with different solutions but is learning something valuable by doing so.	The team hasn't discussed an issue fully.
The team reaches a solution that wouldn't be your first choice but that you think is a viable option.	The team has decided on a solution but has missed a key element that will make the solution unworkable.

You should back off *when*...	*You should* jump in *when*...
The team has substantial experience and understands the broader organizational issues.	The decision is risky and could affect the larger organization negatively in ways the team hasn't explored.
Internal disagreements are generating constructive discussion.	Internal conflict is becoming destructive to team effectiveness.
The team seems to be moving ahead and hitting key milestones and goals.	The team has missed interim goals; a sense of urgency is missing.

Finally, you'll need to give your teams specific and constructive feedback. Unfortunately, many new-team leaders are reluctant or unskilled in this area. They either are fearful of confronting the team with "negative" feedback or are uncomfortable delivering highly positive feedback. They can describe their team's strengths and weaknesses at great length to outsiders, but when asked if they've shared these observations with the teams, they invariably answer no. Sometimes this comes from a mistaken belief that feedback will destroy the team process. On the contrary, feedback is one of the fastest ways to help a team develop. In fact, it's your job to give positive *and* developmental feedback to the team, because teams need balanced feedback to stay on track.

At Cape Coral Hospital, employees in the family birth center completed surveys before teams were formed and again six months afterward. The results showed that teams had become more responsible for eleven of nineteen tasks. The unit director used the survey feedback both as a reason to hold a celebration event and as a way to determine where the group needed to improve.

Buick's team leaders regularly measure their teams' progress at six-month intervals. They assess how teams are doing against the original empowerment schedule, how effectively they're meeting their business plan, and how they're doing on six factors of team success: trust, communication, involvement, purpose, process, and commitment. The leaders then use this feedback to develop action plans with the teams. Leaders at International Paper do this even more frequently by taking time at every meeting to focus on what they could have done differently or better.

WHAT TO DO
WITH YOUR BOSS

While the focus of your preteam progress reviews was on your own needs and concerns, most of your discussions with your boss in the new-team phase will center around staying one step ahead of the teams. For this purpose, many new-team leaders use a team development plan like the one shown in Tool 9.2, which provides a convenient format for you and your boss to anticipate the team's needs and ward off potential problems. You can also use the development plan to discuss where you need your boss's help with resources. Some of the kinds of support you might want to ask for in the new-team phase include the following:

- Arranging celebration events to recognize the team's progress (on adding new responsibilities, completing training, achieving business goals, and so on)
- Arranging customer or supplier visits
- Securing additional training or team-building interventions for the team
- Publicizing the team's achievements throughout the rest of the organization

Not surprisingly, problems crop up between leaders and their bosses at this stage of the implementation. For example, managers are often impatient to see results of the team implementation. Unfortunately, during the first six months of the new-team phase, you're not likely to see significant increases in

Tool 9.2. Sample Development Plan for New Teams.

Team	Current State	Strengths	Needs	Next Three Steps
Jacksonville Sales Team	Getting started. Still getting adjusted to two new members; everyone is excessively polite to one another.	• Strong technical/product knowledge (combined eighty years of experience). • Sue has strong facilitation skills and keeps meetings on track. • The team reached agreement on the office rearrangement quickly and smoothly.	• Leo and Dave still don't completely buy in to the team concept and are holding the team back. • Entire team needs to be more open with one another.	• Ask Leo and Dave to present the six-month update at corporate. • Facilitate a team-building session; get members to discuss the impact of their personal styles on the team. • Ask Sue to facilitate a session on discussing members' concerns at the next regional meeting.
Tampa Sales Team	Going in circles. Have started to openly disagree; three most senior members are on the verge of forming their own faction; major disagreements exist over proposed redistricting.	• All team members support the team concept. • Trust level has improved slightly since they all collaborated on the new-product promotion.	• Senior and junior members still don't completely respect each other's expertise. • The team is no longer objective over the redistricting proposal; it's becoming a contest of wills between those who support it and those who don't.	• Deliver training on valuing differences; use redistricting as a practical example. • Attend the next three Tampa team meetings and provide feedback on how they go about reaching agreement. • Provide refresher coaching on conflict resolution.

production and quality indexes; instead, what you'll see is that the teams are taking on new responsibilities. To help reconcile this situation, discuss behavior and attitude changes with your boss, especially as they might affect bottom-line results in the future. As team members become more comfortable tracking their own performance measures, invite your boss to attend meetings at which the team reviews its performance.

At a General Electric motor assembly facility, a representative from each team, the team managers, and the plant manager held daily production meetings that were facilitated by one of the team managers or representatives. As a group, they discussed major problems (such as machine breakdowns). These meetings had dual benefits: the plant manager kept in touch with team results and problems, and the representatives and managers received direct coaching support from the plant manager.

Another potential problem at this stage is that you and your teams may feel overloaded. You might find that you have to push back or negotiate some items with your boss. For example, it might be impossible to complete all the training and provide all the coaching needed when you're still expected to attend fifteen meetings a week and complete five twenty-page reports. Keep in mind that in a typical team implementation, the number of people reporting to you might increase dramatically as well. You and your boss need to discuss priorities openly for you *and* the teams. If you attempt to do everything, you *and* your teams will burn out.

KEY BEHAVIORS

BE PERSISTENT

Be persistent with your teams, yourself, and your boss. Avoid giving in to initial failures. Keep at it! Almost every successful leader of teams has felt completely discouraged (to the brink of giving up) at least once during the transition. Sometimes it seems that team members are being willfully obstinate or deliberately dense, and nothing you do is improving the situation. Then suddenly there will be a breakthrough. Team members will "see the light"; they'll succeed at a new task, effectively use a new skill, or even express appreciation for your help. Savor each of these small triumphs. And if you aren't getting enough support and reinforcement from your team, try your boss or fellow team leaders.

RECOGNIZE READINESS

When transferring responsibility, consider associates' skills, knowledge, interest, and experience. It isn't so much a matter of when *you're* ready as when *they're* ready. Learn to look for signs that one member (or a few members, or the entire team) could use more of a challenge. Some of these indications might be finishing current tasks ahead of schedule or demonstrating a high level of initiative in a particular area.

CREATE OWNERSHIP

Give team members the freedom to choose their own approach to completing work assignments. Allow individuals to retain responsibility and authority in the face of challenges and encourage them to seek out tasks that increase their level of responsibility and involvement in the organization. Try to give them whole tasks (such as managing the team's safety audit) rather than bits and pieces of tasks (such as calling a vendor to get information on performance standards). The more responsibility the team has for something from beginning to end, and the more involved they are in the big picture, the more excited they'll be about the task.

SET PERFORMANCE EXPECTATIONS

Clearly communicate performance expectations and check for understanding. Sometimes new team leaders mistakenly believe that if they're too definitive about goals or targets, the team will feel unempowered. Actually, the reverse is true: if you're vague about your expectations, the team will feel confused or even paralyzed. If, for example, they must involve

Purchasing for a particular project to be successful, be sure they understand that fact. Before delegating any new responsibilities, it might be helpful for you to examine what you consider minimal conditions for success, discarding any that are personal idiosyncrasies and not really necessary, and then discuss the remaining conditions with the team.

PROVIDE SUPPORT

Offer personal time, ongoing feedback, and an appropriate amount of guidance. Your team needs you during this phase, probably more than you realize. One way to check is to come right out and ask the team whether you are available enough to help, appropriately open to their ideas, and adequate in providing guidance to help them avoid major problems.

BEHAVE CONSISTENTLY

Keep your commitments in regard to meeting times, work assignments, support and assistance, and other agreed-upon actions. Avoid taking out your personal frustrations on others. Consistent, predictable behavior is one of the best ways to build trust. If your team members feel they can count on you, that is one of the highest compliments a leader can receive.

ANTICIPATE SAND TRAPS

What's the ultimate key to success in your new role? We believe that having confidence and being comfortable in the new role will affect how successful you are more than just about anything else. And knowing what to expect will increase your comfort level. Consider the following sand traps and options for getting back onto the fairway.

ESTABLISHED PATTERNS

Falling back into established patterns is the most difficult trap to stay out of, because you might not be able — or willing — to even recognize the trap. You're in this trap if

- You don't feel as if you're learning anything new.

- You notice that your days really haven't changed much.

- You see that many of your tasks are still reactive or controlling in relation to your team.

To get out of this trap, try

- Reviewing the pie chart you developed in the preteam phase to reflect how you intended to allocate your time differently. Use that chart to develop a new daily or weekly schedule.

- Seeking feedback from team members. Ask your team members if they feel that you're doing enough, too much, or too little.

TEAM DEPENDENCE

The team may still be overly dependent on you as their leader, because over the years they've come to rely on you to make all decisions. You're in this trap if

- The team isn't excited about agreements reached in meetings.

- You feel overburdened and overworked.

- The team gets very little accomplished when you aren't there.

If you find yourself in this trap, you need to get your teams out of this habit before you burn out. If you don't take the necessary steps to make your teams more autonomous, you'll only reinforce their dependence on you and not achieve the results you're counting on.

If you find yourself and your team in a dependence trap, consider

- Experimenting with new techniques. For example, try not speaking at all in meetings to encourage others to participate.

- Focusing on your own personal development. If team members have the skills necessary to accomplish tasks on their own, spend time away from the group focusing on your own training needs. This encourages the team to begin making decisions when you aren't there.

- Encouraging the team to select meeting leaders on a rotating basis. By doing this, members will accept more of the leadership responsibility rather than always relying on you.

ENJOYING TEAM DEPENDENCE

Frequently, dependent, immature teams might seem to be more pleasant to work with than teams that challenge your ideas and demand more autonomy. If you find yourself enjoying the dependent team more than the independent team, you may inadvertently foster team dependence. You've succumbed to this danger if

- You find yourself spending significantly more time with dependent teams than with teams that are working through counterdependence or independence and you tell yourself it's because the dependent teams have fewer skills or newer team members.

- You notice a feeling of more power or satisfaction when you work with the dependent teams.

If this sounds familiar, try

- Discussing dependence issues with the teams. Ask them to consider how dependence could affect their effectiveness in the long term.

- Establishing some "withdrawal" goals with the dependent teams. Encourage the teams to schedule some events or activities without your involvement. Provide them with assignments to complete in your absence.

RUNNING INTERFERENCE

If support departments or other teams don't allow your team members to have access to the materials, resources, and support they need to do their jobs, or if they continue to resist team member interaction and insist on working with you directly, you're in a different sort of trap. This trap puts you in the awkward position of running interference between your teams and others in the organization, which can take valuable time away from more important activities.

You're in this trap if

- You receive an inordinate number of calls from support groups or other teams regarding matters you thought the team was handling.

- Meetings between your team and other teams often are rescheduled or postponed.

- When you ask team members how they're coming along with tasks that require others' support, they respond by saying, "Pretty good," "Okay," or "Not too bad."

You can get out of this trap by

- Reassuring other leaders and support departments that you've provided the necessary coaching and direction to the team for their support activities. Assure them that you've discussed specific next steps with team members. Tell them you have confidence in the team to get the job done. This will increase their comfort in working directly with your team.

- Consistently directing others' calls and inquiries to the appropriate team members so that they get in the habit of working with one another directly.

AN ENEMY UNITED

Sometimes the easiest way to create cohesiveness is to band against a common enemy in an us-versus-them mode. Unfortunately, with new teams they're often the *us* and you're the *them*! If your team members test you, challenge you, or attack you, you're in yet another trap: an enemy united.

You're in this trap if

- You detect that the team is becoming counterdependent; that is, they push your help away even when they really need it.

- The team doesn't invite you to their meetings, share information with you, or update you on their progress.

To get out of this trap, try

- Calmly responding with empathy. Try not to become defensive; don't counterattack. You might say something such as, "I can see that you're frustrated about the problems you're facing in doing your own scheduling. Let's take a look at what you've tried so far and come up with some solutions together."
- Acknowledging any mistakes you've made.
- Redirecting the team from attacking you to attacking the problem.
- Developing a partnership progress report for yourself and your team members. This report should specify what you agree to do to support the team and what team members agree to do to support you.
- Remembering that eventually they'll grow out of this stage!

LESSONS LEARNED

To help you benefit from the experience of others, we want to share some lessons learned from successful leaders who survived the new-team phase:

- "Your new role might be more fun and challenging than you expected. Now that we [the managers] interact with a wider span of people, it's a lot more fun and challenging than it used to be" (Pat, Cape Coral Hospital).

- "Be as clear on boundaries and parameters as you can. We were developing a cross-training plan for staff nurses so they could draw blood on the units. We had an implementation team working on this, but we didn't specify clearly how many people we were hoping to get cross-trained or the percent of cross-training we had in mind. We knew in the back of our minds somewhere that we wanted as much cross-training as possible. During the planned development, they became overwhelmed with the paperwork and the liability involved with staff nurses drawing blood. The way we resolved the problem was in an open discussion at the next implementation team meeting. We, the managers, admitted that we didn't do an adequate job in conveying our expectations in regard to cross-training. Through two-way negotiation, we were able to come up with a cross-training plan that was comfortable for everyone" (Pat, Cape Coral Hospital).

- "Don't give up at the first sign of resistance. Keep trying. Eventually, your efforts will pay off" (Sarah, Milwaukee Insurance).

- "There's a lot to do at this point in the implementation. Try to maintain your focus on coaching and developing the team" (Jim, International Paper).

- "Balance your emphasis on teams with a focus on quality or productivity. Otherwise, the first time you have to cancel a team meeting for production, you'll hear, 'Oh, you don't believe in the team concept'" (Diane, Miller Brewing).

- "If it's not a life-or-death matter, try to let the team make the decision" (Diane, Miller Brewing).

- "Realize that you can say no. It's not a dirty word" (Diane, Miller Brewing).

- "You must be patient. You can't rush in and take over. People learn more from their failures than their successes" (Bart, Miller Brewing).

- "We take for granted our ability to make decisions. It's become so easy for us. But remember what it was like when you first were made a supervisor and you were scared to death to make a mistake. That's what your team members feel like now" (Bart, Miller Brewing).

- "You have to have confidence in what you're doing, because your title doesn't mean much anymore. You have to be willing to pick up a wrench and help a technician fix something one minute and sell the plant manager on a new idea the next minute" (Bart, Miller Brewing).

- "Although there's a lot of emphasis on the need for a change in management style, there's also a need for a change in 'hourly style.' It's your job to help technicians accept the responsibilities as well as the freedoms" (Bart, Miller Brewing).

- "Only turn things over to the team when they can prove to you that it's a repeatable event—that they have a process or system in place to make the decision or handle the responsibility" (Bart, Miller Brewing).

- "Structure is good. Don't just open everything up for a team free-for-all. Insist on agendas and use a shared leadership structure like the star point system" (Diane and Bart, Miller Brewing).

- "Concentrate on what you're doing. Otherwise you can get hurt, and you might not bounce back" (Michelangelo, trapeze artist, from his act *The Man on the Flying Trapeze*).

NEW-TEAM
LEADER JOB PROFILE

If you're successful in making the transition, your job should take on the characteristics outlined in Exhibit 9.1. You should

Exhibit 9.1. Job Profile for Leaders in the New-Team Phase.

Time spent on reactive tasks	40 percent
Primary tasks	• Providing resource support and barrier busting • Providing guidance by helping the team connect its activities with the mission and overall organizational values • Helping the team establish measurable goals • Coaching by asking open-ended questions, summarizing progress on the task, and encouraging others to develop solutions
Behaviors required for success	• Recognizing readiness • Creating ownership • Setting performance expectations • Providing support • Behaving consistently
Priorities/problems	• Knowing when to "jump in" and when to "back off" • Helping the team establish its own positive partnerships with others inside/outside the organization • Encouraging teams to take initiative
Parts of the job that are most satisfying at this phase	• Handling activities with greater impact, such as employee development, rather than merely fire fighting • Pride in watching your teams begin the development process, as they grow both as individuals and as a more cohesive unit • Feeling a sense of accomplishment because coaching and leadership skills are improving

notice that you're spending less time on reactive tasks and much more time guiding and supporting teams in handling their new decisions and tasks.

SELF-CHECK

Consider how you spent your time last month. Then use the checklist shown in Tool 9.3 to determine whether you're effectively changing your role in the new-team phase.

Tool 9.3. Self-Check for Leaders in the New-Team Phase.

Last month...	*Done*	*Not Done*
I withheld comments unless I could add significant value to the discussion or the decision.	☐	☐
I commended the team for taking initiative or coming up with new ideas.	☐	☐
I communicated at least 80 percent of the information I received from others.	☐	☐
I told the team and individual team members how valuable they are.	☐	☐
I listened more than I talked.	☐	☐
I avoided jumping in with my own solutions when the team was wrestling with an option.	☐	☐
I avoided taking empowerment opportunities away from the team.	☐	☐
I distributed high-visibility assignments to the team.	☐	☐
I included the team in making new decisions.	☐	☐
I encouraged support departments and others outside my team to deal directly with my team members.	☐	☐

SPECIAL CONSIDERATIONS FOR
SUPPORT PROFESSIONALS

The move to teams has two primary implications for support professionals: changes in support department structures and changes in behaviors. Overall, the new team culture increases the pressure on support departments to become more responsive to the teams' managing the organization's core process.

Structurally, this means that support departments might either become integrated with the core-process teams or create their own home-base team. If the services they provide are in heavy demand by the team or if the team needs technical direction in order to function, then the support professionals might need to be part of that team. For example, Ampex moved its engineering staff offices directly to the plant floor. (Keep in mind that the team will be more likely to follow support suggestions if support professionals eliminate status differences between themselves and the team.) They should attend meetings as members of the team and spend 20 to 30 percent of their time coaching team members to assume some of their tasks.

An analysis of support professionals' activities often reveals that a portion of what support professionals used to do can be done better by line employees (Lawler, 1992). For example, the maintenance department might teach the operators to handle their own preventive maintenance. Engineers might work with operators to improve changeover time. Accountants might help teams understand what overtime costs will do to their team budget. As members of the team, support professionals also should pitch in to help with the day-to-day operations, such as housekeeping (although this, of course, shouldn't become a primary role).

This transition to a new support relationship is usually gradual, as was the case at Tektronix, where engineers used to be traditionally organized along three strong functional lines: research and development, process engineering (liaison with vendors), and sustaining (manufacturing) engineering. As they moved to teams, an effort was made to align engineering more closely with manufacturing, as explained here: "When Tek's new circuit board plant was designed around self-managed work teams, the general manager decided that the engineering functions should be consolidated and that the engineers needed to be more closely aligned with the manufacturing operation. Hence, all three engineering functions reported to one manager and, over several years, all engineers were moved out of the office area and assigned to work with manufacturing teams. This departure from the traditional functional organization proved difficult for the engineering manager, as evidenced by the fact that there were three different managers within four years" (Rosow and Zager, 1989).

Another option is for support professionals to be dedicated as team mentors, retaining a home base in their professional area (Klein, 1993). This option works best when the demand for their technical services doesn't require a full-time support professional on the team but the teams need advice from and consultation with support professionals in order to assume additional responsibilities. Under these circumstances, support professionals become mentors to designated teams. In that role, they provide support by preparing easy-to-understand information and facilitating meetings to coach the teams.

This is what happened at Kodak's Plastic and Metal Products Division in Rochester, New York. Originally, PMP's support personnel were part of the Manufacturing Resources Division, and most of the support functions (financial services, personnel relations, and materials management) were located in a separate building. When they were first invited to manufacturing meetings, the support professionals sat on the periphery and rarely participated (thereby earning the nickname "the wall people"). Eventually, they were invited to become voting members of the meetings and move into PMP offices; they've now evolved to the point that they're true partners with Manufacturing. Although these support professionals still report to a home base, their evaluations are based heavily on their role in mentoring teams. Their primary tasks are to enhance operators' capabilities, transfer technical skill to operators, and involve operators in setting standards for continuous improvement (Rosow and Zager, 1989).

Having a home base also allows support professionals to confer with their technical colleagues about new technical developments and approaches they've used successfully with their teams. They'll want to develop a home-base team charter that states who supports each operation team, the purpose of the mentor relationship, and the mentor's responsibilities. In addition, a logical amount of home-base cross-training will increase support professionals' ability to respond to team needs and business changes. Support professionals should make sure their cross-training is practical, and they should remember that not everyone can be cross-trained in every technical specialty.

SPECIAL CONSIDERATIONS FOR UNION LEADERS

As much as managers are struggling with their new jobs, so too are local union leaders attempting to come to grips with their own drastically redefined role. As Paul Blackman, president of the A. O. Smith Steelworkers Local, put it: "To remain the same is to invite yourself out of a job" (Hoerr, 1989). Fortunately, the changes mean that for once, union leaders will be able to do more than listen to complaints from members. In fact, the new team structure should provide plenty of opportunities to work with members in a more proactive way, not just when they're angry, complaining, or having problems. It also gives union leaders a chance to represent the silent majority, not just the 20 percent who always seem to have problems.

One of the chief reasons for redesigning union leaders' roles is that, typically, fewer grievances follow the move to teams. What problems do occur tend to be resolved informally and earlier in the resolution process. The increasing power of the design team and the decreasing conflicts with management have the potential to leave stewards feeling isolated and resentful—unless their role is redefined as well.

Some United Auto Workers–GM plants have incorpo-
rated the role of committeemen (a combination of steward and
bargaining committee members), who serve as facilitators to
help groups of employees solve problems informally (U.S.
Bureau of Labor Management Relations, 1988). Such is also
the case at Seagrams. If, for instance, a team has a problem
with cleanup at the end of the day, the steward might intervene to get a volunteer. This places new demands on the
steward to know and understand each team's unique rules. If a
team member from Team A complains about job rotation, for
example, the steward needs to understand Team A's agreement about rotation procedures (Bisesi, 1993).

The local leaders at AT&T's Denver Works have under-
gone a similar transformation. Mike Gregorich, president of
the International Brotherhood of Electrical Workers, Local
2300, describes it this way:

> One role of our union people is to be a resource for teams.
> Union people do some team training, for example, which
> is something we bargained for. We were concerned be-
> cause some training personnel haven't been on the shop
> floor in 15 years. When people change environments,
> they tend to change focus. So we wanted training to be
> done by union associates who had actual team experi-
> ence, and who could relate to the problems shop floor
> associates are going through.
>
> Our union resource people are like firemen. When-
> ever a team is having a problem, the associates can call on
> them for help. Slowly, I'm trying to build more union
> resource people rather than only having stewards who
> know how to file a grievance. But we can't ignore the
> contract or fall into the patsy role.

Gregorich goes on to say that "it's difficult to find union
people with facilitation skills who, instead of pushing their
own ideas, can help a team solve a problem" (*Commitment
Plus*, 1992). For this reason, the Grain Millers have recommended specific skills and training for their local leaders working on the introduction of a new work system; these skills

include problem solving, planning, organizational development, communications, and training (Willis and others, 1991).

The United Steelworkers of America also are launching a
major education program to develop leadership skills. They're
teaching their headquarters staff how to negotiate on a
problem-solving basis rather than on a confrontational, adver-
sarial basis, thus equipping them to train local union presidents.

In a similar move, the Communications Workers of
America require officials involved in total quality efforts to pass
a very intensive training program in facilitative skills. This
group continues to emphasize the traditional bargaining skills
but sees the need for developing two kinds of union leaders:
those trained to handle contractual problems and grievances
and those involved in such participative efforts as total quality.

Just as managers might have difficulty making the transition from

| control based on authority | ⟶ to ⟶ | control based on commitment, |

union leaders often have trouble making the shift from

| decision making based on rules and precedents | ⟶ to ⟶ | decision making based on values and commitment. |

Obviously, it's impossible to anticipate everything that
will occur in a new team environment. Union leaders should
let their values about joint processes guide their behavior at
critical junctures when it becomes necessary to make some
form of unfamiliar adaptation.

SUMMARY

This period, when teams are actually getting started, is likely to
be one of the most exciting and frustrating of your entire
career. Many leaders speak of it as a time of life-changing
intensity. Your triumphs and setbacks are likely to affect you
more deeply than ever before. We hope that the advice in this
chapter will help you enjoy the triumphs.

TEN

New-Team Safety Nets: Demonstrating Organizational Commitment and Support

"I'd just as soon sack up bobcats."

That's how one of our Texas clients described the period in her organization's history when teams were just getting started.

Without question, the new-team phase is the most exciting and chaotic time in the team implementation. Even though all the organization's plans are starting to come to fruition, things may feel slightly out of control, especially for the leaders charged with pulling off this immense transformation. This is a critical period for them; it's the time when they'll either succeed or give up in disgust. (Because these people are the ones who had the most to contribute—or they wouldn't have been promoted in the first place—the organization certainly doesn't want to lose them.)

There are six major areas organizations should focus on in the new-team phase: senior-management support, assessment and feedback, training, appraisal and compensation, career development, and team member support. We recommend that top managers use all the resources at their disposal to help leaders make it through this difficult transition.

SENIOR-MANAGEMENT SUPPORT

If senior managers would just do two simple things—demonstrate commitment and pay attention to leaders' needs—they would make leaders' jobs immeasurably easier.

DEMONSTRATE COMMITMENT

Of all the ways top managers can show their commitment, by far the most powerful is to model the behaviors they expect of others. Motivational speeches are nice, and written pronouncements can have some effect, but what people really pay attention to is what top managers *do*, not what they *say*. In a recent survey of high-involvement practices, "leadership commitment" was rated as the most important factor in the success of the change effort, but it was also rated as the factor where there was the greatest gap between what was required and what organizations were able to produce (Wellins and others, 1993).

Modeling empowerment is important to leaders for two reasons. First, more often than not, leaders learn what to do by observing behavior at the top levels of their organization, not by what they hear in some classroom. This means that senior managers must participate in the same training that they expect their leaders to attend. Equally important to modeling the skills learned in training is displaying behaviors supportive of organizational values. For example, they can start each meeting with issues relating to the company's driving value. If customer service is the organization's driving value, they might begin by discussing positive examples of how leaders and their teams have met customer service goals. This behavior reinforces the importance of the value and demonstrates management's commitment.

Top-level managers also need to be visible on the floor. The organization should encourage managers to discuss the vision and direction of the company with leaders and team members not only at meetings but in other work situations. Top managers should plan to spend 20 to 30 percent of their time communicating the vision—in person!

When Bob, the plant manager at an electric motor assembly facility, agreed to spend time walking through the teams' areas every day, the plant was impressed. Unfortunately, after a few short weeks, team members complained that they never saw Bob. In fact, Bob was spending more time than ever glued to his computer, trying to stay in touch with the plant through production reports. Both members and leaders eventually gave up on the team implementation, figuring that if it wasn't a priority for Bob, then it wasn't a priority for them.

Senior managers who model empowering behaviors also help leaders in another way: "walking the talk" reduces the amount of time leaders need to spend explaining or rationalizing senior management's actions. One team leader estimated that in the first six months of the team implementation, he spent 20 percent of his time trying to justify the plant manager's behavior. He was bombarded with questions from team members, such as, "Well, if we're so empowered, why did Ed dictate that we had to work overtime on Saturday? We could have met the production goal by reassigning some of our equipment without incurring the extra cost." This leader was in an untenable situation: he could agree with the team member (and imply that his boss was unempowering), say that he didn't know (which would make him feel—and look—uninformed), or feebly attempt to justify the action (which would cause him to lose the trust of his team members).

Unfortunately, in most organizations no one wants to tell

the emperor he isn't wearing any clothes. That's why it's absolutely imperative for the organization to establish an anonymous feedback system for all leaders — especially senior managers.

Finally, senior managers need to pay attention to the symbolic effect of their actions. Early in team implementation, senior managers' opinions and behaviors still carry a disproportionate weight with the workforce. After a key meeting, subordinates will often ruminate on the top manager's words: "What do you suppose he meant by that?" "Do you think that means she's going to . . .?" Simple plans or communications often have unintended consequences.

For example, when one senior vice president of sales had to cancel a planned tour of three self-directed sites, the teams were thrown into an uproar. They were convinced he was withdrawing his support for the pilot. The teams slipped into a downward spiral of doubt and fear. Finally, when one of the members had the sense to call him and ask for an explanation, it turned out he had a perfectly legitimate reason: a business crisis in another region.

Senior managers must remember that at this point in team evolution, many of their subordinates are going to be reluctant to approach them with "touchy" feedback or concerns. After all, leaders aren't that far removed from the days when they might have had their heads chewed off. It helps to remember that organizational memories are exceedingly long. People will discuss what senior managers did fifteen years ago as if it happened only yesterday.

PAY ATTENTION TO LEADERS' NEEDS

There's an unfortunate, but almost universal, tendency to overlook leaders in the haste of satisfying team needs. Organizations mistakenly assume that team members have the greatest adjustment to make when in fact the transition is probably the most difficult for leaders. This mistake is committed on several different fronts:

- *Communication systems.* In the rush to get team members the information they need, organizations sometimes bypass their leaders completely. What a blow to a group of people who are feeling insecure enough as it is! Senior management should make every effort to include leaders in *any* communication going to the teams.

- *Training.* The universal lament in most team implementations is that the organization didn't spend enough time training leaders. When this happens, it's generally because the organization hasn't recognized that leaders have development needs above and beyond those of team members.

- *Surveys of satisfaction.* Everyone is concerned about the team members: "Are they feeling more empowered than before? Do they have enough input? Are we responding to their suggestions?" Unfortunately, almost no one asks these questions about the team leaders.

The most important need of leaders is for understanding and patience. Top management should remember to give them a chance. This is a difficult (and, for some, a gut-wrenching) transition to make. Managers shouldn't expect changes overnight. Many team implementations go through a period when quality and productivity increases are slow in coming. This means the organization shouldn't expect dramatic increases in the first six to nine months. After all, these trends are the result of adjustments *everyone* is making. Leaders aren't necessarily at fault.

ASSESSMENT AND FEEDBACK

Because leaders are being measured against a new yardstick of acceptable behavior, we recommend that managers be explicit about the new requirements. It's important to set these requirements early in the new-team phase, because leaders need to know how they're doing on their new criteria for success.

We suggest using specific dimensions and behaviors (see Chapter Five for examples) as the criteria for assessment, coaching, and feedback. These behaviors will show leaders exactly what they need to do to be successful. Many of our clients measure these behaviors in anonymous surveys of leaders' empowerment skills. Often called "360-degree feedback" (because leaders get the perceptions of their boss, their peers, and their team members), these surveys can be excellent vehicles for development. Because leaders and employees have had a chance to work together to develop new roles and skills, the 360-degree feedback process should be a comfortable next step in providing each other with feedback. Sample behaviors for the dimension "Building Business Partnerships" are outlined in Exhibit 10.1.

The outcome of the 360-degree feedback process will provide leaders with an idea of how they stack up against the new requirements. For example, leaders will see how team members perceive their effectiveness on each behavior and then be able to compare that with their perceptions of their own performance. Perhaps the most beneficial application of 360-degree feedback is the use of the data in a feedback meeting—a team meeting at which leaders discuss their greatest strengths and greatest development needs. The leader might begin by saying, for example, "The data said that 'preventing our group from becoming isolated' was my greatest strength. What else can I do to expand on this strength?" Similar feedback can be solicited about developmental needs. This type of dialogue is a relatively safe way to begin more face-to-face feedback, which leaders and teams will use frequently in the mature-team phase.

Some organizations go even further with the assessment process. Although the surveys provide a good indication of how leaders are perceived within the organization, they don't tell anything about an individual leader's potential—what he or she *might* be capable of doing. For that purpose, many of our clients use a series of assessment exercises.

**Exhibit 10.1. Sample Assessment Form for the Dimension
"Building Business Partnerships."**

How Often Does This Person
Perform the Behavior?

A = Always or Almost Always	B = Often	C = Sometimes	D = Seldom	E = Never or Almost Never	
					Encourages me to develop partnerships with other teams or groups.
					Makes sure that business partners understand our team's requirements.
					Prevents our group from becoming isolated from the rest of the organization.
					Asks me how I'll involve others to gain alternate perspectives on new ideas.
					Shows me how my work affects other departments.
					Directly involves partners in decisions that affect them.
					Makes sure our team members understand the needs of business partners.
					Works toward improving relationships with partners rather than blaming them for problems.

Assessment activities can simulate tasks and problems leaders will face in each of the phases of their teams' development. Not only do participants have an opportunity to receive feedback on all the appropriate dimensions, but they also get to experience some of the typical situations that probably will arise later in their teams' development. In one assessment program, for example, leaders experience typical problems that come up three weeks after teams have been introduced, and then six, twelve, and eighteen months later. Not only does this information provide a comprehensive picture of the leader's abilities; it also gives them a very realistic preview of what to expect with teams.

In addition to providing feedback on leadership behaviors, the organization can help leaders monitor how they're doing against the original empowerment schedule (the schedule of responsibilities teams take on and by when). Here are some of the questions your organization might ask:

- Are teams assuming responsibilities according to the one-month, three-month, and six-month schedules?

- Are they ahead of or behind other teams in the organization?

- Are leaders taking on more interesting and important tasks as they transfer some of their former responsibilities to their teams?

- Are leaders allotting their time according to the original plan for their new role?

The leaders' shift in roles and responsibilities requires constant vigilance from the organization. Otherwise, it's too easy to rest comfortably in the old roles. Managers can monitor roles and responsibilities easily by using a work team progress survey such as the one shown in Tool 10.1.

Significant glitches in the transfer of responsibilities probably will require the attention of an objective facilitator. Sometimes the problem resides with the leader's boss, who might be holding the leader responsible for things the team should be doing or not giving up enough of his or her own tasks to give the leader something challenging to do.

In one case, in the field sales and service organization of a major automotive manufacturer, a six-month check on the teams showed that they were ahead of schedule on everything

Tool 10.1. Sample Work Team Progress Survey.

Please circle the number that best represents how responsibility is shared between your team's leader and the team. For example, in the first item, if your team is primarily responsible for this activity, you would circle the number 6.

	Leader Has Primary Responsibility		Responsibility Shared Between Leader and Team Members			Team Has Assumed Primary Responsibility	
Prepare and/or manage cost budgets	1	2	3	4	5	6	7
Assign daily tasks to team members	1	2	3	4	5	6	7
Work with external customers and suppliers	1	2	3	4	5	6	7
Work with internal customers and suppliers	1	2	3	4	5	6	7
Stop work process to address quality concerns	1	2	3	4	5	6	7
Select team members	1	2	3	4	5	6	7
Handle vacation scheduling	1	2	3	4	5	6	7
Manage our cross-training plan	1	2	3	4	5	6	7

except the car distribution responsibilities. Team members said that they were ready but hadn't received the go-ahead or the necessary training. Upon further investigation, it became apparent that Bob, the staff manager in charge of car distribution, wasn't letting go of this responsibility for two reasons: first, Bob was sixty-one years old, had been doing this job for the last fifteen years, and was hoping that he might be able to coast to retirement without having to alter his daily routine; second, because eighty percent of Bob's old job was being transferred to the teams, he was supposed to move to a new "business development" role, but Bob's boss didn't have the time to help him with his new, more proactive responsibilities. No wonder he was clinging to his old role!

In time, the situation was resolved by having one of the original architects of the team system work with Bob one-on-one for a week. They established a specific training schedule for team members to learn car distribution, and they worked together on the business development role for four days. After that, Bob required only minor booster shots of encouragement to keep him pointed in the right direction.

TRAINING

"Training? You just can't do enough of it," said one facilitator, expressing the sentiments of team leaders the world over. Organizations are asking their leaders to do more than ever before — and to do it in an entirely different way. Organizations can't possibly expect them to be successful without adequate training.

Assuming that leaders are already proficient at the tactical skills, now is the time for leaders to get into strategies for their new role: leading through vision and values, building trust, facilitating learning, and building business partnerships. In addition to the guidelines for effective training that the organization followed in the preteam phase, there are some other features to look for in training the leaders of new teams:

- *Attention "hooks."* Organizations need something that's going to grab leaders' attention. They might feel they've already spent enough time in the classroom in the preteam phase. Leaders need to be convinced that more training is important and that it applies to them.

- *Discovery learning.* Just being told what to do is unlikely to have any real impact on leaders. If they can discover the principles themselves, however, through experiential exercises or the Socratic method, the training will be much more likely to stick.

- *Modeling.* Most leaders don't have many positive role models when it comes to transferring responsiblitics to teams, so thcy need to be shown an effective model. In addition, they need an opportunity to practice the positive behaviors; just seeing the behaviors isn't enough to do the trick. Practicing and receiving feedback is vital to learning the difficult skills.

- *Expansive thinking.* Ultimately, top management will need leaders to think creatively about new ways to lead, not just mechanically apply techniques. Thus training should encourage leaders to take risks and try new things.

Training modules should be arranged in a logical sequence, with built-in opportunities for leaders to apply the skills they're learning. A sample training schedule is illustrated in Exhibit 10.2.

APPRAISAL AND COMPENSATION

Top managers need to use performance appraisal and compensation systems to drive the behaviors they want, not just to satisfy personnel department requirements.

We strongly recommend that the performance management system should cover both results (*what* was accomplished) and behaviors (*how* those results were achieved). The year-end review will be even more effective if the organizaton involves leaders in setting their own objectives. Leaders (and team members) should have an opportunity both to shape the organization's goals and to translate them into specific team goals. In most cases, leaders' objectives will include areas beyond the team's goals. For example, a leader might have individual responsibility for new technology development— something that isn't expected of the team.

Once goals have been established, top-level managers can discuss how they expect leaders to accomplish the results

Exhibit 10.2. Sample Training Schedule for Leaders of New Teams.

Training	SCHEDULE				Application Assignments
	Q1	Q2	Q3	Q4	
AWARENESS TRAINING					
Technical Training *(for the new areas each leader's teams will encompass)*	X				Explain the technical process to visiting engineers.
Business Analysis *(benchmarking and competitive analysis)*		X			Lead team members in developing a world-class performance board.
Budgeting 101			X		Involve team members in the analysis of last year's performance against budget; coach them through developing a team budget for next year.
Business Planning				X	Develop a long-range plan for staffing, material management, and customer satisfaction.
SKILLS TRAINING					
Leading Through Vision and Values	X				Complete team start-up kit with each team and agree on team charter, operating guidelines, and roles and responsibilities.
Developing High Performers	X				Identify an opportunity to coach each team member.
Facilitating Learning	X				Develop cross-training and team development plans with each team.
Championing Continuous Improvement		X			Lead each team through the problem-solving cycle for at least one improvement project.
Building Business Partnerships			X		Identify a joint project with a customer or supplier.
Facilitating Team Performance				X	Lead the team through the team performance review process using survey feedback.

by identifying appropriate dimensions and being explicit about behavioral expectations. An example of the product of this process is shown in Tool 10.2.

At the end of the performance period, the organization will need to involve multiple sources in the evaluation of leaders' performances. Typically, sources include peers, team members, and customers. Although eventually the organization might progress to the point that those sources can provide face-to-face feedback, at this phase it's generally safer to collect their perceptions via anonymous surveys. The leaders' managers then can assume responsibility for summarizing everyone's observations and ratings, later agreeing on a specific development plan with each leader.

The compensation system also has to be adjusted to account for leaders' new roles. In organizations such as Bausch & Lomb and UCAR Carbon, as much as 40 percent of leaders' compensation is based on skills in leading teams. In Colgate's Technology Division, leaders' bonuses are based on corporate-wide goals, technology team goals, and individual objectives. Each leader prepares specific signed contracts with key customers, and the customers' evaluation is one of the most important components of the year-end review. Notably, a third of each leader's bonus is based on the extent to which the Technology Division's team goals are achieved (McDermott, 1992).

CAREER DEVELOPMENT

At this phase in their transition, most leaders are too busy trying to keep their heads above water to worry about career development. There are, of course, a few exceptions that top management needs to provide for: leaders who clearly are unable to make the transition and leaders who master the new role so rapidly that they're ready for new responsibilities.

Tool 10.2. Sample Objectives for Leaders of New Teams.

Organization's Key Result Area	Leader's and Team's Key Result Areas	Objectives	Leader Dimensions That Support the Key Result Area	Leader's Behavioral Expectations
	Delivery to customers *(team)*	Increase on-time delivery to customers from 89 percent to 95 percent *(team)*	Championing continuous improvement	Solicit improvement suggestions from the team (70 percent of all suggestions should come from the team)
SPEED	New-product introduction *(leader)*	Launch the M82 product by the end of the third quarter with the designated project team *(leader)*	Building business partnerships	Directly involve partners in decisions that affect them (achieve an overall rating of "4" from R&D partners)

LEADERS WHO AREN'T GOING TO MAKE IT

If the organization did an effective job of offering options in the preteam phase, most of the people who didn't *want* to try the new role have probably opted out already. This leaves the company with leaders who are doing well and leaders who, for one reason or another, simply can't adjust to the new role. These latter leaders are the individuals most organizations have the hardest time dealing with, often because these people are genuinely trying to succeed.

To handle this situation effectively, the organization must have a reliable system for assessing leaders' performance. It can't simply wait for team members to stroll into the personnel office to complain about their leaders. A formal performance management process is helpful here, but it's probably not enough (especially if it calls only for annual appraisals). Top managers must create opportunities to observe leaders in action: in team meetings and in training or coaching situations. Between firsthand observation and 360-degree survey feedback instruments, the organization should be able to identify the team leaders who are in trouble.

Once the company has pinpointed the leaders who don't seem to be making the transition effectively, it's very tempting for top management to wait and hope that these leaders will improve on their own. Despite our most fervent hopes, though, this almost never happens. Instead, the organization must take action.

We recommend the following checklist of activities. Top managers should check to make sure:

- ☐ It's a can't-do (skill) problem rather than a won't do (attitude) problem.

- ☐ The company has provided the necessary skill training.

- ☐ There isn't some other barrier (time, lack of information, mixed messages from a boss) preventing the person from using the skills effectively.

- ☐ Top managers have provided one-on-one coaching.

☐ Leaders have "safe," easy opportunities for practice.

☐ Any successes have been reinforced.

☐ There has been sufficient time for the leader to demonstrate changes.

☐ Top management has discussed the alternatives if the situation doesn't improve.

Another way to look at this problem is to examine the number of leaders who are in trouble. If most of the organization's leaders are struggling, chances are they haven't received enough support. If only a few of the leaders are having problems, it's more likely an individual skill issue.

Once the company is sure that it's provided all reasonable support and the situation still hasn't improved, management must remove the ineffective leaders. Otherwise, the teams in their areas will never develop. This is where a formal assessment of the leaders' potential can be invaluable. If top managers have an accurate skill profile for all the leaders, it's much easier to match the ineffective team leaders to other jobs that are better suited to their unique talents.

Consider the case of Karen, a leader in an assembly plant. Her skill profile is shown in Figure 10.1. With the implementation of teams, Karen moved into a leadership role — an obvious mismatch given her skill profile and the job requirements of leading self-directed teams. (An appropriate profile of skill

Figure 10.1. Karen's Skill Profile.

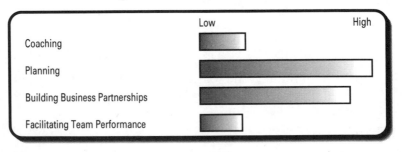

requirements for that job looks more like Figure 10.2-a.) Karen's skill profile *was* a good match, however, with the job of production scheduler. (The profile of skill requirements for that position is shown in Figure 10.2-b.)

In Karen's case, the organization was able to make an effective switch: the former production scheduler took over Karen's job on the line, and Karen became the new production scheduler. Obviously, all situations don't work out this well, but we do recommend that companies make every effort to place failing leaders elsewhere in the organization. After all, the organization changed the rules in the middle of the game by moving to teams—and it wants to keep its good people.

LEADERS WHO MASTER THE NEW ROLE RAPIDLY

To keep the high-performing leaders motivated, organizations need to provide creative development options. Quaker Oats' Topeka plant does this quite effectively by providing multiple special projects for leaders. This way, leaders never run out of

Figure 10.2. Job-Specific Profiles of Skill Requirements.

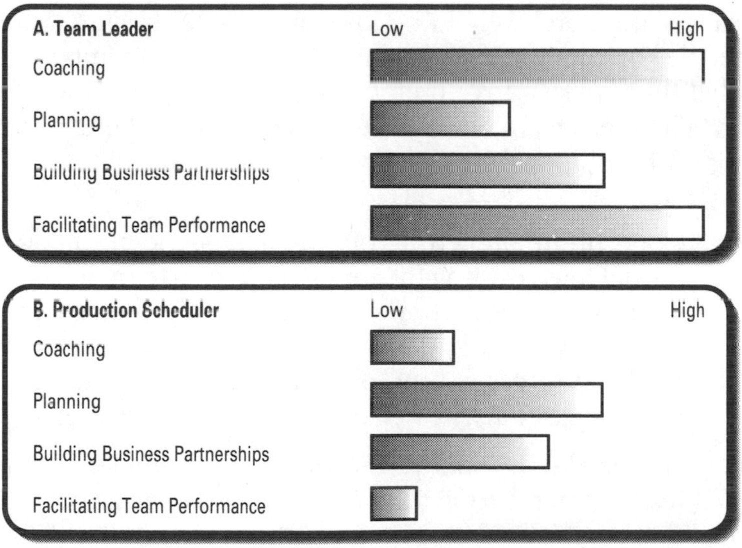

interesting work to do and are able to increase their value to the company.

Successful leaders generally make great trainers, facilitators, and internal consultants, and these areas are where organizations need their strongest performers. It's in these positions that leaders have the potential to influence the greatest number of teams. Top management should resist the temptation to staff these important positions with the leaders who "aren't making it." This can look like an attractive and convenient alternative, but it will mean disaster in the long run.

TEAM MEMBER SUPPORT

While all team members play an important part in their leaders' adjustment to their new role, not all team members are created equal. When team members are tolerant, open to change, and direct with their feedback, leaders tend to feel more secure and are much more likely to be reinforcing with the team. When team members are unrelentingly negative, leaders are more likely to be insecure and controlling. Some people have gone so far as to suggest that "team members get what they deserve." We prefer to suggest that there are some specific things team members can do to ensure a better working relationship with their leaders:

- Concentrate on getting out of the dependent mode of the old role, resisting the temptation to go to their leaders for answers before they've at least thought through their options. When they do go to their leaders, they should be prepared to discuss the pros and cons and timelines of their suggestions, as well as outcomes they expect.

- Help leaders by not overreacting to small problems in the team, remembering that these problems will get worked out, especially if they involve others.

- Give leaders immediate and constructive feedback. Don't build up resentment and then blow up or strike back.

- Assist leaders by learning all they can about teams. They can share articles on teams or plan a site visit to another self-directed organization in the area.

- Let leaders know how things are going. Leaders may be able to use the information to promote the team with a customer or a senior manager.

Leaders themselves spend a lot of time talking about the amount of support they get from team members. One of the favorite topics of conversation with leaders in this stage of evolution is "teams from hell." If a leader accidently ends up with a group that consists of the company's surliest naysayers, by all means the organization should break them up. Under no circumstances should top managers continue to torture a leader by forcing him or her to work in an impossible situation.

TOUGH SITUATIONS THE ORGANIZATION MIGHT ENCOUNTER

Despite the organization's best efforts, senior managers will encounter some tough situations in the new-team phase. Certain problems arise consistently in team-based organizations; a few examples follow, with suggested actions.

EMPLOYEE COMPLAINTS ABOUT ORGANIZATIONAL INACTION

What happens if the teams under a particular leader are hitting their results targets, but the leader isn't demonstrating the desired coaching behaviors?

What could be causing the problem? The leader doesn't believe the organization is serious about changing leadership behavior. Years of watching similar programs come and go without any significant consequences have lulled the leader into a sense of complacency, as well as years of being reinforced for achieving "results at any expense."

What might the organization do? Acknowledge the problem. It helps to send a clear message that:

- Leaders who make their "numbers" but don't share the values need to improve — or they're out.

- Leaders who miss commitments but share the values will be given a second chance.

High Management Turnover

What happens if management turnover is high in the department or facility?

What could be causing the problem? Chances are that either the site is used as a stop on the promotional ladder or the organization isn't selecting people who are a good match with its needs.

What might the organization do? There are several steps you can take to address leadership turnover problems. First, develop the mission and vision statements and the team charters so that they can outlive any one person. Second, involve team members and leaders in selecting replacement managers. Third, make sure that the next level up in the organization supports what leaders are trying to do. (Sometimes this can be done by creating a division-level steering committee.)

Mismatched Leaders Near Retirement

What happens if the organization has one or two leaders close to retirement who just aren't working out as team leaders (but whom the organization is reluctant to retrain in technical jobs)?

What could be causing the problem? After years of being reinforced for an autocratic management style, these leaders are probably incapable of change.

What might the organization do? Don't, under any circumstances, place them in charge of teams if they're not truly motivated to change their leadership style. Instead, try to put them in a job that's a reasonable match with their strengths. If they're motivated to try a more technical job, however, go ahead and provide the extra training; everyone might be pleasantly surprised. (One of our clients ended up with a part-time technical consultant who worked until he was seventy-eight years old!)

SUMMARY

This is usually the phase that makes or breaks most leaders. Therefore, it's imperative that top managers marshal all the organizational support they can for leaders at this critical juncture.

ELEVEN

Mature-Team Leadership: Encouraging Focus, Direction, and Initiative

After all the anticipation of the preteam phase and the intensity of the new-team phase, most leaders look forward to the time when their teams mature and hit a stable stride. Many are surprised, then, to learn that the changes and demands in their own role don't subside as their teams mature. This is not unlike the feelings many parents have when their children depart for college. After eighteen years of looking forward to an empty nest, they might be surprised to find the nestlings back home, asking for money or dropping off laundry. Your responsibilities don't end just because you've successfully guided your teams through their adolescence. Perhaps now more than ever, you have an important and evolving role in the success of your teams.

WHAT'S HAPPENING
IN THE ORGANIZATION?

The honeymoon is over. All the hoopla and unrealistically positive expectations have faded. But gone, too, are the irrational fears and concerns of most of the team holdouts in the organization. Everyone has a more informed, rational view of teams. The advantages and challenges are clear.

By this time, teams have passed through the stages of dependence and counterdependence to arrive at a state of *inter*dependence. They've settled into their roles in the larger business. They trust you and interact effectively with others outside the team. Because the intense conflicts of the new-team transition have subsided, they no longer struggle with you over decision-making and control issues; they're past the need to see everything in us-versus-them terms.

By now, many of the needs that motivated you to move to teams in the first place are being fulfilled. Customers' requirements for quality and delivery are being met. Products and services are being delivered faster and more efficiently. The workforce has become more focused and flexible so that one member's absence doesn't bring the entire process to a screeching halt.

These improvements, however, probably are happening at a slower rate now than in the earlier phase of team evolution. Most of the obvious problems and glaring variances have been brought under control. The excitement associated with making quantum improvements in quality and productivity might have begun to wear off. Fortunately, this situation generally is counterbalanced by the visibility and recognition that teams now receive.

This was certainly the case with the San Diego Zoo, where teams were organized around new bioclimatic zones. Teams of zoo employees now cooperate to run an entire zone, from buildings and grounds to the horticultural and animal collections. When word got out about their initial success, team members were invited to speak at local business schools and at a whole range of companies that have nothing to do with zookeeping (Sony, Pacific Bell, and Northern Telecom, to name a few). The effect was to inspire team members to live up to their growing reputation. David Glines, who's in charge of training and development at the zoo, explained that team members' and leaders' pride helped reenergize the implementation (Glines, Forror, Silva, and Kobert, 1993).

Your implementation need not be located in as exotic a setting as the zoo to garner this much attention. Would-be implementers of teams happily tromp through chemical plants, pulp mills, and waste treatment facilities in the pursuit of knowledge about teams. By the time your teams have matured, chances are you'll be beset with requests from inside and outside your company to talk about your experience. If you encourage your team leaders and members to get involved in conducting tours and speaking at conferences, you'll help sustain some of their early excitement about teams.

At the employee level, teams have probably assumed most of the responsibilities outlined in the original transfer plan. Because team members have become more comfortable and familiar with these tasks by now, the leaders should be freed up to be more fully engaged in their new, value-added responsibilities.

A good example of this shift in leaders' responsibilities is found at Shenandoah Life, which converted to total processing teams back in 1983. The teams consist of five to ten employees who are responsible for providing all policy-related services to customers in a specific geographical area. The teams are cross-trained so that any member can handle any customer request. Now, more than ten years after the initial transformation, leaders spend no more than 10 percent of their time on traditional supervisory functions. Instead, they

- Function as personal computer gurus to the teams as they help the teams streamline operations, often by re-programming PCs, maintaining PCs, and evaluating PC-related equipment for purchase decisions.

- Serve on task forces to increase feedback upward to top management.

- Serve on company-wide product implementation teams that debug new, untested forms of insurance policies and coordinate the new policies through various departments as part of the test procedure.

- Assist the company's security director in ensuring system integrity.

- Test new computer procedures to ensure that the proper amount of tax is paid on each policyholder's investment income.

- Aid the data processing department in providing new procedures and making updating easier.

- Recommend ways of eliminating substantive, costly errors from the company's reports to the Internal Revenue Service.

- Serve on task forces to increase customer satisfaction through corporate and individual service (Forbes, 1989).

A similar transition occurred at A. E. Staley's Sagamore, Indiana, corn refinery. Operating in a new work system since 1979, Staley's area managers (the equivalent of first-line supervisors) have taken responsibility for the following:

- Experimentation that resulted in a dramatic improvement in the color of corn syrup

- Initiating a cooperative venture with another plant to share the costs of a consultant for solving an ongoing technical problem

- Developing corporate support for buying costly state-of-the-art equipment and then arranging training for employees (Barnett, 1989)

Unfortunately, some leaders fail to make this shift successfully and continue to operate in their old comfort zones. Indeed, without a specific plan and concentrated attention, it's relatively easy for some to get left behind. The reasons for this are both practical and personal. In the next section, we examine some of the emotional reasons preventing leaders from growing with their teams.

HOW LEADERS FEEL

Many forces are at work to keep leaders stuck in their old roles:

- *Requests for operational data from above.* Your boss might be sending you mixed signals by expecting you to have up-to-the-minute knowledge of the teams' day-to-day operations.

- *Pressure to act now.* There's nothing like a production or customer crisis to cause otherwise well-intentioned leaders to jump back into the fray.

- *Gunslinger orientation.* Some of us never give up our desire to "ride in and save the day."

- *The impulse to "do something."* The old tasks tended to require action and to result in some tangible outcomes. The new tasks require more thought than action and might not produce any visible results for months:

Old Tasks	*New Tasks*
Current	Long-term
Specific	Nebulous
Well defined	Undefined
Organization-initiated	Leader-initiated
Internal focus	External focus

You'll have to examine whether you're finding too much gratification in doing your team members' work. Ralph Stayer, the former CEO who moved Johnsonville Sausage into highly successful self-directed teams, finally had to own up to this tendency and take some radical corrective action. He scheduled himself out of many meetings, forcing others to make their own decisions. He also stopped collecting data about daily operations, recognizing that if he had information about shortages and yields, he would feel compelled to get too involved (DuBrul, 1993).

On the other hand, leaders who've attempted to make this role shift might still be experiencing that all-too-familiar feeling of not knowing what they're doing. This shift isn't unlike the transition they made many months ago with new teams, after all. In both cases, leaders have had to give up tasks that enabled them to feel progress and mastery and step into the unknown. With the earlier transition, though, they probably received some training and attention from the organization. Unfortunately, that assistance often doesn't exist in the mature-team phase, because most organizations don't recognize the challenges leaders experience in moving from new teams to mature teams.

TALES OF THREE LEADERS

Leaders' reactions to the role transition in the mature-team phase vary tremendously. Consider the actual cases of Deb, Mike, and Bill, all of whom were department supervisors before the transformation to teams (as illustrated in Figure 11.1).

In their organization, teams were created to include lab, compounding, and production employees on the same team. Each team handled all the functions to produce a particular family of products: all the way from compounding (mixing the raw materials) to shipping the finished product. Star points on each team assumed many of the supervisors' former lead-

Figure 11.1. Original Organizational Structure.

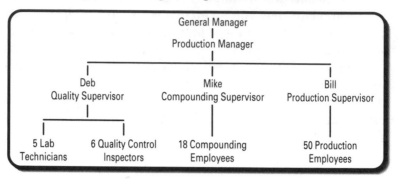

ership and administrative responsibilities, while Deb, Mike, and Bill assumed technical resource roles.

After two years in the new roles, Deb, Mike, and Bill were primarily responsible for continuous technical improvements across all five teams. This responsibility was intended to include training of team members, coordination with the appropriate star points on each team, and proactive improvement programs (such as applying for Q1 certification from a major customer). During the new-team phase, the three former supervisors were very busy training team members and providing direct technical support to each of the lines.

It was only as the teams matured and the technical resources had less of an opportunity to provide hands-on support that any significant problems emerged. Once teams had assumed 60 percent of the leaders' old duties and the leaders were freed up to begin handling the more proactive responsibilities in their new job descriptions, the leaders were faced with a second role transition. Each of them reacted in a different way.

- Deb was quite excited about the chance to work on larger projects. In her former role as a quality supervisor, she had never found the time to take action on many of her grander-scale improvement ideas. And although her boss had never said anything to her, Deb had always felt that management was slightly disappointed that she hadn't done more with the quality function. She saw her changing role as an opportunity to make a significant impact on the operation.

Deb wasted no time in transferring the more routine quality tasks to the team. She not only developed an effective training schedule, but she also delegated much of the training responsibility to the quality star points. If anything, team members complained that Deb "pulled away" too fast.

Bill had a much tougher time with this phase of the transition. He had handled the new-team phase fairly well, when he was out on the lines training team members and answering their questions about new responsibilities; but as the team members became more self-sufficient, Bill found himself at loose ends. His reaction was to insinuate himself into team meetings and production crises until team members finally complained that he wouldn't leave them alone. After he was gently "banned" from team meetings, Bill sulked in his office for several weeks. No amount of coaching or explaining could get him to take the initiative on production improvements across the five lines.

Finally, Bill admitted that he was a "people person," not a "project person." He genuinely liked the day-to-day interactions with employees and couldn't get excited about sitting in his office plotting out Gantt charts. This disclosure led the company to carve out a modified technical resource role for Bill. The production manager agreed to handle the technical innovations component of Bill's role (a secret vice of his anyway), and Bill assumed more responsibility for "human" innovations: leading the design team, developing additional team training, and facilitating peer review sessions.

■ Mike, who had had the most difficulty with the first part of the transition, believed that his compounders were incapable of making many of the decisions he had always made for them. And this was true at first, of course. Mike had never shared information with his employees or included them in his analyses, so their first decisions on the new teams were near-disasters. But once the compounders grew into their new responsibilities, Mike relaxed and started working on changes in compounding procedures and a more cooperative development process with the R&D lab.

Mike's only remaining difficulty was in seeing the big picture. He tended to try to maximize compounding efficiency at the expense of the filling and packing operations. He steadfastly resisted taking a broader perspective until the company finally rotated him to the production supervisor position at a sister plant for half a year. After six months of being in a production position and trying to cope with the consequences of the compounding department's decisions, Mike came back a reformed man. Even though his lack of planning and organizing skills prevented him from becoming an outstanding technical resource, Mike settled in to what became an acceptable niche for himself and the organization.

After initial adjustments, most leaders find the mature-team phase of the transition a very rewarding time. Freed from the reactive aspects of their old role, they derive a great sense of accomplishment from developing others and mastering new tasks.

WHAT TO DO
FOR YOUR TEAMS

Remember that teams might be peaking about now. To help them avoid the stagnation associated with burnout or complacency, you'll need to

- *Help them reexamine their charter.* Two or more years into a team implementation, it's possible that the team's purpose will have evolved and that operating guidelines or norms will need to change. The evolution in one team's operating guidelines is illustrated below:

New-Team Guidelines *(three months)*	*Mature-Team Guidelines* *(three years)*
We won't talk behind each other's backs.	We agree to give each other honest feedback in the interests of individual and team development.
We'll make decisions by consensus.	
We'll assist each other when members get busy.	We value each other's differences and will actively work to use these differences to the benefit of our work.
	We have fun at work and take our tasks, but not ourselves, seriously.

As a leader, it's your job to help team members progress beyond the basic maintenance commitments they made as a new team and move on to more sophisticated agreements that "stretch" their team dynamics.

- *Help them identify new task challenges.* By now, the team probably is comfortable with most of the tasks in the original empowerment schedule, so it's time for you to reexamine what you're still doing that the team could be doing just as well. As Al Douglas, a leader of mature teams at KG Packaging, put it, "If the team can do it even 70 percent as well as you can, let it go." Some typical responsibilities that leaders shift to the team at this stage of the game include performance feedback and appraisal; selecting new members; attending meetings in your place; and developing, not just administering, their own budgets.

Some leaders find it impossible to objectively identify new jobs for their teams. If this is the case for you, ask for help. Spend a day or two documenting the tasks and decisions that you handle as part of your job. Then sit down with a trusted adviser and reassess each one, using the format shown in Tool 11.1. Remember that new challenges for the team don't have to originate with your job. Because support departments are often fertile ground for interesting new tasks, you might try the same exercise with them.

- *Continue to arrange celebration events.* Twelve to eighteen months after they're formed, most teams notice a sharp decline in the internal recognition and attention they receive. If you've continued to "push" your teams, there still should be plenty to celebrate.

- *Give them increasingly sophisticated feedback about their team dynamics.* One team leader we know devised a meeting-feedback checklist with the help of her teams. It not only gave team members some structure to overcome the awkwardness of feedback at the end of each meeting, but it also helped to keep the team leader focused on

Tool 11.1. Sample Mature-Team Assessment Form.

Tasks/Decisions	Not Value-Added	Team Could Do Now	Team Could Do with Training
Completing the 495 production report	✔		
Taking the customer representative out to lunch		✔	
Conducting training on the personal-style indicator for new team members			✔

team interactions and avoid getting embroiled in technical discussions. The content of the checklist changed as the teams matured, as the following sample items illustrate:

New Teams	Mature Teams
Followed an agenda	Discussed the right things; had the most important and urgent items on the agenda
Started and ended the meeting on time	
Shared information	Took advantage of members' known styles and preferences in making assignments
Involved all team members	
	Spent more time making decisions than simply reporting information
	Included internal partners, customers, and suppliers in the meeting

Now this team leader drops in on meetings only occasionally; and when she does, she always asks the team which interaction skills they're working on so that she can include them in her feedback.

WHAT TO DO
FOR YOURSELF

This is the phase where you get a break from the all-consuming demands of the team and get to devote more time to your own development. Take advantage of this opportunity!

SEEK NEW DEVELOPMENT RESPONSIBILITIES

Many team leaders are so conditioned to think only about what the team needs that they neglect their own development. Don't wait for the organization's top managers to hand you a development plan; chances are they're too busy with other aspects of the change. You need to take the initiative here. You could, for example, try the following:

- Assuming responsibility for things your boss does now that you'd like to take on.

- Increasing depth in an area you enjoy. You could, for example, offer to become the benchmarking expert for your organization.

- Increasing breadth in areas you've traditionally avoided. If you've managed to escape so far with virtually no understanding of the organization's accounting system, perhaps now is the time to tackle a project that requires detailed budgets and forecasts.

- Leading cross-functional process improvements.

- Coming up with new ideas that could add significant value to the organization or your customers.

With any of these options, you need to be fairly aggressive. Be prepared to sell the need for the change. Consider the cases of Bob and Sally, both team leaders. Since the move to teams in their insurance company four years ago, both Bob and Sally have had time to contemplate what they should be doing next. Each of them mentally developed a pet project to spend more time on.

Sally wanted to experiment with video teleconferences for her organization's agents in the field instead of constantly bringing the agents to corporate headquarters for training and meetings. She'd always had an interest in new technology (she was the first in the firm to install a local-area network, for example), and her preliminary estimates indicated that the company might be able to save as much as $150,000 over the course of a year by implementing her idea. When Sally approached her boss with the idea, he wasn't very encouraging, but she pressed on, planning what the next steps should be. She put together a comprehensive plan for the entire company and presented it to the top-management team. When they rejected the idea, she was disappointed, because she remained convinced it was the right thing to do; but rather than give up, she sold her boss on a smaller-scale pilot in their own area.

Bob had a different interest. Having visited another progressive organization that used a peer review process at all levels, Bob hoped that his organization could replace its antiquated ranking system with a more team-oriented feedback process. He, too, put together a proposal for his boss, who offered encouragement to take it to the next level. However, when the top team hemmed and hawed, Bob threw in the towel. He figured that he'd given it a shot and that someday they might come around to his point of view.

To be successful in the role of mature-team leader, you have to be more like Sally than Bob. You must discard old notions that if you work hard, don't make too many waves, and keep your nose to the grindstone, management will reward you with increasingly important assignments and promotions. In today's organization, you must create your own opportunities.

REQUEST ADDITIONAL FEEDBACK

Asking for increasingly sophisticated feedback on your leadership behaviors from the team serves two purposes: it provides an excellent model for your team members on being receptive to feedback, and if you do it right, it also gives you some of the most accurate feedback you'll ever receive.

With advanced teams, members might feel comfortable giving you face-to-face feedback. One common approach to this is the "more of, less of, same of" format. For instance, a team member might say

- "Joan, what I'd like you to *do more of* is running interference for us with corporate departments, like Purchasing. If we could get our spending limits increased by $1,000, we'd be a lot more efficient."

- "What I'd like you to *do less of* is damning an idea with faint praise. If you don't like something, just come out and say so. We're big kids now; we can take it."

- "What I'd like you to *keep doing* is finding opportunities to give us visibility — like that time you pushed me to make that presentation to the division vice presidents. That was a real ego boost."

As with all input, it's important for you to summarize the feedback you've received and explain to the group what you're planning to do about it.

WHAT TO DO
WITH YOUR BOSS

Since much of your future development will depend on the cooperation of your boss, don't stop having regular progress review meetings now. You can continue with the same format you used in earlier phases; only the topics for discussion change. A sample discussion plan for leaders at this stage is shown in Tool 11.2.

Now is a good time to take stock of your personal preferences and career plans. You've had an opportunity to try on the new role long enough to determine whether it's a good fit for you. If you're still having fun at work and feel sufficiently challenged, you might want to ask your boss for additional development within your current role. If you're not enjoying the job or you feel that it doesn't make the best use of your skills, now is the time to consider a change.

Once again, you'll need to take the initiative. Because most organizations are in a near-constant state of change, you

Tool 11.2. Sample Mature-Team Leader Discussion Plan.

	Now	*Next*
What do I need from you and the organization?	• Honest feedback on career potential • More intra-organizational consulting opportunities (would like to be assigned to help the 1080 team)	• The opportunity to start an internal SWAT consulting team to help other units within the organization start up teams
What do my teams need?	• Redefined charter and operating guidelines • More interesting responsibilities from my plate (for example, the quarterly trip to visit our major customer)	• A meeting with Purchasing and Human Resources to see what additional responsibilities they could turn over to the teams • Pizza party to celebrate teams' preparing first successful budgets
What actions should I take?	• Ask for feedback from the team on what I can do to make their jobs better • In preparation for upcoming building expansion project, set up meeting with Barb in Engineering to understand more about our internal facility design capabilities	• Lead the upcoming task force on the building expansion, focusing on redesign of the internal facilities

can often capitalize on that fluidity to make a creative proposal for a new job or a position.

Once you've agreed on a plan, you can reassess what you're doing and divide the tasks in a logical way. Susan, a service manager to whom several self-directed teams of sales and service professionals reported, decided that she wanted to be ready to move into a zone manager position when one became available. She and her boss (himself a zone manager) agreed that Susan needed more sales management experience; so when they held their semiannual review, Don agreed to give Susan some of his own sales management duties, and they transferred to the teams some tasks that Susan could do in her sleep. That way, Susan was freed from the tyranny of daily warranty expense logs and service training audits and was able to get into planning more creative sales promotion events.

KEY BEHAVIORS

Several key behaviors become much more important in the mature-team phase of your role transition.

PROVIDE FOCUS AND DIRECTION

Now that you've backed out of the day-to-day operations of the team, the best thing you can do for team members is keep them pointed in the right direction. As one team leader put it, "It's like taking a family trip. My job is to say we're headed to Los Angeles. How they choose to get there is up to them. But if they start veering off toward Houston, my job is to point that out and help them get back on track."

The best ways you can provide focus and direction are these:

- Make sure your team members understand the company's vision and how your unit's mission "nests" within it. (It's your job to paint a picture of what Los Angeles will look like when you get there.)

- Ask how team plans and actions support the vision, mission, and goals. (For example, ask, "How will stopping in Fargo help us get to Los Angeles?")

- Help team members get rid of extraneous tasks that divert their attention from their real purpose. ("I know you've been doing daily gas and mileage charts, but they're taking up a lot of time and they're not helping us get there any faster or smarter.")

TAKE INITIATIVE, INITIATIVE, INITIATIVE

Like the three L's of real estate (location, location, location), initiative is what really counts. If you don't exercise initiative, you could end up with only half a job. In fact, your new tasks require almost pure initiative — planning large-scale improvements, researching trends in your industry, working with suppliers to anticipate problems, and so on.

You're also going to be bumping up against the catch-22 of empowerment: top managers keep control until leaders show significant initiative and strategic thinking, and leaders wait for top managers to loosen the reins so that they can demonstrate some creativity and strategic thinking.

Stop waiting. Get on with it! In the final analysis, who do you think the organization is more likely to keep: the people who never did anything they hadn't been told to do or the people who did more than was expected?

The new role requires a change in mindset. It's no longer appropriate to "go with the flow." Alan Ross, responsible for setting up the first self-directed teams in sales and service at Buick, uses a good test. He suggests examining what you do when top management proposes an idea that you think is a big mistake. The old definition of a team player meant that you would work very hard to make the idea work. Using the new definition of a team player, you would question the idea before it gets started. If you have mature teams, your organization should be long past shooting the messenger.

Remember, don't wait for someone to tell you what to do. Leadership is taken, not given.

WORK TOWARD LATERAL INTEGRATION

An interesting thing happens as decision-making responsibility is pushed downward in the organization: responsibility for integration also moves downward. Think about it: in the old days, only the top managers were responsible for integration;

everybody else was supposed to be concerned with his or her own function and nothing else.

In a typical plant structure, this often meant that only the plant manager worried about the overall success of the plant. Everybody else was too busy managing individual technical specialties. The engineering manager wasn't expected to worry about the impact of a proposal on Distribution, for example. And if a supervisor ever asked, "Well, what about Purchasing?" she was told, "Don't worry, we'll take care of it."

Now teams often cross those functional barriers. And teams are making decisions (regarding purchasing, selection, and supplier certification, for example) that require their leaders to be able to act in the organization's best interests, not just those of their team. Suddenly the responsibility for integration has moved down to the team leader's level.

This is a tremendous transition for most leaders, because historically leaders functioned in vertical roles. They communicated primarily with their bosses and their subordinates. Translating organizational messages for the masses and carrying complaints back up, they were message carriers and funnels. When times got tough, senior managers figured that they didn't need intermediaries. Today one real value that leaders can add is to take responsibility for integration—in other words, make decisions for the good of the entire organization, not just some of its parts. As one leader put it, "I'm a lot more concerned with the sales and shipping implications of the manufacturing schedule than ever before. I talk to some of the sales reps on a daily basis now. A while ago, I didn't even know we *had* sales reps."

The best ways you can succeed at integration are to

- Develop a broader perspective; take time to understand your peers' needs and develop collaborative relationships.

- When faced with a decision, ask yourself what would be in the best interests of the organization as a whole.

- Start spending more of your time (approximately 60 percent) developing partnerships and communicating laterally (to other functions and other areas) instead of just to your boss and your team members (the remaining 40 percent).

- Work on your conflict management skills. Responsibility for integration means responsibility for resolving conflicts.

ADOPT A LONG-TERM ORIENTATION

The new components of your role demand a longer planning horizon. You have to "helicopter up" from the daily fire fighting and think in terms of tasks that can be accomplished in weeks or months. This shift is illustrated in Exhibit 11.1.

This is precisely what happened to Steven Gagnon, former operations manager at A. E. Staley's Sagamore facility. Gagnon had always been in charge of three work areas (the wet mill, the starch department, and the syrup refinery), but his job changed dramatically as employees assumed more responsibility. Before, he used to spend a lot of time on direct, hands-on supervision and fire-fighting tasks. After, most of his time became consumed with budgets, marketing, and sales. Gagnon's time and energy became focused beyond the current to the future operations (Barnett, 1989).

Exhibit 11.1. Shift in the Planning Horizon.

Phase	Tasks	Planning Required
Preteam	Handling employee problems	Daily
	Completing production reports	Daily
	Planning overtime	Daily
	Responding to production crises	Hourly
New Team	Scheduling/providing training	Weekly
	Facilitating team meetings	Daily
	Developing star points	Weekly
Mature Team	Setting up a supplier certification process	Quarterly
	Developing a customer satisfaction index	Monthly
	Working on a major business process reengineering project	Quarterly

ANTICIPATE SAND TRAPS

Although there aren't as many hazards to watch out for when your teams mature, the traps that do exist can be difficult to get out of.

BURNOUT

Some team leaders feel exhausted, overworked, and underappreciated one to two years into the implementation. This burnout can be caused by a variety of factors:

- Not giving enough tasks to the team as you take on new responsibilities.

- Working so hard to get your team recognition that you neglect to publicize your own efforts and initiatives.

- Sacrificing yourself for "the good of the team," as Richard Walton (1977) discovered when he went back to check on a team implementation two years after teams had started up. Working long hours without any expectation of promotion while the teams are getting all the attention can be quite debilitating. In this case, Walton found that it had become acceptable for the operators to express strongly held views, but the team leaders still felt that they had to keep their opinions to themselves.

  If you see these things happening to yourself, consider

- Forming a support group with other team leaders to discuss common experiences and any counterproductive norms that might have developed. Several companies around the country refer to such groups as AA groups (for Autocrats Anonymous). These groups can provide a forum for discussing the pressures that might cause you to fall back into old habits.

- Reassessing how you spend your time. Stop doing things that the teams could be doing or that don't add value.

- Finding ways to get recognition for your own work. Not every idea has to come from the team. You're allowed, and even expected, to come up with things on your own. Be sure that your leader and your team know what you're working on. One group of team leaders developed its own awards, which group members bestow on each other at quarterly celebration ceremonies. Some of the awards are humorous ("Most Reformed Autocrat"), but most are serious efforts at peer recognition.

COMPLACENCY

Having survived the struggles of the new-team phase, leaders might find it tempting to coast for a while. Having transferred many responsibilities to the team, you could theoretically get by for a while just doing what was left of your old role, without picking up any new responsibilities. If you choose to do that, two things will happen: first, you'll find yourself unconsciously trying to fill your time by interfering in tasks that you've transferred to the team; second, management and the team will begin to wonder what you're getting paid to do.

You can counteract complacency by

- Periodically asking your boss and the team what else you can do to make their jobs easier.
- Regularly assessing how challenged you feel at work and, when you start to feel too comfortable, seeking out new responsibilities. One team leader we know set up a batch file on her laptop so that every time she flips the computer on, she's greeted by the following reminder: "Each morning in Africa when a gazelle wakes up, he knows he must run faster than the fastest lion or he'll be killed. Each morning when a lion wakes up, he knows he must outrun the slowest gazelle or he'll starve to death. So you see, it doesn't matter whether you're a lion or a gazelle. When the sun comes up, you'd better be running."

You'll have to strike your own personal balance between burnout and complacency.

Do We Really Need a Leader?

As your role shifts and you do less hands-on work with the team, team members will begin to wonder what you're doing and whether it really adds any value. This is something of an ongoing problem at Shenandoah Life, where team members complain that "directors don't know what we do, and we don't know what they do." Moreover, team members appear to resent the fact that leaders are paid more but don't have all the technical knowledge that members possess (Forbes, 1989).

To head this problem off at the pass, you might want to consider

- Openly discussing the transition with your team before you start to take on large-scale improvement projects.

- Giving a progress report on your activities and results at team meetings.

- Switching jobs with team members periodically. There's nothing like walking in another person's shoes for a few days to appreciate what he or she is going through.

LESSONS LEARNED

Leaders who've lived to tell about their experiences with mature teams offer the following advice:

- "Keep your eye on the big picture. Be sure to take the time to analyze how well the team is working toward the vision. That's what you should focus on now" (Bart, Miller Brewing).

- "Watch out for 'group think' taking over your teams. As groups get to know each other better, they're more likely to assume they know what the others are thinking. You have to be especially vigilant about them coming to premature agreement" (Walt, manufacturing manager).

- "Take advantage of requests to learn about your teams' implementation. It can be very rewarding to speak to outside groups or see your pearls of wisdom in print in the local paper or business publications. Divide these opportunities among leaders and members" (David, San Diego Zoo).

- "Don't stop paying attention to the little stuff—like thanking someone for a job well done or arranging lunch with the president" (Sarah, Milwaukee Insurance).

- "Distinguish yourself by taking a broader perspective, not just maximizing your own teams' effectiveness. Get involved in projects that benefit the plant as a whole" (Al, KG Packaging).

- "Ask your teams whether they see you too much or not enough. It's a hard balancing act. You can find yourself swinging from one extreme to the other" (Susan, sales manager).

- "You have to realize when the teams experience level changes and accept their approaches to the business, which by now have matured; in many cases, their ideas are now better than yours. This can be hard to take" (Bart, Miller Brewing).

- "As teams mature, they need you less. This allows you to grow in other areas, if you choose. Our problem is that many leaders see themselves as managing the 5 percent who aren't mature and they forget those who are" (manager, GE Bromont).

- "Once you're good at it, you can go on to a whole new level of excitement. Now that you're not so tense, you can relax and have fun" (Michelangelo, trapeze artist, from his act *The Man on the Flying Trapeze*)

MATURE-TEAM LEADER JOB PROFILE

If you're successful at making the transition to mature-team leadership, your job should take on the characteristics outlined in Exhibit 11.2. By now you should be spending very little time on reactive tasks. Much of your time and activities will focus on projects outside the teams.

You've come a long way from the days when most of your time was consumed with endless fire fighting and you were plagued by deep anxiety over the teams' abilities to handle their new responsibilities. Now you have a greater opportunity to make a substantial contribution to the organization's success.

SELF-CHECK

Consider how you spent your time last month. Use the checklist shown in Tool 11.3 to determine whether you're effectively changing your role to keep up with the demands of the mature-team phase of evolution.

Exhibit 11.2. Job Profile for Leaders in the Mature-Team Phase.

Time spent on reactive tasks	20 percent or less
Primary tasks	• Leading continuous improvement projects that cut across team boundaries • Advancing or maintaining team development • Partnering with other departments to make quantum improvements
Behaviors required for success	• Providing focus and direction • Employing initiative • Furthering lateral integration • Adopting long-term orientation
Priorities/problems	• Battling burnout • Counteracting complacency
Parts of the job that are most satisfying at this phase	• Reveling in team accomplishments • Making a significant impact on organizational functioning • Learning about other functional specialties

Tool 11.3. Self-Check for Leaders in the Mature-Team Phase.

Last month...	Done	Not Done
I spent at least 50 percent of my time doing things I didn't do three years ago, including proactive improvement projects.	☐	☐
I redirected requests for operational data to the teams.	☐	☐
I avoided reinserting myself into the teams' work even during production or customer crises.	☐	☐
My teams would say that I was accessible without being overbearing.	☐	☐
I helped my teams develop more sophisticated norms.	☐	☐
My teams took on new responsibilities.	☐	☐
I arranged at least one celebration event.	☐	☐
I asked for feedback on new leadership behaviors from my boss and my team.	☐	☐
I told my superiors when I thought they were making a mistake.	☐	☐
I spent at least 60 percent of my time working horizontally in the organization.	☐	☐
Most of my time was spent working on things that won't come to fruition for more than a month.	☐	☐
The work I did last month stretched my skills and abilities as much as it did a year ago.	☐	☐
I worked on developing at least one new skill.	☐	☐
I provided more sophisticated feedback to my teams, including a check on possible "group-think" tendencies.	☐	☐

SPECIAL CONSIDERATIONS FOR SUPPORT PROFESSIONALS

For those support team leaders who remain in a central support function (that is, who aren't permanently attached to any operations teams), now is the time to focus on their own team development. Up to this point, much of their energy has been devoted to the development and coaching of operations team members. Now it's their turn. Most support team leaders find it helpful to borrow some of the team design techniques used in other parts of the organization. For example, they might

- *Create a vision for the entire support function.* The support professional's vision should support the overall organization's vision and inspire the group to greatness. At Tektronix, the manager of the Organizational Development Group developed a compelling vision with his team: "To become the premier organization development group in America." They even went so far as to identify a similar group at TRW that they could benchmark against (Rayner and Klein, 1989).

- *Reassess status barriers.* Support professionals also need to pay attention to whether the "symbols" in the support group are contributing to, or getting in the way of, achieving the vision. These symbols include everything from titles and approval limits to how space is arranged. Many team-oriented support groups find that having their cubicles arranged in a circular fashion around a central meeting area is more conducive to team functioning.

- *Continue to spend time on team development.* Support teams should spend as much time as operations groups do in assessing how members' styles interact, working on joint problem-solving projects, and monitoring their own progress through the phases of team development.

    This also applies to individual development. If a support professional happens to be Patton of Purchasing or Conan the Controller, it isn't too late to get help. There are special training programs devoted to the changing role of the support professional that can help reorient support team members.

- *Develop a cross-training plan.* The support professional's plan should cover specialties inside and outside the group. Support professionals shouldn't be deterred by protests from specialists that no one could possibly learn *their* jobs. Often there are many "core functions" that the entire group can learn, resulting in a much more flexible unit.

The objective of the cross-training plan outside the support professional's group should be to develop a broader business focus among the members of the team. For this purpose, many support functions establish internal internships: they send a team member out on "loan" for a period of days, weeks, or even months. This approach can work quite effectively to help control variances between related departments (such as variances between Accounting and Purchasing or between Engineering and R&D).

If support professionals follow these guidelines, they'll have a department that's more than a loose collection of individual contributors and in which the whole is greater than the sum of the parts.

SPECIAL CONSIDERATIONS
FOR UNION LEADERS

It's at the mature-team phase that the union leader's role as the "conscience of the implementation" becomes most critical. If any backsliding occurs, it tends to happen after teams start to hit a steady pace. Union leaders should watch for these signs:

- Declining commitment to training (suddenly people can't leave their work stations for cross-training or team training).

- Lack of union involvement in decisions or meetings in which the union had previously participated.

- Impending moves among key stakeholders — a problem that can submarine a team's implementation faster than almost anything else. We've observed numerous cases where the key team visionary (sometimes the general manager or the human resource manager) was transferred two to three years into the team's implementation and the whole process unraveled. (Such changes can, of course, have the opposite effect. At one Procter & Gamble plant, the local union president sees signs that the new plant manager is actually building improved bridges with the union and attempting to revive a dying team implementation [Firenze, 1993].)

Even Saturn has begun to experience some problems. Despite objections from its United Auto Workers leaders, Saturn has reduced the training time for new members by more than 50 percent. This, according to Saturn employees, seems to have led to new members' making up a disproportionate share of the 29 percent who recently voted to return to a more traditional labor-management relationship (Woodruff, 1993a).

If union leaders haven't already implemented it, now is the time to consider approaching contract negotiations in a new way. What the Grain Millers have recommended to their locals is this:

> Negotiations may also be conducted in a different manner. With a stated goal of problem-solving, negotiations become "interest-based." The union's legitimate interests include fair income for members, employment security, career mobility, safety on the job, and fair treatment. But, these interests and others are approached as problems to be solved rather than "postures." Management, too, has its interests.
>
> Thus, in NWS [New Work Systems], contracts are not rigid. The more general nature of the contract language in a new work system means that the contract is "written" as practices develop, decisions are made, and problems are solved.
>
> Pay, vacations, and benefit grievances are spelled out in detail, not in general [Willis and others, 1991].

In such cases, the agreement is more likely to cover processes for getting issues resolved than to cover the actual decision-making rules.

Union leaders can also act as the "organization memory," helping to sustain advances beyond the life cycle of the current management team, because union leaders tend to stay in one place and managers are more mobile.

SUMMARY

The mature-team phase should be a time of growth and development for all leaders in the organization. By offering leaders and their teams ongoing support and reinforcement, senior leaders will help assure everyone's success.

TWELVE

Mature-Team Safety Nets: Sustaining and Refreshing the Efforts of Mature-Team Leaders

If the organization has been lucky enough or skillful enough to have sustained teams to this phase, it has a real obligation to maintain them. It's like owning a home on a national historic register: to let it fall into ruin is practically a crime. Maintaining it, though, requires constant vigilance so that little problems don't develop into permanent damage or require time-consuming and expensive repairs.

There are five primary vehicles for sustaining leaders of mature teams: senior-management support, assessment and feedback, training, career development, and team member support. Chances are that the organization will need to employ a variety of techniques from each of these areas in order to keep leaders and their teams from falling into disrepair.

SENIOR-MANAGEMENT SUPPORT

The main contribution senior managers can make in the mature-team phase is to sponsor organizational renewal. The new team structure shouldn't be viewed as an end state. Rather, the organization should constantly reevaluate its purpose, goals, and structure in light of the changing business climate. Those organizations that don't adapt will face extinction. Leaders of teams at all levels should be involved actively in renewal activities such as those described below.

Ongoing Environment Scan

Although many organizations begin their team implementation with a comprehensive analysis of business conditions and customer requirements, they fail to establish an ongoing mechanism to monitor the external environment, which, of course, is changing constantly. As your teams mature, one or more team leaders can be involved in facilitating this scan.

In one midsized manufacturing plant, the senior managers created a standing committee for assessment, which meets monthly to analyze the plant's situation. Their responsibilities include the following:

- Completing long-term analyses of quality, cost, market share, and profitability
- Checking the corporate mission, vision, and values periodically
- Reassessing key variances in the processes and how they're controlled
- Reviewing levels of morale and empowerment
- Recommending changes in organizational structure and design

The standing committee regularly presents recommendations at the plant's quarterly state-of-the-business meetings for all employees (Taylor and Felten, 1993).

If the organization chooses not to involve leaders in this type of organized environment scan, it needs to find some other mechanism to help leaders and the teams appreciate the big picture, because it's important for leaders to integrate the teams' efforts and decisions for the greater good of the organization. Organizations have attempted to do this through a variety of other ways:

- Sending leaders to industry conferences

- Providing leaders with subscriptions to industry publications

- Involving leaders in top-management meetings

- Asking leaders to fill in for top managers on vacation

- Arranging three-month sabbaticals for leaders to pursue a special industry research project

REDESIGN

Leaders should be actively engaged in reengineering the structure and boundaries of the organization. Consider the case of one organization that packages aerosol products. As the design team originally conceived the organization's teams, they handled everything from mixing the chemicals to filling, "gassing," and packing the cans. At the time of implementation, this controlled 90 percent of the company's key variances. Teams purchased the caps, however, from an outside vendor. When one of the leaders reanalyzed the process two years into the new team arrangement, she discovered that 40 percent of the variances could be linked to defective caps. She worked with the teams to study alternatives for bringing this variance under control and, after testing several alternatives, convinced the plant to bring the cap-making operation in-house and under the control of the teams.

In order to encourage this kind of innovation, organizations need to make it an explicit expectation of leaders' new roles by providing training in sociotechnical systems analysis.

They then need to follow up by rewarding leaders who model innovation and initiative.

CELEBRATION EVENTS

If the organization can help arrange certain standard celebrations, it makes the team leaders' jobs infinitely easier. This is because it can be taxing to come up with new, creative ways to recognize team members all the time.

One of the most interesting forms of team celebration we've observed is the "team open house." At this event, teams host visitors through their areas and explain their team structure and accomplishments. The invited guests often include family members, customers, suppliers, and employees from parts of the organization that haven't yet converted to teams. The teams often realize quite a motivational boost in the process of preparing charts and posters to explain their team processes and results. Additionally, these events offer the dual advantages of recognizing team members and educating the key people with whom they interact.

Of course, celebrations don't have to be company-organized events. Some organizations allot each team a pool of money to spend on team celebrations as part of the regular budget. The teams at Toyota's Georgetown, Kentucky, plant, for instance, receive $100 each quarter to spend as they see fit for celebrating team accomplishments. In another vein, Boeing's Corinth, Texas, plant, which has been involved with self-directed teams for six years, sends thank-you notes to recognize the extra efforts of individuals and teams (Campagna, O'Fallon, and Gilbert, 1993).

In addition to helping leaders recognize their teams, the organization needs to have some mechanism for rewarding team leaders themselves. In developing such recognition systems, it's helpful to keep in mind the new behaviors that the organization expects of its leaders. That's why one of our favorite examples is Hewlett-Packard's award for "meritorious defiance." This term is inscribed on a plaque that's given for "contempt and defiance above and beyond the call of engineering duty" (Frohman and Johnson, 1993). What a great way to reward the risk taking and initiative that the organization wants to encourage in leaders of mature teams!

NEW LEADERSHIP STRUCTURES

Senior managers may also want to consider radical new leadership structures. Many organizations have begun to experiment with a team of managers running the operation (instead of a single general manager acting as the final authority). This is the case at Drypers, a fast-growing manufacturer of disposable diapers. Instead of having a single chief executive, Drypers is run by a team of five managing directors, all with equal power. Each of the five individuals has a functional responsibility, but all work together as a team to share information and make overall decisions about the enterprise. No major decision is made until all five individuals arrive at a consensus.

In such situations, the initial decision-making process might take a little longer, but the actual implementation occurs much more swiftly and smoothly. Using this structure, Drypers was able to get a new product (disposable training pants called "Big Boy" and "Big Girl") to market in six months — an industry record. So far, Drypers seems to be flourishing under this new arrangement, with sales growing at 24 percent annually (Dumaine, 1993).

At the very least, by this point in the team implementation top leaders need to be past the point where they're just a collection of functional managers who are permitted to speak and have opinions only about their own functions. GE's Bromont, Canada, plant is run by a senior management team (SMT), whose members spend 50 percent of their time on external demands, 25 percent on long-term vision, and 25 percent on day-to-day operations (Rosow and Zager, 1989). GE's lighting business is run by a senior team of nine to twelve managers who allocate resources and ensure coordination of programs and processes. Similarly, Eastman Chemical replaced the head of manufacturing with a team composed of all the plant managers. The president of Eastman Chemical says this is the most dramatic change in the company's history and that "it gives people a much broader perspective and forces decision making down at least another level" (Byrne, 1993, p. 81).

ASSESSMENT AND FEEDBACK

Having provided some assessment of leaders' skills for the new-team phase, it's tempting to check that activity off the list and move on to the next project. But leaders of mature teams need *ongoing* feedback about their leadership skills. Not only do the key behaviors change over time as teams mature, but, as one manager put it, "Some of the leaders just don't get it the first time around."

By this point in the team implementation, the organization should have established a regular system of multiple-source feedback for each leader. The best systems allow for changes in the categories of behaviors that are evaluated. At this stage in their development, most leaders should no longer need extensive feedback about their meeting-management skills. They should be moving toward working on how clearly they provide a direction and focus for the teams. The organization's feedback system should accommodate and even encourage this shift.

The system also should reflect the change in primary interaction patterns that occurs for leaders of mature teams. In the earlier team phases, it was entirely appropriate for leaders to be assessed by their team members and their bosses: that was where most of their energy and interactions were focused. By now, however, the project-oriented nature of team leaders' jobs precludes the team members from observing much of what their leaders do. Thus leaders' evaluations should be handled primarily by their peers and by the customers and suppliers with whom they have the most interaction.

The other service some organizations are beginning to provide is a team assessment center. At these centers, an entire team (with or without the leader) can elect to participate in a special series of simulations designed to assess their patterns of interaction and decision making. For instance, team members might participate in a group discussion exercise to evaluate how effectively they share information, value each other's perspectives, and involve everyone in their deliberations. They might also try a team problem-solving simulation so that they can get objective feedback on the extent to which they respect each other's ideas and include everyone in the solution. These activities can be particularly helpful in cases where there are dysfunctional dynamics between leaders and their teams or where the leaders believe they've reached the limits of their effectiveness with team feedback.

TRAINING

At this point in the implementation, leadership training should focus on two objectives: refreshing skills that might be starting to deteriorate and establishing new skills and abilities to correspond with leaders' expanding role. Senior managers should be careful not to commit the mistake of one insurance company executive who, when approached about additional training for the team leaders, said, "What? I thought we already fixed them!" In fact, they had been "fixed" five years earlier, and some of them were starting to unravel.

The exact content of the company's refresher training will vary with the needs the organization uncovers through its assessment and feedback systems, but common topics include building trust, creating partnerships, coaching, and encouraging initiative.

An even more powerful way for companies to approach the reinforcement of skills is to train leaders to train others. This strategy works for several reasons:

- Training others sets up leaders as models, which reinforces the appropriate behaviors for the leaders *and* their teams.

- Regularly delivering the training provides a constant reminder and reinforcement of the skills.

- Leaders often learn from the comments and experiences of others during training.

- There's considerable overlap between the skills it takes to be a good trainer and the skills it takes to be an effective coach. Leaders benefit from practicing clear explanations, demonstrating skills, and reinforcing learners.

In addition to providing refresher training, the organization will want to plan training in the new skills it expects its leaders to demonstrate at this point in their role transition. On the team development side of their job, most leaders benefit from specific training in maintaining high-performance teams. Developing mature teams requires a different focus and set of skills than getting teams up and running in the first place did. Leaders must be able to recognize any signs of backsliding in their teams and know how to get the teams back on track. And they must be prepared to deal with the special challenges of motivating a mature team. For the technical side of leaders' jobs, most organizations focus on training in project management and business planning. One plan that integrates all these new skill requirements is shown in Exhibit 12.1. As you can see, it is important to integrate on-the-job applications with the formal training.

Top management shouldn't assume that leaders will pick up these skills naturally. If they do, they could find themselves in the position of one general manager who—after two calls from angry suppliers who were so frustrated that they were ready to quit, a phone message from the corporate finance department asking, "What the *!? are Fred and Barry [team leaders] up to?" and an on-site accounting department ready to revolt—had to face up to the fact that something wasn't going as planned. Upon further investigation, the general manager discovered that about half of the twenty team leaders were actively initiating improvement projects with unrealistic deadlines, involving the wrong people, and setting ill-defined goals.

Exhibit 12.1. Sample Training Plan for Leaders of Mature Teams.

Training	SCHEDULE				Application Assignments
	Q1	Q2	Q3	Q4	
REDESIGN SKILLS					
Environment Scans	X				Report on business conditions at semiannual all-plant meeting.
Sociotechnical Systems Analysis	X				Identify key variances in customer service.
Process Reengineering				X	Reengineer the distribution process.
NEW SKILLS					
Advancing Teams	X				Facilitate manufacturing council meetings.
Project Management		X			Set up supplier certification program.
Train the Trainer for Team Skills		X			Train five teams from Plant 2 in Team Skills.
REFRESHER TRAINING					
Encouraging Initiative			X		Lead the M85 product development team.
Building Trust			X		
Creating Partnerships				X	
Coaching				X	Mentor one newly appointed team leader.

The other half, who didn't have a clue how to start a project, were sitting on their hands waiting for someone to instruct them. It was hard to tell which was worse.

Senior managers need to be sure this doesn't happen. They should be clear about the new role expectations. It may be helpful to revisit the pie charts and role agreements set up in the new-team phase and revise them to reflect the new expectations. Then leaders can be involved in developing or selecting the training necessary to meet the new requirements; of course, they'll require coaching and support from top management to help them over the rough spots.

Occasionally, even when a company has provided formal classroom training in basic and advanced skills, some leaders still won't quite get it. Most often, this failure will manifest itself in the form of complaints from team members or peers. Before top managers give up on these leaders, though, they might want to try using an "empowerment coach" — someone who can follow recalcitrant leaders through the day, offering advice and feedback on decisions and interactions. Often people who haven't internalized the message during formal training sessions have several "aha!" experiences with this kind of intensive, one-on-one assistance.

CAREER DEVELOPMENT

The organization's primary career development goal with leaders of mature teams is to enable them to develop an "integrating perspective" so that they can facilitate decisions and actions in the best interests of the larger organization, not just their own functions or units. There are a couple of ways to accomplish this:

- *Assignments to lead cross-functional teams.* These assignments can range from taking charge of improving the organization's order-fulfillment process to spearheading a new-product development team. By all means, top managers should be explicit about the purpose of the assignment: to develop leaders' knowledge and rapport with other functions. Follow-up, with debriefing and feedback about how it's going, is essential. Cross-functional forums of leaders are a variation on this approach. These forums should be designed to remove leaders from their functional silos and encourage them to cooperate with other leaders to get things done. For example, they could overhaul the budget process to make it more team-oriented, establish an employee-assistance program, or plan the reallocation of building space.

- *Rotational assignments across department boundaries.* This approach is the equivalent of a functional cross-training plan for team leaders. It enables leaders to develop an in-depth appreciation for other departments' perspectives. It also allows the organization to move those leaders around who might be mismatched with their teams' needs. Occasionally, organizations go so far as to install leaders on-site with customers or suppliers for an extended period of time, not only to fix problems but to develop a broader perspective.

If the company's appraisal system also involves cross-functional peers in providing feedback, leaders will be inclined to cooperate rather than compete with other departments. In the new organization, as in hockey, "assists" should count as much as goals.

Our discussion so far might seem to have implied that it's the organization that's primarily responsible for career development, but this isn't true. Enlightened companies put their leaders in the driver's seat on career development concerns. Boeing's Corinth, Texas, plant is a good example. Corinth is a 500-person greenfield site that started with self-directed teams in 1987. Several years into the implementation, managers were hit with a lot of career questions and concerns, particularly from the support team leaders; so they implemented a system that allowed interested individuals to identify career paths that matched their personal interests and the company's needs, using a three-phase process.

In the first phase, individuals complete an assessment of personal values, interests, and skills; then they check the results of the assessment with their bosses. Armed with a better understanding of their own needs, they go on in the second phase to study the organization's and the teams' strategic development plans, and they create a personal business plan (matching their skills to organizational needs) and check it out with their bosses. Finally, in the third phase, they seek developmental assignments to match the personal business plan that they and their bosses have agreed on (Shenberger and Killingsworth, 1992). Obviously, one of the advantages of this plan is that it puts the most interested parties — leaders themselves — in charge of the process.

Even if top-level managers do all this, they'll still be faced with two traditional promotion dilemmas: how do they get qualified people into team leader positions, and what do they do with the outstanding team leaders they have?

Fortunately, the first question is easier to handle in a team-based organization than in traditional structures. Many empowered organizations use shared leadership structures (such as star points or coordinator positions) to enable team members to learn and practice leadership responsibilities over time. At AT&T's Denver Works, for example, the teams elect five coordinators — one each for cost, quality, production, environmental health and safety, and employee relations and training. Each of the coordinators receives an additional thirty hours of training in helping the team and serving as a conduit between teams (*Commitment Plus*, 1992). These coordinators function as junior team leaders and are easily promotable into a team leader spot. This sort of program is especially helpful in the mature-team phase because the company might be losing leaders to other parts of the organization: good performers might be transferred or promoted and poor performers might be outplaced or reassigned.

The more difficult part of the equation is what to do with outstanding leaders in a flattened organization. One unique solution to this dilemma comes from James River's Kendallville, Indiana, plant, where managers solved the problem by creating an interim promotion opportunity they call the "alchemists." This is a special team of up to five outstanding leaders who serve as the core group for starting up other team-oriented plants. Candidates for alchemist openings are interviewed by a board made up of managers, current alchemists, and team members; they're selected on the basis of technical, interpersonal, and leadership characteristics. Once in this position, alchemists receive a small salary increase and serve as technical resources and facilitators for all three shifts. They provide extra help to the teams and develop their own coaching and consulting skills in the process (Campagna, O'Fallon, and Gilbert, 1993).

Ultimately, the organization needs to redefine success so that it no longer means increasing one's span of control but instead means increasing one's decision-making power and ability to influence the business. With mature teams, status should be based on contribution rather than on rank in the ever-diminishing hierarchy.

This redefinition of success is what Southern Bell had to do in the eighties when that organization reduced its mid-management ranks from 1,200 to 400. The task force studying the problem recommended several approaches to minimizing the importance of level in the hierarchy. The following changes were implemented: lateral transfers were changed from something the organization did to poor performers to a regular part of the High Potential Development Program; training for new managers was changed so that it emphasized increasing responsibility, not increasing status; and special pay bands were developed for highly valued jobs so that Southern Bell could reward leaders for their skills, not necessarily their position in the hierarchy (Rosow and Zager, 1989).

TEAM MEMBER SUPPORT

Team members themselves can play an active role in supporting leaders of mature teams. Some of the most important contributions they can make are these:

- *Provide honest and direct feedback.* There's nothing more unnerving to team leaders than to think that team members talk about their leadership skills behind their backs.

Leaders will feel much more secure if they know where their employees stand — even if it's negative.

- *Ask for what they want or need.* Now that leaders are spending more time engaged in activities outside the team, they must be able to rely on team members to ask for help when they need it.

- *Involve leaders in key events.* Even though team members are probably feeling technically self-sufficient, leaders can still add value in decision-making and problem-solving meetings (as a result of their broadening organizational perspective). When team members include their leaders in key events, they're also helping them maintain a feeling of "connectedness" with the team.

TOUGH SITUATIONS YOU MIGHT ENCOUNTER

By now organizations will be experiencing fewer "tough situations" involving leaders. Ironically, some of the difficult situations that tend to arise in the mature-team phase are often by-products of success with teams.

Although it's impossible to anticipate all the situations organizations might face with leaders of mature teams, it's possible to plan for the most common situations. We offer a summary of those below.

"EXCESS" LEADERSHIP

What happens if the organization runs out of creative positions for former supervisors and managers as teams need less direct coaching and attention?

What could be causing the problem? If top managers aren't focused on truly strategic activities, they may not have let go of enough responsibilities.

What might the organization do? Whatever you do, never create a position the organization doesn't really need. Everyone will see through this—especially the person being "helped." Look for areas of real need: unless all the variances are under control and the company has achieved world-class performance in all critical success factors, there's still work to be done. Examine who's overworked and redistribute tasks as needed.

PROMOTION IMPEDIMENTS

What happens if the organization is having a hard time promoting team leaders out of the facility because the rest of the organization is suspicious about what's happening?

What could be causing the problem? There are a couple of possible answers. The rest of the organization may not really understand what's going on at the facility, and that ignorance may be breeding fear. Alternatively, the rest of the organization may resent the "elitist" attitude the organization has adopted and be punishing the leaders for it.

What might the organization do? Managers can look for opportunities to have leaders work with other parts of the organization on joint projects. In general, managers should open the doors and share information (but without proselytizing).

SUMMARY

The organization should pull out all stops to support leaders of mature teams. Why? It's simple. Look at where the company was. Look at where it is now. Much of this movement and achievement is the result of leaders' good work, and they will remain the key to maintaining and advancing team success.

THIRTEEN

Virtual Teams
in Virtual Organizations:
A Look at the Future

In the future, we see the job of leading teams going beyond the new realities described in Chapter One, because leaders will be dealing with teams that don't exist on most present-day organizational charts. While the preceding chapters have focused on leading natural or redesigned teams that have a high degree of power, have a common purpose, and are relatively permanent (they can make at least two- to five-year business plans), this chapter describes the challenge of leading teams that are just as powerful, but not as permanent.

As organizations attempt to become even more responsive to ever-changing customer needs, the organizations themselves are becoming more fluid and flexible. This trend has spawned a new type of team structure, the *virtual team*. Virtual teams are temporary teams made up of a cross-section of the organization, and sometimes even its customers or suppliers, that are formed to take highly important action, such as the development of a new product or the reengineering of a major organizational process. In general, these teams function more like movie production companies than traditional departments, in that people with diverse skills are brought together, form a team, create something, and then scatter to the winds (Brown, 1993).

Virtual teams get their name from the *virtual organization* that has been envisioned by notable authors (Davidow and Malone, 1992; Hirschhorn and Gilmore, 1992). The virtual organization is made up of many teams, which may extend beyond the traditional organizational boundaries. Figure 13.1 contrasts a traditional organization with a virtual organization. As shown, virtual teams are different shapes and sizes, depending on the assignment. Team boundaries indicating areas of responsibility and authority sometimes overlap — that is, they don't have the rigidity associated with traditional teams. New teams are created and dissolved as needed to meet changing customer needs and directions; and members, leaders, customers, and suppliers move in and out of teams as new teams are created or reconfigured. An individual might be a member of one team and a leader of another. As with self-directed work teams, teams in a virtual organization are characterized by a great deal of shared leadership, with individual team members assuming responsibility for various team functions and subprojects and leading the team in their respective areas of expertise.

Jack Welch, CEO of General Electric, describes the virtual organization as a "boundary-less company...where we knock down the walls that separate us from one another on the inside and from our key constituencies on the outside" (Welch and Hood, 1991).

The goals of virtual teams are to move ideas through the organization faster, to be more responsive to customers, and to react more quickly to competition. These goals are reached by

Figure 13.1. Stylized Depiction of Team and Individual Role Boundaries in a Traditional Organization and a Virtual Organization.

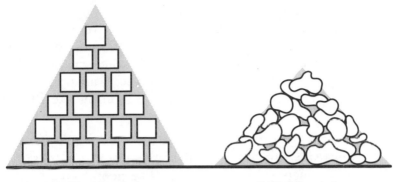

A. Traditional Organization   B. Virtual Organization

joining together on one team all the people necessary to perform a function or a process and then empowering that team to make the requisite decisions to accomplish its task.

For most companies, the virtual organization is a long way off, but virtual teams are not. In fact, most of today's leaders can expect to face the challenges of leading virtual teams sometime in their careers. Examples of present-day virtual teams follow:

■   At Apple Computer, the Information Systems team is developing systems that reach beyond the company's own boundaries to external distributors to gather "channel information" that the company needs but can't gather by itself (Davidow and Malone, 1992).

■   At James River, where self-directed teams have operated for ten years, the company took the next step and created customer teams with their largest customer, Kellogg's. One week every month, a James River team moves on-site to a Kellogg's plant and assumes the responsibility for any quality issues related to James River (Macy, 1993).

- Modicon, Inc., a maker of automation control equipment, uses virtual teams for its product development process. Instead of having an engineering group develop the product with some minimal input from marketing, they've formed a team of fifteen people from engineering, manufacturing, marketing, sales, and finance. This has allowed the company to take six software products to market in one-third the time it would usually take (Byrne, 1993).

- Even American auto manufacturers are employing virtual teams to get their cars to market faster. At Chrysler, a multifunctional team of eighty-five people created the Viper in only three years (half the usual time and half the development cost of the Mazda Miata) (Woodruff, 1991b). General Motors used a similar strategy to form a virtual team of engineers, manufacturing leaders, marketing specialists, and production people to create an electric car in just under four years (Woodruff, 1991a).

- Bell Atlantic formed a virtual reengineering team they called the "core team," to completely redesign their carrier access service (CAS) process (supplying the link between commercial or residential customers and their selected long-distance carriers). The team started with a well-respected leader, who assembled a team of experts cutting across all the disciplines involved in CAS. She and the team took the process (the time from receiving an order to turning the service over to the customer) from fifteen days down to hours, in some cases (Hammer and Champy, 1993).

And, of course, there are hundreds of other examples of synchronous engineering teams, new-product launch teams, and reengineering teams currently at work on increasing speed and responsiveness to their customers.

The primary differences between virtual teams and more permanent self-directed work teams are illustrated in Exhibit 13.1. The differences between self-directed, empowered work teams and virtual work teams present special leadership challenges. Unquestionably, it is more difficult to lead a virtual work team, for the following reasons:

■ *The leader has little or no "position power."* Pay and appraisal decisions usually are made by the part of the organization where team members are permanently assigned. While a leader's appraisal of a team member's performance can affect that individual's future in the organization, this power is seldom used, because complaining about a team member makes the team leader look bad and runs the risk of exacerbating problems within the team. Furthermore, the team leader has little or no responsibility for the career path of team members after the team's work is accomplished; if customers or suppliers are on the team, the leader has even less relative control.

Exhibit 13.1. Characteristics of a Self-Directed Work Team Compared with a Virtual Team.

	Self-Directed Work Team	*Virtual Team*
Responsibility Boundaries	Relatively clear, particularly with other work teams	Usually overlapping with various functions and sometimes with other teams
Leadership	Shared leadership among team members	Single leadership, usually designated within the team (to an individual who shares tasks and decision making with members, but maintains his or her position throughout the project)
Duration	Permanent	Usually temporary (for the life of a project)
Reporting Arrangement	All team members reporting to the same person	Team members on loan from other departments or organizations that typically retain responsibility for pay and appraisal

- *Conflicts arise over team member time and resource requirements.* Ideally, members of virtual teams are on full-time assignments. Sometimes, though, they're not; they might be expected to perform their full-time jobs in addition to their virtual team assignments. This situation puts pressure on team members, and problems must be handled by the leader. Because of the makeup of virtual teams, the mere act of scheduling a team meeting can become an ordeal. In one virtual development team, meetings had to be scheduled on Saturdays to accommodate the fact that the development project was only a part-time assignment for the customer-member. The rest of the team took off Monday mornings to balance the regular Saturday meetings.

- *Organizational boundaries are unclear.* By their very nature, virtual teams overlap in responsibility with various functions inside and outside of the organization. Thus a major challenge for the team is to do its job with the cooperation of the other important departments. A team isn't effective unless its ideas are *implemented*; and because the team has no power over the rest of the organization, dealings with other organizational functions are extremely important. The alternatives to cooperation are turf wars and as-needed appeals to higher authorities to resolve issues, both of which usually work out to no one's benefit in the long run.

- *Time and organizational pressures abound.* Everywhere there's pressure for results, and virtual teams often are formed for the explicit purpose of improving speed (reducing product development or service delivery cycles). Therefore, an effective virtual team leader must be sure that an adequate time frame is negotiated so that the team has a realistic opportunity to experience a "win."

- *Team members don't know one another.* Frequently, teams are faced with the need to get off to a fast start. The challenge is that team members come from varied backgrounds and experiences, and team members don't know others very well or understand their unique skills and motivations. Also, the *leaders* don't know the team members. Recognizing that producing something in record time requires unprecedented levels of trust and openness, this situation obviously presents a problem. One virtual team leader put it this way: "I had a hard enough time getting people back in my own department to admit that we had quality problems. And they all knew each other. Now I'm faced with people from three different departments and an engineer on loan from our customer. It took me almost six weeks to get them to feel comfortable enough with each other so that we could honestly discuss the causes of our delivery problems."

- *Team members often are independent and self-motivated.* In many cases, team members have their own agendas and loyalties to a functional team, profession, or special technology. This "loyalty to others" can present a special challenge as different team members begin forming a cohesive, effective virtual team.

This was a particular problem in one start-up team that we observed. They were charged with planning (not operating) the first new plant this manufacturing company had built in twenty years. The team was composed of professionals from the human resources, engineering, sales and marketing, and production departments. They had fourteen months to locate a site while the operations leaders were being identified and freed from their existing responsibilities. It took the planning team more than eighteen months to accomplish their task, because each of the functions had its own axe to grind. Human Resources refused to consider any states with what they considered to be low-literacy levels, and Marketing insisted on location in several such states to minimize distribution time. Each member saw it as a contest to "win for their side," and they never developed a common vision or shared understanding. In the end, members suboptimized their choice "just to get it over with."

It's difficult to get people to leave their functional hats at the door and think more broadly. According to Terry Ennis, who leads a team at DuPont, "This is very unsettling and threatening for people. You find line and function managers who've been honored and rewarded for what they've done for decades" (Byrne, 1993).

LEADER TASKS

To accomplish results under such difficult circumstances, leaders of virtual teams must focus on using unique strategies. This section reviews some of the tasks and responsibilities necessary for a leader to start, maintain, and disband a virtual team.

First, virtual teams need a form of turbo-start. Leaders must create instant cohesiveness, because virtual teams can't afford to chart a three-year development plan. Team members must get to know one another and learn how different members like to operate — their foibles, motivations, areas of knowledge, and personal goals. Often it's appropriate to hold a modified version of a visioning conference to speed up this process. At such a conference, the entire team can learn about customer requirements (sometimes directly from the customers) and the mission and goals for the group (if possible, directly from management). At the same time, the leader might want to use personal-style questionnaires to help the team get to know one another and to understand their diverse styles and approaches to solving problems.

Dr. Edward Prichard used such a conference at Tektronix when he assembled a virtual team for a new-product development effort. His vision was to beat the company's major competitor to the market by developing the product in just seven months. But he needed a way to bring the twenty hardware engineers, software engineers, and marketing professionals together as a team. In an off-site session, they developed the following concepts (Rayner and Klein, 1989):

Teamwork Principles

- Shared power
- Consultative decision making
- Motivational culture
- Professional code
- Trust
- Expertise over status or position

Goals

- All involved hooked into bringing it off
- A clean, crisp, real-product introduction

In addition to the principles by which the group will operate, another output of the visioning conference should be a team commitment to the purpose and goals for the group. If the team doesn't have a clear mandate with measurable results, it can't possibly measure its achievements and automatically will be devoid of a sense of completion and success. Without clarification about purpose and goals, team members will be extremely frustrated, because the team will be going in the wrong direction and working hard on the wrong things. The leader is responsible for seeing that the team's vision is clear and that it's translated into key result areas, measurement methods, and goals, usually in the form of a team charter.

Another objective is to inspire a sense of belonging in the team. Although leaders of virtual teams are *assigned* team members, they must *earn* followers. So, the leader must create a connection between each member's personal goals and the goals of the team. By focusing team members on the team goals, and on how those goals relate to individual goals, the leader encourages team members to build a sense of responsibility to one another to be successful as a team and, at the same time, determine how they will meet their own achievement needs. This is important, because high-visibility virtual teams often have a lot of high achievers as members.

Team goals should deal with personal development needs as well as team output. For example, a team member who wants to improve his or her leadership skills will be more accepting of leading a task force when the personal development opportunities are pointed out. Similarly, a team member who's just completed a course on process mapping will appreciate an opportunity to apply those skills in a team project.

As with self-directed teams, when virtual projects involve many people, the leader must work with team members to develop and communicate role clarity about who does what by when and what level of involvement each team member will have in tasks and decisions. The leader can help team members incorporate those responsibilities into their performance plans so that individual efforts are acknowledged as part of the organization's performance management process. Often it's appropriate to circulate to all team members a list of each member's responsibilities, goals, measurement methods, and development plans. This serves as a means of clarifying roles and providing information so that team members can coach and support one another.

Once the virtual team is under way, the leader can do a variety of things to ensure smooth functioning and improved results. Chief among these tasks is keeping the team focused and on track. As an example, a client's new-product launch team had problems that threatened the successful completion of a phase of their assignment. The leader found that team members often couldn't see the forest for the trees, panicked easily, and felt as if the only solution was to change the deadline, when in fact a radical shift in thinking about the processes was what was really needed. This situation was especially challenging because

- The team of high achievers was afraid of failing.
- Excessive anxiety and pressure kept team members from thinking creatively about alternative approaches.

- Time was in short supply, as usual, and it seemed easier for the leader to dictate what needed to be done.

- The last thing the leader wanted was for the team to agree verbally to a process that they weren't convinced would work.

The leader needed to ask questions to get the team thinking creatively; then the leader needed to make suggestions in order to prime the brainstorming pump. Once the team developed a process, the leader asked all the team members to "show their cards" regarding belief in the plan. The leader agreed not to move ahead until full commitment was a reality. Using this approach, team members were able to agree on a completely different process that allowed them to meet customer requirements on the original schedule.

It's also the leader's responsibility to make sure the team understands when and how management wants to have input or review progress. The leader should set up opportunities for team members to share what they've accomplished and to gain valuable input from other people in the organization; this process shouldn't be seen as a check or as a second-guessing of the team.

The leader also must help members keep a balance between their team and functional responsibilities. This typically causes a lot of tension. Often team members need counseling about how to deal with their functional leader and regulate time-sharing. Even if this situation has been worked out at the beginning of a team assignment, the need for a reconfirmation usually arises—particularly when the functional unit is under pressure for output.

As a result of the speed requirements of most virtual teams, one of the leader's primary responsibilities is to coach members on how to overcome organizational barriers to success. It's always tempting for leaders to "save the day" by picking up the phone and intervening at a high level on behalf of a team member. This shows your organizational power, but it deprives team members of the ownership feelings that come from being able to do things on their own. Team members should be given every chance to solve a problem before you intervene. If you *do* have to intervene, it should be done behind the scenes. For example, you could call a manager to ask if he or she will see one of your team members and listen openly to that member's ideas.

At Tektronix, one of the barriers the team encountered was the lengthy purchasing process. It required that the purchasing department be directly involved in all expenditures — often delaying the acquisition of critical items for a week or more. When team members began making purchases with their own credit cards, their leader helped them explain to Purchasing the reasons for the practice (Rayner and Klein, 1989).

Time constraints on the team also make it challenging for the leader to handle any performance problems that crop up. Some team members won't have the skills or motivation to pull their weight; other team members will be obstinate about their ideas, to the extent that they hold up decisions. A common tendency for leaders is to avoid dealing with such problems, because the members eventually will return to their home teams. We'd argue, however, that because the team will be together for a relatively short period of time, the virtual leader must be especially vigilant and decisive about handling performance problems or team conflict.

Celebrations are even more critical for virtual teams, because it's important for the team and all the people who work with it to receive credit and perceive progress toward goals. Several kinds of celebrations of a team's accomplishment are usually required: public celebrations for everyone who contributed and private celebrations for the team itself.

As part of the winding down process, some methodology must be in place for team members to provide supportive developmental feedback to one another and for the leader to provide individual feedback as well. This is a unique opportunity to enhance the personal development of all involved. Unfortunately, in the rush of winding down a team and moving on to other things, this opportunity is missed more often than not.

If properly handled, being on a virtual team can be exciting. Team members deal with important issues and often take on greater responsibilities than is typical in their regular jobs. Not surprisingly, leaving the virtual team and going back to the normal job can be a letdown. So it's the responsibility of the leader and the organization to ameliorate problems as much as possible. A formal "reentry" meeting between the returning members and their home teams can help reestablish home-team bonds.

In one organization, these reentry meetings are called "Prodigal Events," to celebrate the return of a "lost" member. The home team reviews its mission and progress on goals. The returning member describes the project experience and lessons learned. The complete home team then reviews and recommits to its own operating guidelines.

A final responsibility of the virtual team leader is to share what is learned from the process with other managers and other teams. One of the biggest risks of the fluid nature of virtual organizations is that teams will be created and disbanded with such speed that they never have an opportunity to learn from one another. If that happens, the organization is condemned to repeating the same mistakes over and over again. In order to avoid that, a leader should *make* the time to generate (with all the members) a list of lessons learned, as one of the team's final "deliverables" to the organization.

LEADER SKILLS AND MOTIVATIONS

Obviously, the leader of an empowered virtual team has an even more challenging role than that of leading more permanent self-directed teams. To meet the challenges associated with leading a task-oriented virtual team, leaders will need to rely to a greater degree on their leadership skills. No *new* skills are needed — just a more advanced application of skills already covered in previous chapters.

When asked about the experience of leading a new-product development team, one product manager remarked, "It was the hardest test of my life. I had headed up plenty of teams before, but this required total concentration. Before, I had always been able to react and do what came naturally, with pretty good results. But for the last one-and-a-half years, I've had to go home and plan how to keep the team focused, how to influence other departments, and how to help each of the different functions respect each other's needs and perspectives." She went on to explain that she had used skills such as coaching, building trust, and creating a shared vision before, but that they took on a new dimension in a virtual team environment.

Coaching was different because she had no position power. In several cases, she was coaching team members who could be considered her organizational peers and, in one case, a team member who would be considered her "superior" in a traditional organizational hierarchy. Establishing trust was a challenge because she couldn't wait for it to develop over a long period of time. The first time a team member violated the team's operating guidelines (by bad-mouthing the project back in his home department), she learned that the team's agreements couldn't be taken for granted or allowed to sort themselves out over time. They needed to be reinforced constantly. There wasn't enough time for team members to learn to trust each other again after that episode, and the offending team member was never fully accepted by the team.

Her biggest surprise, though, was in the amount of energy it took to maintain a shared vision. All her previous work had been with teams from a single functional area, where members had a common history and similar values. Although this development team had jointly created a mission that involved producing the product in record time, she found she was constantly mediating conflicts between engineering team members (with an ethic of "if we take the time to do it right now, we'll save time in the long run") and marketing team members with a bias for action (who erected a big sign over their cubicles that proclaimed "Just do it"). So although she used the same skills she had used with previous teams, she found that she used them more frequently (eight to ten coaching discussions a day) and more deliberately (planning events to refocus on the vision).

One of the best ways to learn to apply leadership skills in a virtual environment is to be a member of a virtual team led by an effective leader. Such team membership provides the opportunity for everyone to use leadership skills over the course of the project and observe the role of an effective, empowering leader in action.

In addition to enhanced leadership skills, success in virtual organizations requires a new set of motivations and tolerances:

- *Tolerance for horizontal moves in the organization.* Some people are still fixated on an upward career path and don't see the advantages of horizontal moves. Given the flattening of most organizations, however, such horizontal moves will become much more common. People need to think more in terms of a *learning* path than a *career* path. In a learning path, individuals determine what knowledge and skills they need to acquire and plan a series of assignments to achieve these learning objectives. Often leadership of or participation in a virtual team is a wonderful way of accomplishing such personal goals. To succeed in a virtual organization, people have to use each new team assignment to develop needed skills, not to plot how to get promoted.

- *Tolerance for organizational ambiguity.* Virtual teams seldom have clean areas of responsibility. A team can seldom claim that an area of responsibility is *"our turf."* For this reason, leaders have no choice but to learn tolerance. Respond by seeking clarity and helping to define areas of team responsibility and shared responsibility. Becoming frustrated or paralyzed by overlapping responsibilities will only inhibit your ability to make things happen for the customer.

- *Tolerance for playing both a member role and a leader role within a team.* In a virtual environment, power comes from what an individual accomplishes for the "customer"—not from position within the hierarchy.

    Leaders should take advantage of every new team assignment to sharpen their leadership and problem-solving skills, even if they're not in a formal leadership position.

The most effective players in the virtual organization of tomorrow will be those people with the broadest technical knowledge who have learned how to make things happen by involving others. If you not only are good at these things but enjoy them as well, you'll be a valued contributor, regardless of how the organization's structure might change.

SUMMARY

Most organizations either have or will have empowered, virtual teams assigned to various important projects; they're becoming a virtual necessity! The traditional method of establishing a team to give advice to management while management retains authority and responsibility too often has failed and tragically prolonged decision making within the organization. Virtual teams, and the people who lead them, are the wave of the future.

Hang In There:
The Change Is Worth It

One of our clients' team leaders has a sign on his desk that broadcasts the following message:

"Change or Die"

Maybe the reality isn't *quite* that dramatic. Some organizations still operate with a hierarchical structure and a traditional management style, but their numbers are dwindling rapidly. A more accurate ultimatum might be "Change, or flee to one of a shrinking number of companies still using early twentieth-century management methods." The point, of course, is that we *all* have to make a choice: to change or not to change, that is the question. We conclude here by reviewing some of the advantages for making the change to high-involvement leadership.

Because this is a deep personal change, it's important to consider the personal impact on leaders who've made the transition. For starters, they're a happier bunch. Two different sets of survey results confirm that the more empowered teams become, the more satisfied their leaders are. The more self-directed our teams become, the more likely it is that we'll be satisfied, well adjusted in our new role, and confident of positive evaluations by team members (George and Pavur, 1992).

Why? One of the primary reasons this transition has been so satisfying for leaders is that it creates new opportunities at work. Chief among these opportunities is the chance to do more interesting things:

- "It used to be that I'd go home and dread the question, 'What did you do at work today, honey?' I mean, how exciting was it to complete a production report or scream at maintenance over some breakdown? Now I have much better things to talk about."

- "I have to admit, this is the first time I've felt challenged in years. I actually have to *think* about what I'm doing. I've learned how to negotiate with a regulatory agency, and I put together my first business plan this year."

You can almost hear the collective sigh of relief from converted leaders all over the country. Their days are no longer consumed by an endless stream of complaints and crises. With their team members involved and working toward a common purpose, leaders can actually accomplish something meaningful, because all their energy isn't wasted struggling to get employees to "do what they're told." By creating an environment where commitment comes from within, leaders find that they expend less energy getting the same—or better—results.

The transition to high involvement also results in

increased visibility for leaders, both inside and outside the organization:

- "I found I really enjoy working with the higher-ups. It gives me a chance to show them what I can do — and I've actually learned something from them at the same time."

- "I couldn't believe what a rush it was to present at my first conference. I admit I thought I'd get sick beforehand, but after it was over, everyone came up to ask me questions as if I was the expert."

The move to teams has resulted in a new crop of talent surfacing. Although this effect usually is discussed in relation to team members, leaders also have a lot more to offer. Often the talent and enthusiasm that caused them to be selected as leaders in the first place was lost in the limited, custodial nature of their old jobs. However, as leaders gain more exposure inside and outside the organization, these hidden skills are being rediscovered. Occasionally, this also results in promotion:

- "After all those years of practicing participative management on the sly for fear of being viewed as soft, it feels like a real vindication to be promoted."

- "Managers who master skills such as team building and entrepreneurship and who acquire broad functional expertise will likely be in the best position to get tomorrow's top corporate jobs. That's because the role of the top exeutive is becoming more like that of a team player and broker of others' efforts, not that of an autocrat" (Dumaine, 1993, p. 80).

Along with these increased opportunities comes the chance to really make a difference — to have a significant impact on the organization. That wasn't so easy under the old structure:

- "All I used to do all day was essentially baby-sit eighteen adults — prod them, remind them, and scold them."

- "I didn't realize it until I sat down one day to put my resume together: What could I say I had really accomplished? Now I can point to the introduction of a new product and a completely overhauled preventive maintenance system."

Finally, as trite as it might sound, there's real enjoyment in helping others grow. Some leaders develop near-cultlike followings. Employees are almost embarrassingly grateful for the coaching and support they receive from their leaders:

- "Even though I left the organization three years ago, I still get Christmas cards from some of my old team members."

- "When one of my former team members was assigned to lead a rather large project, she came to me and said, 'I thought about whose leadership skills I really respected, and who I could model myself after, and I thought of you.' That comment alone was enough to keep me going for the next two years."

Reformed leaders speak with the most enthusiasm (and surprise) about the organizational wallflowers who've blossomed under this new approach:

- "We had one guy everybody used to call Elmer Fudd — I guess because he was so bumbling and ineffectual. Well, my greatest sense of accomplishment came the day he led his first team meeting. He really didn't want to do it, and it took days of coaxing and coaching on my part to get him up there. But it turned out to be a real turning point in the respect he got from the other employees."

If you're still not convinced, consider the alternatives.

Teams are rapidly taking over most of the operations in this country (in fact, around the world). Only 18 percent haven't yet converted (Gordon, 1992), and even in those cases, management jobs are being eliminated. Management jobs account for only 5 percent of the workforce but a whopping 22 percent of the layoffs in recent history (Dumaine, 1993), so traditional leaders are competing for a dwindling share of a declining pie.

What about trying to wait it out? Lie low and look inconspicuous? Not likely:

- "If you can't say why you actually make your company a better place, you're out."

- "We can't afford to pay people just for watching others anymore."

Everywhere, at all organizational levels, people are feeling the need to justify their existence. We must make ourselves valuable to the organization, and we won't accomplish that by doing the wrong things. Unfortunately, this is what too many leaders attempt to do: they simply work harder at doing what they've always done. They come in earlier, go home later, yell louder, and demand better results; and they're surprised when their organizations don't appreciate their efforts. But the rules have changed. What got leaders recognized and rewarded in the past now is more likely to "put them out to pasture." Good intentions aren't enough; we must adapt to the changing requirements of leadership.

The chain of change in workplace operations has a domino effect. As the business climate changes, organizations must change their structures and processes in order to accommodate the demands for increased speed and quality. And as the internal organizational landscape changes, the remaining jobs are redesigned radically, ultimately requiring fundamental personal change from the people who fill them.

Although much has changed, the need for good leaders remains a constant. In fact, good leaders are more important than ever before. Only through outstanding leadership will we achieve the levels of effort and commitment needed to compete in the world economy.

We believe that most leaders can and will make the leadership transition successfully and that their organizations have an obligation to provide the support necessary for them to be successful. Those leaders who succeed at this difficult and demanding transformation will find themselves in new roles that are much more rewarding, both personally and professionally.

REFERENCES

American Management Association. *AMA Survey on Down-sizing.* New York: American Management Association, 1992.

American Society for Training and Development. *HRD Executive Poll.* Alexandria, Va.: American Society for Training and Development, May 1991.

Barnett, J. K. "A. E. Staley's Sagamore Refinery: New Roles for Supervisors." In J. M. Rosow and R. Zager (eds.), *New Roles for Managers: Part I. A Work in America Policy Study.* Scarsdale, N.Y.: Work in America Institute, 1989.

Bednarek, D. I. "Go, Team, Go." *Human Resource Executive,* Apr. 1990, p. 45.

Bennis, W. *An Invented Life: Reflections on Leadership and Change.* Reading, Mass.: Addison-Wesley, 1993.

Bennis, W., and Nanus, B. *Leaders: The Strategies for Taking Charge.* New York: HarperCollins, 1985.

Benson, T. E. "America's Best Plants." *Industry Week,* Oct. 19, 1992, p. 45.

Berger, S. *Working Papers of the MIT Commission on Industrial Productivity.* Vol. 2: *The U.S. Textile Industry: Challenges and Opportunities.* Cambridge, Mass.: MIT Press, 1989.

Beyerlein, M., Beyerlein, S. C., and Richardson, S. *1993 Sur-*

vey of Technical Professionals in Teams. Denton: University of North Texas, 1993.

Bisesi, F. "Moving from Traditional to Teams at the House of Seagrams with Distillery Workers Local 34." Paper presented at the Ecology of Work Conference, Baltimore, June 1993.

Block, P. *Flawless Consulting: A Guide to Getting Your Expertise Used.* San Diego: University Associates, 1981.

Brown, T. "Think in Reverse." *Industry Week*, July 19, 1993, pp. 14–22.

Byham, W. C. *Zapp! The Lightning of Empowerment.* New York: Harmony Books, 1991.

Byrne, J. "The Horizontal Corporation." *Business Week*, Dec. 20, 1993, pp. 76–81.

Campagna, B., O'Fallon, T., and Gilbert, R. D. "Making a Self-Directed Team Organization." Paper presented at the Ecology of Work Conference, Baltimore, June 1993.

Cernero, J. "A Strategy for Succeeding with Self-Managed Work Teams in a Union Manufacturing Work Environment." Paper presented at the International Conference on Self-Managed Work Teams, Dallas, Oct. 1991.

Charlier, M. "Magma Copper Heals Its Workplace and Bottom Line: Improved Labor Relations Lead to Lower Production Costs and Less Debt." *Wall Street Journal*, April 4, 1992, p. B-4.

Collins, J. C., and Porras, J. I. "Organizational Visions and Visionary Organizations." *California Management Review*, 1991, 34(1), 30–52.

Commitment Plus, Apr. 1992, pp. 1–4.

Cummings, T. G., and Huse, E. F. *Organizational Development and Change.* (4th ed.) West, 1989.

Davidow, W. H., and Malone, M. S. *The Virtual Corporation: Structuring and Revitalizing the Corporation of the 21st Century.* New York: Harper Business, 1992.

Denton, D. K. "Multi-Skilled Teams Replace Old Work Systems." *HRMagazine*, Sept. 1992, p. 52.

DePree, M. *Leadership Is an Art.* New York: Doubleday, 1989.

"Diary of an Anarchist." *Economist*, June 26, 1993, p. 78.

Doucette, R. W. "Charting Our Course for Tomorrow: Milwaukee Insurance Group, Inc." In 1992 *Annual Report.* Milwaukee: Milwaukee Insurance Group, 1993.

DuBrul, R. J. "Management Coordination." Paper presented at the Ecology of Work Conference, Baltimore, June 1993.

Dumaine, B. "Who Needs a Boss?" *Fortune,* May 7, 1990, pp. 52–55, 58, 60.

Dumaine, B. "The New Non-Manager Managers." *Fortune,* Feb. 22, 1993, pp. 80–84.

Faltermayer, E. "Poised for a Comeback." *Fortune,* Apr. 19, 1993, p. 175.

Farrell, C., and Schiller, Z. "Stuck! How Companies Cope When They Can't Raise Prices." *Business Week,* Nov. 15, 1993, pp. 146–155.

Fields, M. "The Impact of Involvement on Unions: A No-Lose Proposition?" Paper presented at the Ecology of Work Conference, Baltimore, June 1993.

Firenze, B. "The Role of Unions in New Work Systems." Panel presentation at the Ecology of Work Conference, Baltimore, June 1993.

Fisher, K. *Leading Self-Directed Teams.* New York: McGraw-Hill, 1993.

Fisher, K. "Managing in the High Commitment Workplace." *Organizational Dynamics,* Winter 1989, 17(3), 31–50.

Forbes, D. "The Impact of Total Processing and Autonomous Teams on Supervisors: Shenandoah Life Insurance Company." In J. M. Rosow and R. Zager (eds.), *New Roles for Managers: Part I. A Work in America Policy Study.* Scarsdale, N.Y.: Work in America Institute, 1989.

Frohman, A. L., and Johnson, L. W. *The Middle Management Challenge.* New York: McGraw-Hill, 1993.

Frohman, M. "What They Really Do: A Profile of Participative Managers." *Industry Week,* Aug. 1, 1988, pp. 51–53.

"From Supervision to Coaching at AT&T Denver Works." *Commitment Plus,* Dec. 1992, pp. 1–4.

Garvin, D. "Building a Learning Organization." *Harvard Business Review,* July/Aug. 1993, pp. 78–91.

George, J. "Impact of Team Leader Behavior on Team Effectiveness: A Leader-Member Exchange Theoretic Perspective." Unpublished doctoral dissertation, University of Tennessee, 1994.

George, J., and Pavur, E. *The Changing Role of the Supervisor Survey: Results and Summary.* Pittsburgh, Pa.: Development Dimensions International, 1992.

Glines, D., Forror, S., Silva, G., and Kobert, M. "Tiger River, Sunbear Forest and Gorilla Tropics: Teams at the San Diego Zoo with Team Local 481." Paper presented at the Ecology of Work Conference, Baltimore, June 1993.

Gordon, J. "Work Teams: How Far Have They Come?" *Training,* Oct. 1992, pp. 59–65.

Hall, R., and Tonkin, L. (eds.). *Manufacturing 21 Report: The Future of Japanese Manufacturing.* Wheeling, Ill.: Association of Manufacturing Excellence, 1990.

Hammer, M., and Champy, J. *Reengineering the Corporation: A Manifesto for Business Revolution.* New York: Harper-Collins, 1993.

Harding, S. P. "Employee Expectations and Opinions: Changes in Western European Organizations." Paper presented at the Institute of Personnel Management's National Conference, Harrogate, U.K., Oct. 23, 1991.

Hill, L. *Becoming a New Manager: Mastery of a New Identity.* Boston: Harvard Business School Press, 1992.

Hirschhorn, L. *Managing in the New Team Environment.* Reading, Mass.: Addison-Wesley, 1991.

Hirschhorn, L., and Gilmore, T. "The New Boundaries of the 'Boundaryless' Company." *Harvard Business Review,* May/June 1992, pp. 104–115.

Hoerr, J. "The Cultural Revolution at A. O. Smith." *Business Week,* May 29, 1989, pp. 66–68.

Hoerr, J. "What Should Unions Do?" *Harvard Business Review,* May/June 1991, 69(3), 4–12.

Houston, P. "Timmberrr." *Business Month,* Dec. 1989.

Howard R. "Values Make the Company." *Harvard Business Review,* Sept./Oct. 1992, pp. 133–144.

Hutzel, T., and Varney, G. "The Supervisor's Role in Self-

Directed Work Teams." *Journal for Quality and Participation*, Dec. 1992, pp. 36–41.

Jellison, J. M. *Overcoming Resistance: A Practical Guide to Producing Change in the Workplace.* New York: Simon & Schuster, 1993.

Katzenbach, J. R., and Smith, O. K. *The Wisdom of Teams.* Boston: Harvard Business School Press, 1993.

Kirker, T. B. "America's Best Plants — Edy's Ice Cream." *Industry Week*, Oct. 18, 1993, pp. 29–32.

Klein, J. "Integrating Maintenance into the Redesign Process." Paper presented at the Ecology of Work Conference, Baltimore, June 1993.

Klein, J. A., and Posey, P. A. "Good Supervisors Are Good Supervisors — Anywhere." *Harvard Business Review*, Nov./Dec. 1986, pp. 125–128.

Koestenbaum, P. *Leadership: The Inner Side of Greatness.* San Francisco: Jossey-Bass, 1991.

Kullburg, J. "Welcome to the Real World: The Transition to Team Based Operations at the Corning Erwin, N.Y., Plant with A.F.G.W.U. Local 1000." Paper presented at the Ecology of Work Conference, Baltimore, June 1993.

Labich, K. "Making Over Middle Managers." *Fortune*, May 8, 1989, pp. 58–64.

Lawler, E. *The Ultimate Advantage: Creating the High-Involvement Organization.* San Francisco: Jossey-Bass, 1992.

Lazes, P. "Unions and the Choice of Employee Involvement Activities." *AFL-CIO Department of Economic Research*, Dec. 1993, 2(2), G-79–G-83.

Lee, C. "The Vision Thing." *Training*, Feb. 1993, pp. 25–34.

Levinson, M. "Playing with Fire." *Newsweek*, June 21, 1993, pp. 46–48.

Lewis, C., and Elden, M. "How Union-Management Strategic Partnering in Organization Design and Change Management Pay Off Big Time at Magma Copper." Paper presented at the International Conference on Self-Managed Work Teams, Cincinnati, Sept. 1992.

McDermott, L. C. *Caught in the Middle*. Englewood Cliffs, N.J.: Prentice-Hall, 1992.

McKenna, J. F. "America's Best Plants." *Industry Week*, Oct. 19, 1992, pp. 33–66.

Macy, B. "North American Organizational Design and Work Innovation." Paper presented at the International Conference on Self-Managed Work Teams, Dallas, 1993.

Manz, C. C., and Sims, H. P., Jr. *Superleadership*. Englewood Cliffs, N.J.: Prentice-Hall, 1989.

Miller, W. H. "America's Best Plants — Unisys Corp." *Industry Week*, Oct. 18, 1993, pp. 33–34.

Moskal, B. "The Wizards of Buick City." *Industry Week*, May 7, 1990, p. 27.

Nasar, S. "Do We Live as Well as We Used To?" *Fortune*, Sept. 14, 1987, p. 62.

Neff, R. "Fixing Japan." *Business Week*, Mar. 29, 1993, pp. 68–74.

Nelson-Horchler, J. "The Magic of Herman Miller." *Industry Week*, Feb. 18, 1991, pp. 11–17.

Noyelle, T. *Services and the New Economy: Toward a New Labor Market Segmentation*. New York: National Center on Education and Employment, Teachers College, Columbia University, 1989.

Pasmore, W. "Getting Everyone Involved in Redesign: The Conference Method and Fact Cycle Approaches." Paper presented at the Ecology of Work Conference, Baltimore, June 1993.

Peters, T. *Liberation Management*. New York: Knopf, 1992.

Peterson, T. "Leadership Power and Transformation at Seattle Metro." In J. M. Rosow and J. Casner-Lotto (eds.), *New Roles for Managers: Part V. A Work in America Policy Study*. Scarsdale, N.Y.: Work in America Institute, 1993.

Posey, P., and Nota, B. "GE Bromont: The Supervisors' Story." In J. M. Rosow and R. Zager (eds.), *New Roles for Managers: Part II. A Work in America Policy Study*. Scarsdale, N.Y.: Work in America Institute, 1989.

Rapasort, R. "To Build a Winning Team." *Harvard Business Review*, Jan./Feb. 1993, p. 112.

Rayner, S. R., and Klein, J. A. "Managing Knowledge Worker Involvement at Tektronix: Three Managers' Stories." In J. M. Rosow and R. Zager (eds.), *New Roles for Managers: Part I. A Work in America Policy Study.* Scarsdale, N.Y.: Work in America Institute, 1989.

Rosow, J. M., and Casner-Lotto, J. *New Roles for Managers: Part V. A Work in America Policy Study.* Scarsdale, N.Y.: Work in America Institute, 1993.

Rosow, J. M., and Zager, R. (eds.). *New Roles for Managers: Part I. A Work in America Policy Study.* Scarsdale, N.Y.: Work in America Institute, 1989.

Schonberger, R. J. *Building a Chain of Customers.* New York: Free Press, 1990.

Semler, R. "Managing Without Managers." *Harvard Business Review,* Sept./Oct. 1989, pp. 76–84.

Senge, P. M. *The Fifth Discipline.* New York: Doubleday/Currency, 1992.

Sheahan, M. "Preparing Local Leaders for Their Role in Joint Programs and Work Restructuring: Keep It Complicated." Paper presented at the Ecology of Work Conference, Cincinnati, Apr. 1993.

Shenberger, R., and Killingsworth, L. "Career Development in a Team-Based Culture." Paper presented at the International Conference on Self-Managed Work Teams, Dallas, Tex., Sept., 1992.

Sheridan, J. H. "America's Best Plants — Exxon Chemical Company." *Industry Week,* Oct. 18, 1993a, pp. 42–44.

Sheridan, J. H. "America's Best Plants — Honeywell, Inc." *Industry Week,* Oct. 18, 1993b, pp. 26–28.

Stalk, G., Jr., and Hout, T. M. *Competing Against Time.* New York: Free Press, 1990.

Sundstrom, E., and others. "Work-Team Context, Development and Effectiveness in a Manufacturing Organization." Paper presented at the Society for Industrial/Organizational Psychology (Division 14) Conference, Miami, Apr. 1990.

Taylor, J. C., and Felten, D. F. *Performance by Design: So-*

ciotechnical Systems in North America. Englewood Cliffs, N.J.: Prentice-Hall, 1993.

Teresko, J. "America's Best Plants." Industry Week, Oct. 19, 1992, pp. 55–56.

U.S. Bureau of Labor Management Relations. The Changing Role of Union Leaders. Washington, D.C.: U.S. Government Printing Office, 1988.

Walton, R. E. "Work Innovations at Topeka: After Six Years." Journal of Applied Behavioral Sciences, 1977, 13(3), 422–433.

Walton, R. E. "From Control to Commitment in the Workplace." Harvard Business Review, Mar./Apr. 1985, pp. 77–84.

Webber, A. "What's So New About the New Economy?" Harvard Business Review, 1993, 71(1), 24–42.

Weisbord, M. Productive Workplaces: Organizing and Managing for Dignity, Meaning, and Community. San Francisco: Jossey-Bass, 1987.

Welch, J. F., Jr., and Hood, E. E., Jr. Letter to Shareholders. In General Electric's 1991 Annual Report. Schenectady, N.Y.: General Electric, 1991.

Wellins, R., Byham, W. C., and Dixon, G. Inside Teams: How 20 World-Class Organizations Are Winning Through Teamwork. San Francisco: Jossey-Bass, forthcoming.

Wellins, R., Byham, W. C., and Wilson, J. Empowered Teams: Creating Self-Directed Work Groups That Improve Quality, Productivity, and Participation. San Francisco: Jossey-Bass, 1991.

Wellins, R., and others. TQM: Forging Ahead or Falling Behind? Pittsburgh, Pa.: Development Dimensions International, Association for Quality and Participation, and Industry Week, 1993.

Wellins, R., and others. Self-Directed Teams: A Study of Current Practice. Pittsburgh, Pa.: Development Dimensions International, Association for Quality and Participation, and Industry Week, 1990.

"What Workers Want: The Gap in Management's Perception." Behavioral Sciences Newsletter, June 27, 1988.

Willis, R., and others. The Grain Millers' Role in Creating

Labor/Management Partnerships for New Work Systems: A Statement of Policy and Guidelines for Local Unions. Minneapolis: American Federation of Grain Millers, 1991.

Woodruff, D. "GM: All Charged Up over the Electric Car." *Business Week,* Oct. 1991a, p. 106.

Woodruff, D. "The Racy Viper Is Already a Winner for Chrysler." *Business Week,* Nov. 1991b, pp. 36–38.

Woodruff, D. "At Saturn, What Workers Want Is...Fewer Defects." *Business Week,* Dec. 2, 1991c, pp. 117–118.

Woodruff, D. "Saturn: Labor's Love Lost?" *Business Week,* Feb. 8, 1993a, pp. 122–124.

Woodruff, D. "Chrysler's Neon: Is This the Small Car Detroit Couldn't Build?" *Business Week,* May 3, 1993b, pp. 116–126.

Wriston, W. B. "The State of American Management." *Harvard Business Review,* 1990, 68(1), 78–83.

INDEX

A

A. E. Staley, 207, 223
A. O. Smith Steelworkers Local, 180
Air Products and Chemicals Inc., 19
American Flint and Glass Workers Union, 125
Apple Computer, 251
Assessment process: mature-team, 239–240; new-team, 164–165, 187–192; peer, 239; preteam, 139–143. *See also* Feedback
AT&T, 121; Denver Works, 157, 181, 245; Operator Services, 64
Autocratic leadership, 60–61

B

Barnett, J. K., 207, 223
Bausch & Lomb, 195
Bednarek, D. I., 3
Bell Atlantic, 252
Bennis, W., 73
Benson, T. E., 19
Berger, S., 21
Bisesi, F., 181
Blackman, P., 180
Block, P., 106

Boeing, 237, 244–245
Brown, T., 250
Buick, 221
Burnout, 224–225
Byham, W. C., 26, 34
Byrne, J., 252, 256

C

Campagna, B., 237, 246
Campbell Chain, 156
Cape Coral Hospital, 46–50, 107, 150, 164
Career development: integrating perspective in, 243–246; in mature teams, 216–220, 243–246; in new teams, 195–200; preteam, 138–139
Celebration events, 237–238
Cernero, J., 122
Champy, J., 74, 252
Charlier, M., 125, 126
Charter, team, 149
Chrysler, 252; Neon design team, 22
Coaching skills, 158–159, 162; proactive, 71. *See also* Training
Cohesiveness, team, 173
Colgate's Technology Division, 195

Collins, J. C., 73
Communication skills, of high-involvement leader, 69
Communications Workers of America, 121, 182
Compaq Corporation, 22
Compensation, team leader, 195
Competing Against Time, 19
Continuous improvement, 20; as team vision, 71–72, 104–105
Corning, 122, 125, 126–127, 130
Cost improvements, 21–23
Cross-functional teams, 26–28, 243–244
Cummings, T. G., 99
Curtis Screw Company, 58
Customization, rise of, 21

D

Davidow, W. H., 251
Delegation, 160–161
Denton, D. K., 3
Dependence, of team members, 170–172
Design team, 31–33; empowerment schedule in, 33; sociotechnical systems analysis in, 32; team leader role in, 130
Development Dimensions International (DDI), 19–20
Dixon, G., 34
Doucette, R. W., 39
Douglas, A., 213
Drypers, 238
DuBrul, R. J., 209
Dumaine, B., 3, 36, 78, 238, 267, 269
DuPont, 256

E

Eastman Chemical, 25, 238–239
Eastman Kodak Company's Customer Assistance Center, 34
Edy's Grand Ice Cream, 19
Elden, M., 135
Empowerment, 23, 71–72, 168; and delegation, 160–161; and

modeling behaviors, 184–185; team leader's role in, 19
Ennis, T., 256
Environment scan, 235–236
Exxon, 20

F

Faltermayer, E., 19, 22
Feedback, 139–143, 164; anonymous, 186; face-to-face, 246–247; in mature teams, 239–240; in meetings, 214–215; by team members, 217–218; "360-degree," 188
Felten, D. F., 235
Fields, M., 126
Fifth Discipline, The, 78
Firenze, 232
Fisher, K., 75, 102
Forbes, D., 207, 226
Forror, S., 206
Frohman, A. L., 238

G

Garvin, D., 77–78
General Electric, 80, 167, 238, 250
General Motors, 181, 252
George, J., 36, 95, 159, 266
Gilbert, R. D., 237, 246
Gilmore, T., 250
Glines, D., 206
"Good Supervisors Are Good Supervisors—Anywhere," 68
Gordon, J., 34, 269
Grain Millers, 181, 232
Gregorich, M., 181
Grimm, G., 156

H

Hall, R., 21
Hammer, M., 74, 252
Harding, S. P., 23
Health care, self-directed teams in, 46–50
Hess, R., 73–74
Hewlett-Packard, 237

Hill, L., 132
Hirschhorn, L., 159, 250
Hoerr, J., 122, 125, 180
Honeywell, 20
Hood, E., 57–58, 250
Houston, P., 3
Hout, T. M., 19
Howard, R., 74
Huse, E. F., 99

I

Intellectual capital, 23
International Brotherhood of
    Electrical Workers, 127, 181
International Paper, 43–46, 79
ISO 9000, 20

J

James River, 245–246, 251–252
Japanese manufacturing, 21; work-
    force empowerment in, 23
Jellison, J. M., 133
Job security, of team leaders, 132
Johnson, L. W., 238
Johnson & Johnson, 121–122
Johnsonville Sausage, 209

K

Katzenbach, J. R., 25
Kellogg, 251–252
KG Packaging, 213
Killingsworth, L., 245
Kirker, T. B., 19, 22
Klein, J., 68, 179
Klein, J. A., 230, 256, 260
Knowledge explosion, 18–19
Kobert, M., 206
Kodak's Plastic and Metal
    Products Division, 179
Koestenbaum, P., 76
Kullburg, J., 122

L

Labich, K., 36
Lateral integration, 221–223

Laurentian Technology, 70–71, 80
Lawler, E. E., 23, 24, 118, 178
Lazes, P., 121
Leaders: analysis and judgment
    skills, 70–71; autocratic, 60–61;
    coaching role of, 71, 97, 158–
    159, 162; and commitment, 97–
    99; evolving role, 57–65; and
    faulty self-perception, 112; fear
    of responsibility, 95–96; "invisi-
    ble elements" of role, 102; mis-
    conceptions about, 4–16;
    participative, 61–63; power and
    influence gains, 8–10; proactive
    role, 6–8, 71; resistance and
    skepticism of, 99–103; role defi-
    nition, 134–138; strategic skills,
    68, 72–80; successful transi-
    tions, 10–12, 38–56, 266–270;
    tactical skills, 68–72; team di-
    rection role, 12–13; vul-
    nerability of, 13–16. See also
    Leaders, new-team; Leaders,
    mature-team; Leaders, preteam
Leaders, mature-team, 90–92,
    204–233; assessment of, 239–
    240; burnout, 224–225; career
    development, 216–220, 243–
    246; complacency trap, 225; job
    profile, 227–228; key behaviors,
    220–223; new responsibilities
    and tasks, 206–208, 213–214;
    performance feedback, 214–
    215, 239–240; self-check, 228–
    229; and support staff, 229–231,
    235–239; team member support
    for, 246–247; training of, 240–
    243
Leaders, new-team, 89–90, 153–
    203; assessment of, 164–165,
    187–195; career development,
    195–200; coaching skills, 158–
    159, 162–164; compensation,
    195; job profile, 176; key behav-
    iors, 167–169; needs satisfac-
    tion of, 186–187; performance
    feedback, 187–192; relationship
    with boss, 165–167; and senior
    management, 184–187; and

stress, 157–158; and support staff, 177–180; and team dependence, 170–172; and team empowerment, 160–161, 168; and team member support, 200–201; training for, 192–193, 194; transition failures, 197–199

Leaders, preteam, 88–89, 93–127, 128–152; accountability fears, 97–99; assessment and feedback, 139–143; career options, 138–139; and development plan, 109; and employee resistance, 104–107; employee support for, 150–151; empowerment setbacks, 112–113; job profile, 115–116; key behaviors, 108–111; and personal resistance, 99–103, 113–114; relationship with boss, 107–108; responsibility fears, 95–96; role definition and clarification, 134–138; self-check, 116–118; and senior-management, 129–134; and support staff, 118–121; and team vision, 94–95

Leadership: The Inner Side of Greatness, 75–76

Leadership structures, innovation in, 238–239

Learning paths, 138–139

Lee, C., 73

Levi Strauss, 73–74

Lewis, C., 135

Long-term orientation, 223

M

McDermott, L. C., 195

McKenna, J. F., 35

Macy, B., 251

Magma Copper, 125, 126, 135

Malcolm Baldrige National Quality Award, 20, 25

Malone, M. S., 250, 251

Managers: layoffs of, 36–37; turnover of, 202

Manz, C., 78

Middle managers, job threat to, 3–4

Miller, W. H., 19

Miller Brewing, 50–55

Milwaukee Insurance Group, Inc, 39–42

Mission, team, 25

Modicon, Inc., 252

Monsanto, 75

Motivation, 71–72

Murray, M. R., 18

N

Nanus, B., 73

Nasar, S., 19

Neff, R., 23

Noyelle, T., 21

O

O'Fallon, T., 237, 246

"One-size-fits-all" approach, 20–21

Operating guidelines, 213

O'Rourke, J. T., 22

P

Participative leadership, 61–63

Partnership-building, business, 79–80

Pasmore, W., 130

Pavur, E., 36, 95, 266

Performance evaluation, of team leaders, 193–195, 196

Performance facilitation, team, 76–77

Performance goals, 168–169

Performance management skills, 69–70

Peters, T., 24

Peterson, T., 101

Pexco, 104–105

Porras, J. I., 73

Posey, P., 68

Prichard, E., 256

Proactive coaching, 71

Procter & Gamble, 232

Productivity, 21–23
Promega, 94

Q

Quaker Oats, 199
Quality improvement programs,
 20, 40–41, 45; statistical approach to, 70

R

Rapasort, R., 77
Rayner, S. R., 230, 256, 260
Redesign, product, 236–237
Reengineering the Corporation, 74
Retirement, and team leaders,
 202–203
Rippe, R., 21
Rosow, J. M., 179, 238, 246
Ross, A., 221
Rothweiler, F., 123–124
"Running interference," 172

S

San Diego Zoo, 205–206
Saturn, 232
Scott Paper, 127
Seagrams, 181
Seattle Metro, 101
Self-assessment worksheets,
 81–83, 144
Senge, P., 78
Senior-management: mature-team
 support, 235–239; new-team
 support, 184–187; preteam sup-
 port, 129–134; and vision plan-
 ning, 129–130
Sheahan, M., 124
Shell Sarnia, 122
Shenandoah Life, 206, 226
Shienberger, R., 245
Sheridan, J. H., 20
Silva, G., 206
Sims, H., 78
Smith, O. K., 25
Sociotechnical systems (STS), 32
Southern Bell, 216

Speed to market, 19–20
Stalk, G., 19
Stayer, R., 209
Steelworkers International Union,
 125
Stress, of team leaders, 157–158
Sundstrom, E., 150
Superleadership, 78
Supervisors, job threat, 3–4
Support professionals: in mature-
 team phase, 229–231; in new-
 team phase, 177–180; in
 preteam phase, 118–121; vision
 for, 230

T

Taeger, M., 58
Taylor, J. C., 235
Team(s): as competitive strategy,
 17–37; concept, clarification of,
 145–146; development plan,
 165–166; organizational case
 for, 94–95; variables, 25–26. *See
 also* Leaders
Team(s), self-directed: in design
 phase, 31–33; in implementation phase, 33; monitoring of,
 34; unique characteristics of,
 26–30; and visioning process,
 30–31
Team-based organizations, versus
 traditional organizations, 29–30
Tektronix, 178–179, 230, 256–257,
 260
Tennessee Eastman Chemical, 25
Teresko, J., 22
Texas Instruments, 153–154; Defense System and Electronic
 Group (DSEG), 25
Tonkin, L., 21
Total processing teams, 206–207
Toyota, 237
Training, team leader: coaching
 skills, 158–159, 162; in mature
 team, 240–243; in new team,
 192–193, 194; and on-the-job
 applications, 241–243; one-on-

one assistance, 243; preteam, 143–150; refresher, 240–241
Training, team member, 77–80, 130
Trust-engendering behavior, 74–76
"Turbo-empowerment," 35

U

UCAR Carbon, 105, 195
Ultimate Advantage: Creating the High-Involvement Organization, 23
Union leaders: as "conscience of implementation," 231–233; in new teams, 180–182; in transition phase, 121–127
Union Pacific Railroad, 75, 131, 132–133
Unisys Corporation, Pueblo, Colorado, 19
United Auto Workers (UAW), 22, 121, 125–126, 181, 232
United Paperworkers International, 127
United Steelworkers of America, 181–182
United Textile Workers of America, 122

V

"Value pricing," 21–22
Values, organizational, 73–74
Varian Associates, Inc., 22
VF Corporation, 19
Video conferencing, 18
Virtual organization, 250, 251
Virtual teams, 26, 249–264; leader skills and motivation in, 261–264; leader tasks in, 256–261;

present-day, 251–252; versus self-directed work teams, 252–256
Vision, organizational, 73–74
Vision, team: creation of, 30–31, 71–72; leader involvement in, 129–130; and motivation, 104–106; support function of, 230

W

"Walking the talk," 75–76
Walsh, M., 75
Walsh, W., 77
Walton, R. E., 24, 224
Webber, A., 23, 75
Weisbord, M., 130
Welch, J., 57–58, 250
Wellins, R., 26, 34, 140, 184
Westinghouse Electric Company, 34
"What Workers Want," 96
Willis, R., 182, 232
Wilson, J., 26
Wilson's Golf Ball, 35
Woodruff, D., 252
Work team progress survey, 190, 191
Workforce, changing values in, 23
Wriston, W. B., 18, 19, 23
Wyatt, S., 125–126

X

Xerox, 123

Y

Younkin, J., 22

Z

Zager, R., 179, 238, 246